States of Credit

THE PRINCETON ECONOMIC HISTORY OF THE WESTERN WORLD

Joel Mokyr, *Series Editor*

Growth in a Traditional Society: The French Countryside, 1450–1815,
by Philip T. Hoffman

The Vanishing Irish: Households, Migration, and the Rural Economy in Ireland, 1850–1914,
by Timothy W. Guinnane

Black '47 and Beyond: The Great Irish Famine in History, Economy, and Memory,
by Cormac Ó Gráda

The Great Divergence: China, Europe, and the Making of the Modern World Economy,
by Kenneth Pomeranz

The Big Problem of Small Change, by Thomas J. Sargent and François R. Velde

Farm to Factory: A Reinterpretation of the Soviet Industrial Revolution, by Robert C. Allen

Quarter Notes and Bank Notes: The Economics of Music Composition in the Eighteenth and Nineteenth Centuries, by F. M. Scherer

The Strictures of Inheritance: The Dutch Economy in the Nineteenth Century,
by Jan Luiten van Zanden and Arthur van Riel

Understanding the Process of Economic Change, by Douglass C. North

Feeding the World: An Economic History of Agriculture, 1800–2000, by Giovanni Federico

Cultures Merging: A Historical and Economic Critique of Culture, by Eric L. Jones

The European Economy since 1945: Coordinated Capitalism and Beyond, by Barry Eichengreen

War, Wine, and Taxes: The Political Economy of Anglo-French Trade, 1689–1900, by John V. C. Nye

A Farewell to Alms: A Brief Economic History of the World, by Gregory Clark

Power and Plenty: Trade, War, and the World Economy in the Second Millennium, by Ronald Findlay and Kevin O'Rourke

Power over Peoples: Technology, Environments, and Western Imperialism, 1400 to the Present, by Daniel R. Headrick

Unsettled Account: The Evolution of Banking in the Industrialized World since 1800, by Richard S. Grossman

States of Credit: Size, Power, and the Development of European Polities, by David Stasavage

Creating Wine: The Emergence of a World Industry, 1840–1914, by James Simpson

States of Credit

SIZE, POWER, AND THE DEVELOPMENT
OF EUROPEAN POLITIES

David Stasavage

PRINCETON UNIVERSITY PRESS

PRINCETON AND OXFORD

Copyright © 2011 by Princeton University Press
Requests for permission to reproduce material from this work
should be sent to Permissions, Princeton University Press

Published by Princeton University Press, 41 William Street,
Princeton, New Jersey 08540
In the United Kingdom: Princeton University Press,
6 Oxford Street, Woodstock, Oxfordshire OX20 1TW

press.princeton.edu

Library of Congress Cataloging-in-Publication Data

Stasavage, David.
States of credit : size, power, and the development of European polities /
David Stasavage.
    p. cm. — (The Princeton economic history of the Western world)
ISBN 978-0-691-14057-5 (hardcover : alk. paper)
1. Debts, Public—Europe—History.   2. Credit—Europe—History.
3. Europe—Politics and government.   4. Europe—History.
5. Middle Ages.   I. Title.
HJ8615.S857 2011
336.3′4094—dc22   2011006917

British Library Cataloging-in-Publication Data is available

This book has been composed in AdobeGaramondPro

Printed on acid-free paper. ∞

Typeset by S R Nova Pvt Ltd, Bangalore, India
Printed in the United States of America

10 9 8 7 6 5 4 3 2 1

TO MY CHILDREN

Rivka and Ezra

Contents

Illustrations   ix

Acknowledgments   xi

CHAPTER ONE
Introduction   1

Representation, Scale, and Control   6
The Evolution and Importance of Public Credit   9
Representative Assemblies in City-States and Territorial States   11
Geographic Scale and Merchant Power   14
Broad Sample Evidence   16
Origins of City-States   18
Case Study Evidence   20
Plan of the Book   24

CHAPTER TWO
The Evolution and Importance of Public Credit   25

Why Credit Was Important   25
When Did States First Borrow Long-Term?   29
The Cost of Borrowing   38
Economic Explanations for the City-State Advantage   43
Summary   46

CHAPTER THREE
Representative Assemblies in Europe, 1250–1750   47

Origins of Representative Assemblies   48
Prerogatives of Representative Assemblies   54
Who Was Represented?   61
The Intensity of Representation   65
Summary   68

CHAPTER FOUR
Assessing the City-State Advantage   70

Representation and Credit as an Equilibrium   72
Representative Institutions and the Creation of a Public Debt   77
Representative Institutions and the Cost of Borrowing   84
Variation within City-States   90
Summary   93

CHAPTER FIVE
Origins of City-States   94

    The Rokkan/Tilly Hypothesis   95
    The Carolingian Partition Hypothesis   95
    Empirical Evidence   100
    Reassessing the City-State Advantage   106
    Summary   107

CHAPTER SIX
Three City-State Experiences   110

    Merchant Oligarchy in Cologne   111
    Genoa and the Casa di San Giorgio   117
    Siena under the Rule of the Nine   125
    Summary   131

CHAPTER SEVEN
Three Territorial State Experiences   132

    France and the Rentes sur l'Hôtel de Ville   132
    Revisiting Absolutism in Castile   142
    Accounting for Holland's Financial Revolution   150
    Summary   154

CHAPTER EIGHT
Implications for State Formation and Development   156

    The Debate on War and State Formation   156
    Information, Commitment, and Democracy   158
    Understanding Early Modern Growth   161

Bibliography   167

Index   187

Illustrations

TABLES

2.1.	Dates of First and Last Observed Long-term Loans	31
2.2.	Revenue Volatility for Different States	45
3.1.	Sources on Representative Institutions	56
3.2.	Geographic Scale as a Determinant of Meeting Frequency	67
4.1.	Probability of Creating a Long-term Debt (Probit Estimates)	82
4.2.	OLS Estimates of the Cost of Borrowing	86
4.3.	Fixed Effects Estimates of the Cost of Borrowing	92
5.1.	Sample Means for Initial City Conditions	101
5.2.	The Correlates of City-State Development	102
5.3.	Instrumental Variables Estimates of the City-State Advantage	108

FIGURES

2.1.	Establishment of Long-term Debts	32
2.2.	Interest Rates on Debts of City-States and Territorial States	39
2.3.	Returns on Land Rents in Five European Regions	41
2.4.	Difference between the Observed Interest Rate on Public-Debt and the Return on Land Rents	41
3.1.	Representative Assemblies by Historical Period	58
3.2.	Representative Assemblies in City-States and Territorial States	58
3.3.	Merchant Representation in City-States and Territorial States	63
5.1.	The Carolingian Partition	97
6.1.	Interest Rates on the Public Debt in Genoa	123
7.1.	Issues of *Rentes sur l'Hôtel de Ville*	135

Acknowledgments

A number of people have been kind enough to give comments and advice related to this book during the process of research and writing. In particular, I would like to thank Daron Acemoglu, Neal Beck, Carles Boix, Deborah Boucoyannis, Mark Dincecco, Mauricio Drelichman, Jim Fearon, Jeff Frieden, Steve Haber, Pierre-Cyrille Hautcoeur, Susan Hyde, Margaret Levi, Bernard Manin, Abdul Noury, Jim Robinson, Ron Rogowski, Ken Scheve, Michael Sonenscher, Konstantin Sonin, Mike Tomz, as well as several anonymous readers for Princeton University Press.

I had the opportunity to present the manuscript to seminar audiences at Princeton University, Yale University, the Paris School of Economics, Harvard Business School, and Stanford University, all of whom gave invaluable reactions and comments. I also had the opportunity to present portions of work from the manuscript to audiences at Harvard University, New York University, Duke University, the University of British Columbia, the University of Pittsburgh, and Washington University in St. Louis, who were similarly generous with comments. In addition, my colleagues in the Department of Politics at NYU were a constant source of insight and encouragement. Also at NYU I would like to thank Chris Bowman, Sonke Ehret, James Hollyer, SunJeong Lee, and Tolga Sinmazdemir for excellent research assistance.

At Princeton University Press I would like to thank Seth Ditchik, Chuck Myers, and Janie Chan for all of their advice at each step of the editorial and production process. Also at Princeton University Press, Linda Truilo as copy editor offered extensive suggestions greatly helping to improve the final manuscript. I am particularly indebted to Joel Mokyr, the series editor, who at each step served as a patient guide as I sought to fashion a book that would address broad intellectual debates.

Finally, my greatest thanks go to my wife, Emmanuelle Ertel, who, in addition to pursuing her own projects, was always willing to listen and offer encouragement during the long period it took to bring this project to fruition.

States of Credit

CHAPTER ONE

Introduction

Among the many distinctive features of European state formation two have received particular attention—the invention of the concept of political representation and the development of a system of public credit. It is a matter of some debate whether Europe was unique in having a system of political representation—certainly rulers in other regions met with councils or assemblies—but it is probably not an exaggeration to say that this phenomenon initially advanced to its greatest extent in Europe. Likewise, while rulers in other regions developed mechanisms for deferring payment for goods or for receiving advances on tax collections, there seems little doubt that the most extensive early development of a system of public credit occurred in Europe. This parallel development of representation and credit suggests that a causal link might have existed between the two. Within Europe, states such as Venice or the Dutch Republic that are seen as models in the development of representative institutions can also be viewed as pioneers in the development of public credit, whereas polities such as France are considered as having trailed on both of these dimensions. Did the presence of an intensive form of representation facilitate access to credit for the former, allowing them to survive and their economies to prosper? If so, why did this intensive form of representation emerge in some places but not others? Finally, how did this joint development of credit and representation affect broader trends involving war, state formation, and economic growth? Despite the importance of these questions, no existing scholarly study examines these issues in a broad comparative context. This book is designed to fill that gap.

I will argue that the presence of an intensive form of representation characterized by an assembly that could monitor and modify expenditures was critical in facilitating access to credit by European states. But the existence of an assembly that would function in this manner was itself dependent on two underlying conditions. First, in an era of high communications and travel costs this intensive form of political representation could be maintained only in polities of limited geographic scale.[1] Second,

[1] The importance of geographic scale in conditioning the type of political representation that could be sustained in medieval Europe has been emphasized by the medieval historian Wim Blockmans (1998, 1978).

assemblies of this sort were more likely to take actions consistent with the interests of state creditors in polities where the same merchants who invested in government debt were also predominant among the political elite. These two underlying conditions were most frequently, but not exclusively and not always, met in city-states where assemblies could be convened by devices as simple as the ringing of a town bell and where the same merchants who purchased public debt also served as magistrates on town councils. In the territorial states of Europe, in strong contrast, geographic scale often proved to be a fundamental obstacle, making it costly to sustain a representative assembly that would meet frequently enough to monitor public expenditures. Assemblies in European territorial states could be powerful, but their influence was of a more passive form involving the ability to veto requests by monarchs for taxation. The social composition of territorial state assemblies was also fundamentally different from that of the city-states. Merchants—those who lent most frequently to government—played a more limited role within them, a fact that had significant consequences for the behavior of these institutions.

In making the above argument about representative institutions, I am not suggesting that the dominance of mercantile interests necessarily led to democracy within city-states.[2] Certainly, none of the city-states considered within this study had the full characteristics of either a modern representative democracy or an ancient direct democracy. But more importantly, even within the group of city-states considered here, I will show that those that were more oligarchical in form tended to have better access to credit than did those with more open systems of political representation. Both my broad sample statistical tests and my qualitative case studies suggest that having a merchant oligarchy was the best recipe for obtaining access to credit. In contrast, when popular pressures led to city-states adopting more open political systems in which those who were less likely to own public debt gained seats on city councils, then access to low-cost credit was less certain. This points to a trade-off: a certain set of political institutions could reinforce the credibility of debt repayment, but

---

[2]Authors have held very different views on this issue with some, such as Guizot (1838), seeing those who governed medieval cities as the ancestors of the French revolutionaries while many others following Pirenne (1910, 1925) have taken a more skeptical view. The subject of medieval and early modern city-states has been an issue of concern for a wide number of authors including Guizot (1838), Sidgwick (1903), Weber (1921), Clarke (1926), van Werveke (1963), Rokkan (1975, 1973), Tilly (1990), Tilly and Blockmans (1994), Spruyt (1994), and Finer (1995), to name but a select list.

these institutions were inherently undemocratic (even by the standards of the time), and, as I will argue, closed political institutions may in the long run have helped to stifle economic innovation.

My conclusions have implications for three debates involving state formation and economic development. The first debate involves the role of warfare in state formation, and in particular the proposition that as military technologies changed, the optimal size of a polity increased and the city-state became outmoded as a form of political organization. The second debate involves the sources of early modern economic growth and the question whether free cities were engines of innovation during this period. The third debate involves the question whether the adoption of representative or democratic institutions can helped solve commitment problems. I will first briefly introduce each of these debates before revisiting them in greater detail in the concluding chapter to this book.

In the first debate on war and state formation, conflict was according to a common narrative, the primary force driving state development within Europe. A key part of this argument is that exogenous changes in military technology—firearms, mass infantry, new styles of fortification— meant greater fixed costs in war-fighting, leading to an increase in the optimal size of states.[3] Many authors also suggest that war was a powerful force prompting rulers to alter the structure of their polity's political and bureaucratic institutions.[4] I will suggest that large size had both costs and benefits when it came to war mobilization, and therefore the effect of changes in military technology on the distribution and organization of European states was more muted than is commonly believed. As the size of armies required to engage in war increased, large states gained an advantage to the extent that they had large populations. However, in an era when armies were paid, rather than being conscripted, efforts to raise large armies also required the rapid mobilization of large sums of money. Access to credit was of the essence to meet this objective, and

---

[3]The clearest exposition of this argument can be found in Bean (1973), and his analysis was also adopted by North (1981). The same argument has been used by Boix, Codenotti, and Resta (2006) as a basis for their analysis. See Finer (1975) for an account of the relationship between state formation and what he calls the "format of the military forces."

[4]This has been emphasized at least since Hintze (1906) and more recently by authors such as Tilly (1975, 1990), Downing (1992), Ertman (1997), Mann (1986), and in a formal setting by Besley and Persson (2009, 2010). See Hui (2005) and Herbst (2000) for interesting accounts of the impact of war (or its absence) on state formation in other contexts.

here I will show that the smaller city-states had an advantage, because they established an intensive form of political representation in which merchants played a primary role. This same form of representation could not be maintained within the much larger geographic scale of a territorial state. It was arguably their better access to credit that allowed many city-states to survive far longer than we would expect, given the conventional "war and state formation" explanation. In the words of the noted German scholar Richard Ehrenberg (1928), "The credit of the cities therefore was accordingly their most powerful weapon in the struggle for their freedom."

The second debate with which this book engages concerns the sources of early modern growth.[5] Precisely because it is known that many economic innovations in Europe took place within politically autonomous cities, any explanation of how autonomous cities survived may aid our understanding of the political context for preindustrial growth. Discussions of city-states often emphasize their engagement in long-distance commerce. But many autonomous cities in Europe were also centers for technological innovation, and it may have been the case that political independence was necessary for this innovation to take place. One exposition of this idea is found in Mokyr (1995), who emphasizes that the initial development of Venice was attributable to its glassblowing industry, that other Italian towns were leaders in the production of textiles, that autonomous German cities were centers of instrument-making in the fifteenth and sixteenth centuries, and finally that Holland, in addition to being a trading state, was also an important site for invention.[6] Economic activity in autonomous cities may have been less subject to dynastic ambitions of a territorial ruler.[7] My study will not determine empirically whether autonomous cities did in fact experience higher average growth rates; instead my analysis of representation and credit will help account for the growth trajectory observed in many European autonomous cities—an initial period of innovation followed by one of economic stagnation. If those

[5] Acemoglu, Johnson, and Robinson (2005), Bosker, Buringh, and van Zanden (2008), Jones (1981), Mokyr (1995, 1994, 1990), North and Thomas (1973), North (1981), DeLong and Shleifer (1993), Epstein (2000), Voigtlaender and Voth (2009), Greif (2006), and Kohn (2008).

[6] See Hicks (1969) for an earlier expression of this idea with regard to the development of trade, and van Zanden (2006) as well as Bosker, Buringh, and van Zanden (2008) for empirical evidence. Many of the ideas about the economy of free cities can be traced back to Weber ([1921] 1958).

[7] Their institutions may also have facilitated enforcement of contracts for the reasons emphasized by Greif (2006). We should also recognize though that cities within territorial states also often had guild institutions or city councils that could have played a similar role.

cities that were the most closed and oligarchical in form had the best access to credit, then they may have been particularly likely to survive. Then again, oligarchical institutions may have created barriers to entry for groups or individuals with new innovations.[8] Over time, members of a sitting oligarchy may have shifted their investments from engagement in active commerce toward investments in lower-risk assets like land and government debt, prompting them to favor more inward-looking policies, again potentially leading to economic decline. Oligarchic politics may explain why, by the end of the early modern period, numerous autonomous cities continued to survive, but as rentier republics. These cities continued to have access to credit at excellent rates, but they were no longer engines of economic innovation.

The third debate for which my conclusions are relevant concerns the effect of institutions on commitment, and in particular the idea that one group or individual in society can concede a degree of control to another group and so solve a commitment problem. It has long been suggested that in the European historical context a strong representative assembly served as a commitment technology; it provided a guarantee against opportunistic actions involving the property rights of state creditors, or the property rights of private individuals more generally.[9] More recently, related arguments have been made about modern democracy being characterized by universal suffrage; it is viewed as a technology that allows commitment to a certain policy (in this case the economic policies preferred by the median voter).[10] Common explanations offered for why we do not observe such institutional solutions whenever a commitment problem emerges refer either to the power of vested interests or to the fixed costs involved in creating an institution. My conclusions remind us of a third possibility—maintaining an institution may also have important ongoing costs. If for exogenous reasons these costs are too high, then either the institution will not emerge, or emerge but fail to solve the commitment problem. In medieval and early modern

---

[8]This idea is nearly as widely expressed as is the argument that city institutions facilitated growth; see Mokyr (1995, 1990), Epstein (2000), and Hicks (1969). See Acemoglu (2008) for a formalization of this idea in a more general context and Dessi and Ogilvie (2004) and Ogilvie (2007) for considerations of the stifling effect of municipal guild institutions on growth.

[9]North and Thomas (1973), North (1981), Levi (1988), North and Weingast (1989), Delong and Shleifer (1993), and Acemoglu, Johnson, and Robinson (2005). This argument is not without its critics including Epstein (2000), Clark (1996, 2007), and Sussman and Yafeh (2006).

[10]Acemoglu and Robinson (2006, 2000).

Europe the ongoing costs of maintaining an intensive form of political representation were prohibitively high in large polities, given the state of communications and travel technology. Today, for much (but not all) of the globe, geographic scale is no longer as much of an obstacle as it once was, but the underlying point remains; for representative government to function effectively individuals need access to information, and acquiring information can be costly - in some cases prohibitively so.

As a final step before proceeding further, given that my analysis places heavy emphasis on the difference between territorial states and city-states, it is worth pausing to say exactly how I will define a city-state for the purposes of this book. In its medieval and early modern European form a city-state was a city that exerted a substantial degree of autonomy over its economic and judicial affairs while also playing a key role in organizing its own defense. A city state might control territory outside the city walls, but political rights were restricted to inhabitants of the core city (a key difference with the classical polis). While it is useful to have an abstract definition of a city-state, it is important to recognize that autonomous cities within Europe each had their individual characteristics and relationships with outside powers, and in practice cities had varying degrees of autonomy with respect to princely overlords. The question is at what point should we say that a city with a degree of autonomy should nonetheless not be included in my dataset because it lacked sufficient independence? In constructing my sample I have chosen deliberately to cast a wide net, including both cities such as Florence and Venice that had essentially total autonomy, together with several Flemish and other cities that had much autonomy in practice but also a degree of subservience to princely overlords. The motivation for this choice is to avoid a potential bias in which I draw a general conclusion while focusing only on a restricted set of cities that come the closest to approximating a city-state in its ideal form. I will also discuss how my statistical results change when those cities that lacked full autonomy are dropped from the sample. In practice this sample change actually strengthens the results in favor of my main arguments.

REPRESENTATION, SCALE, AND CONTROL

Before proceeding with the historical analysis, it may first be useful to describe the problem I seek to analyze in a more abstract fashion. In chapter 4, I will provide a very simple game theoretic formalization of the following problem. Consider a polity in which an executive, who might be either a monarch or a ruling magistrate, seeks to borrow money to wage war, either of an offensive or defensive nature. In this polity some individuals hold liquid wealth that can be readily invested in debt. In order for these individuals to purchase debt, they need some expectation that once money is lent, any policy actions taken will be consistent with the goal of eventually repaying the debt. This could, for example, imply that the executive cannot use too much of the money for personal consumption, should not engage in overly expensive military engagements, and must raise sufficient revenues. Finally, it may also be necessary for the executive to alter policies in response to unforeseen events, such as a dramatic shortfall in revenues. A potential solution to this contracting problem between the executive and lenders would be for the lenders to specify in advance a full course of action that the executive should take. But even if such a contract could be enforced, the difficulty is that the ideal future course of action may not be known in advance.

Given the infeasibility of such a contract, one alternative might be for the executive to concede a degree of control over future policy to the lenders. In the event, for example, that there is an unexpected shortfall in revenues, then lenders would have an assurance that a corrective action, such as reducing military expenditures or raising revenues, would actually be taken. In the literature on corporate finance this is often referred to as granting a control right. Granting control rights can improve access to finance when investors anticipate that a manager would face incentives not to follow their desired course of action, yet investors do not know in advance precisely what action they prefer.[11] In the historical context that I am considering, a representative assembly that has a prerogative to monitor and modify public expenditures might serve this function. Without third-party enforcement, in order for such a system to induce individuals to lend they would need to anticipate that the executive would actually be willing to let an assembly exercise control in this fashion. This is perhaps the most obvious reason why conceding a control right might have

---

[11]On the importance of control rights in corporate finance two canonical contributions are Hart and Moore (1998) and Aghion and Bolton (1992). For recent text book treatments see Tirole (2006: ch.10) and Bolton and Dewatripont (2005: ch.11). As discussed by Tirole, the importance of control rights is often demonstrated by referring to a situation where contracts are incomplete, but this does not have to be the case.

little effect in facilitating access to credit. But there may also be a second obstacle that is equally important and that is less frequently recognized—it may be prohibitively costly to maintain the intensive form of political representation that would be implied by this arrangement. If the literature on corporate finance emphasizes that allowing monitoring increases access to finance, it also emphasizes that engaging in monitoring may be costly.[12]

In the historical context that I am considering, where travel and communications costs were substantially higher than they are today, there is ample reason to believe that geographic scale could be a fundamental obstacle to lenders exercising a control right. If lenders are geographically dispersed then there may be substantial costs involved in sending representatives to an assembly. Even if these costs could be overcome, for example, by paying representatives and by sharing this cost among a large number of people, there would remain the issue of monitoring the representatives. As long as representatives are subject to moral hazard, say because they can be bribed by the executive, then monitoring of this sort will be necessary. Nor would concentration of lenders in a country's capital necessarily solve the problem if the activities they need to monitor are geographically dispersed.

In addition to the costs imposed by geographic scale, the cost that lenders face in exercising a control right will also depend critically upon their relative influence within a representative assembly. Medieval and early modern assemblies sometimes resembled committees of state creditors, but in many cases they were instead dominated by other social interests. In large territorial states the more common phenomenon was to have an assembly in which those holding landed wealth were the preponderant element. In such cases merchants would find it costly or impossible to influence policy.

The above discussion leads to the following conclusion: a high cost incurred by a representative for exercising a control right, as brought about by geography, for example, will have three effects: (1) a lower likelihood of an intensive form of political representation, (2) higher interest rates on debt, and (3) less likelihood that debt will be issued. This book will test each of these three predictions empirically.

---

[12]For an example see Holmstrom and Tirole (1997) for a model where monitoring improves access to finance but monitoring is costly, and these costs are passed on to borrowers.

THE EVOLUTION AND IMPORTANCE OF PUBLIC CREDIT

When considering medieval and early modern Europe, it is widely argued that imperatives of war drove states both to improve revenue collection and to seek access to credit. What presents a potential puzzle about public borrowing is that despite its general usefulness, some European states succeeded in establishing a public debt much earlier than others, and in addition, the relative cost of debt finance for different states varied enormously.[13] While the imperatives of war existed from an early date, European states before 1000 initially faced a constraint in that there were few private individuals or entities with liquid wealth that could be used to provide credit. Between 1000 and 1300, Europe experienced an economic expansion, accompanied by growth of commerce, that altered this picture. With some simplification, we can say that two forms of public borrowing then emerged.[14] Some states, especially territorial monarchies, began to contract loans directly from international merchants.[15] These loans had two main characteristics: they were short-term, and they were contracted at very high rates of interest. The loans from Italian bankers to Edward III during the Hundred Years' War provide a well-known example. Other states, especially city-states, succeeded in taking the further step of establishing a long-term debt. In the case of the Italian city-states, this involved forced loans that nonetheless paid interest, and for which an active secondary market soon developed. Outside of Italy, city-states obtained finance by issuing annuities (referred to as *rentes* in French or *renten* in Dutch and German). Strictly speaking, these were not loans. The contracts involved the permanent transfer of a specific sum to the "borrower" in exchange for the "lender" receiving a regular income stream, alternatively for one lifetime, several lives, or in perpetuity. One reason why this type of contract was preferred was that since the principal was never repaid, it did not run as easily afoul of usury restrictions as

---

[13]Hicks (1969), Parker (1974), and, more recently, Macdonald (2003) have also emphasized the idea that the timing of the establishment of a long-term public debt in different states presents an important empirical puzzle.

[14]See Usher (1943), Ehrenberg ([1928] 1963), Munro (2003), Tracy (2003), Homer and Sylla (1996), Fryde and Fryde (1963), and Macdonald (2003) for surveys of the evolution of public credit in Europe.

[15]Loans from Jewish lenders also served as a short-term high-interest source of loans for European monarchs. However, by the end of the thirteenth century, monarchs instead found it preferable to heavily tax, and eventually confiscate, Jewish assets.

was the case with conventional loans.[16] Contracts based on rentes also became a major source of finance for those seeking to make agricultural improvements, again based on the exchange of a sum in exchange for a future income stream. In what follows I will compare the rates at which governments could issue rentes against rates prevailing for private finance. The Northern European model of the rentes in fact became the model for public debt in Europe up to the end of the nineteenth century. Within city-states merchants were major purchasers of these long-term debts. It has been argued that after establishing themselves in commerce, merchants had an incentive to diversify their asset holdings by purchasing public annuities that would provide a regular stream of income.[17] It was also critical that merchants held wealth that was liquid and which could thus be swiftly converted into government annuities if a city-state suddenly needed to expand its level of borrowing.

While the idea of long-term public borrowing emerged at an early date, either following the Italian model or the annuities model, the speed with which European states gained access to this type of finance varied tremendously, as did the financial terms that states found it necessary to concede to lenders. We have numerous records of self-governing cities in Italy, the Low Countries, and northern France issuing debt starting in the thirteenth century, and cities or towns in Germany, Switzerland, and Catalonia in the fourteenth century. In contrast, among larger territorial states, Castile did not begin to issue long-term debt until the very end of the fifteenth century, and the French monarchy did not establish a long-term debt until 1522. In the words of Geoffrey Parker, "It was a surprisingly long time before princes were able to emulate their towns."[18] When they did establish a long-term debt, territorial states also appear to have paid significantly higher interest rates than did their city-state counterparts.

One possible explanation for this differential development is that there were greater legal and technical obstacles to the development of long-term debt in territorial states, but important studies by Ehrenberg ([1928] 1963) and Fryde and Fryde (1963) both argue that princes in medieval

[16] See Munro (2003) for an extended discussion of this point, as well as a review of other barriers to the development of markets for public annuities.

[17] See Postan (1952: 216–18) for an example of this argument, as well as the discussion in Kohn (1999).

[18] Parker (1974: 567). The significant time lag between the establishment of long-term debts in city-republics and in territorial monarchies has also been emphasized by Hicks (1969: 94).

territorial states had from a very early date evolved the principle of granting specific individuals a fixed income stream from their revenues in exchange for a service. Evidence reviewed by Usher (1943) demonstrates that the French monarchy was paying annuities to certain bodies as early as 1332, yet it took another two centuries before French monarchs used this same system to establish a long-term public debt.[19] So, it remains to be explained why princes were so slow to take the logical next step of granting a fixed income stream in exchange for a financial service. It also seems unlikely that princes would have preferred to opt for short-term borrowing, given the clear constraints implied by this type of finance, both in terms of its high cost and limited ability to leverage current resources. The more likely explanation I will pursue is that territorial rulers did not establish a long-term debt earlier because no one was willing to lend to them on such terms.

The financial advantage enjoyed by city-states had several important implications. The most direct of these was that access to credit allowed city-states to survive in an era of constant warfare and in the face of larger enemies. Access to borrowing was particularly important. Armies needed to be paid, because from an early date methods of raising forces through obligatory means—either feudal obligations or militia membership in cities—proved insufficient for the task at hand. The need for defense expenditures also often appeared suddenly and unexpectedly, and it was generally impossible to substantially augment tax revenues within a sufficiently short time frame.

REPRESENTATIVE ASSEMBLIES IN CITY-STATES AND TERRITORIAL STATES

While the English parliamentary experience is the most frequently studied, it is now recognized that a very large number of medieval and early modern

---

[19] See Usher (1943: 162–63), who draws his evidence from de Boislisle (1875). In terms of legal obstacles, some authors also refer to the fact that credibility of the debts of city-states was reinforced by a principle whereby individual merchants within a city could be held personally liable by third parties and have their assets seized if their municipality defaulted on its financial obligations. However, as Greif (2006) demonstrates, this "community responsibility system" undergirded trade and commerce in a very wide number of medieval European communities. As a result, it was not specific to city-states. The unlimited liability principle also had less applicability when debts were held by a city's own residents, as was usually the case.

European political entities had representative assemblies that often had significant prerogatives. The period between 1250 and 1500 in particular is highlighted as having experienced a flowering of assemblies across Europe, both in self-governing cities and in larger territorial entities.[20] While territorial states tended to have a single assembly with varying procedures for selecting members, city-states often had a hierarchy of representative bodies, including a general city council made up of a broad membership, as well as one or more smaller bodies of magistrates chosen through a variety of means. Georges de Lagarde (1937, 1939) referred to this period as a "corporatist age" characterized by spontaneous action of different social groups seeking recognition from princes. For the period after 1500 until the end of the eighteenth century, scholars often point to a progressive weakening of representative institutions, in particular in the larger territorial states of Europe. Historians like de Lagarde (1937) have referred to this later era as the "age of the territorial state."

Historians have given much attention to the development of representative institutions in Europe during the two above periods, producing detailed studies of individual assemblies, general overviews, as well as studies comparing a small number of states. But there have been few attempts to provide a broad and systematic empirical picture of the evolution of representation in Europe. Drawing on existing historical work, this book presents a new dataset that provides systematic information about the prerogatives and level of activity of representative assemblies in a broad number of European states. These data help to show how representative institutions evolved over time, and how they varied across different types of states. They also allow us to examine specific prerogatives, such as the ability to refuse new taxes, to intervene in the administration of tax collection, or to monitor both state debt and expenditures. Finally, the data also provide some insight into the selection of members for an assembly and the representation of different social groups. Such information will be particularly important for distinguishing between those city-states that had more oligarchical institutions and those in which participation was more open. The data that I present certainly contain errors and misinterpretations for individual cases. I cannot pretend to be

[20] See Bisson (1973), de Lagarde (1937, 1939), Lousse (1937, 1966), Marongiu (1968), Major (1960), Blockmans (1978, 1998), Gilissen (1969), and Graves (2001). This pattern of representation has also been emphasized in more general treatments of medieval state development, such as the classic study by Strayer (1970). See also the fascinating recent study by Boucoyannis (2006).

a historian of medieval and early modern Europe, let alone a specialist of each of the 31 entities considered in constructing this dataset. Future observations by commentators may help to correct mistakes in my coding or spur efforts toward the collection of more detailed and accurate data. With this said, the evidence presented here still provides a broad and systematic picture of political representation of a sort that has not existed before. With regard to errors and misinterpretations of individual cases, the most important question to ask is whether they are pervasive enough to bias my broad conclusions.

The evidence I have collected demonstrates how representation within city-states took on a much more intensive form than was the case in territorial states. Representative bodies in city-states met frequently, and they played an active role in monitoring not only taxation but also public spending and borrowing. If a representative body is to exert a degree of control over public finances to this extent, then it seems plausible to suggest that the assembly will need to meet frequently. In larger territorial states it was rare to see assemblies meet even annually. A representative assembly that did not meet frequently could still play a powerful role, for example, by refusing to consent to taxation, but this power should be distinguished from the more intensive type of political representation found in city-states. Those territorial state assemblies that came the closest to city-state assemblies in terms of the prerogatives they exercised tended to exist in small polities.

While representative institutions in city-states had strong commonalities in terms of their control over public finances, there were also very significant differences within this group of states, with some cities having more open institutions and others having more closed, oligarchical regimes. Many city-states were dominated by merchant oligarchies. A small group of merchants held control of a city's key decision-making body, with this power often reinforced by a formal stipulation that members of this group should hold a preponderance, or even the totality of seats, on the council. In such cases representatives were often selected by a system of cooptation; an outgoing group of representatives would choose the incoming group, a procedure that tended to reinforce the dominance of one group. Other independent cities had more open constitutions where representatives were selected by a broader electorate of the citizenry and where rules of procedure stipulated that members of the craft guilds should also hold a significant share of positions, instead of reserving these predominantly for merchants. The structure of city-state constitutions was often a source of bitter conflict among these different groups. It was also directly related to the question of public debt, because merchants tended to own debt whereas members of the craft guilds bore a significant part of the tax burden necessary to service this debt. One of the main conclusions I will arrive at in this study is that those city-states with more oligarchical institutions actually tended to have better access to credit than those with more open regimes.

GEOGRAPHIC SCALE AND MERCHANT POWER

Ultimately, if representative bodies in city-states were more effective mechanisms in providing access to credit than were those in territorial states, this is not something that happened by accident. I will argue that it was an outcome dependent on two underlying conditions: the small size of these polities and the wealth composition of their political elite. My emphasis on the importance of the types of wealth held by a state's political elite fits closely with the arguments made in my earlier work on public debt and political representation in France and Great Britain during the eighteenth century (Stasavage 2003). But while my earlier work investigated the structure of political coalitions within two territorial states, the present book has as its goal to make a broader comparison between two different types of political entities that coexisted within Europe. By considering the importance of geographic scale, I also hope to shed light on the origins of representative institutions in a way that my earlier work did not.

Given premodern technologies for communications and transport, geographic scale posed a substantial obstacle to regularly convening a representative assembly. In this respect, city-states had an undoubted advantage over their larger neighbors.[21] Within many cities it was possible to have an assembly that was summoned by a simple device like a bell. So, for example, the General Council in thirteenth-century Siena was also known as the "Council of the Bell" for precisely this reason.[22] In a large territorial state this was obviously not possible. We have abundant historical evidence pointing to transport and communication costs as a hindrance to frequent meetings of premodern European assemblies. In chapter 3, I will present systematic evidence suggesting first that assemblies in city-states met more frequently than assemblies in territorial states.

---

[21] As noted above, the importance of scale in conditioning the development of representative institutions in Europe has been emphasized by Blockmans (1978, 1998).

[22] See Bowsky (1981: 85)

I will then show that within the group of territorial states, we also observe a strong negative correlation between state size and meeting frequency.

The proposition that either democracy or republican government is more likely to be sustainable in small polities is a very old one, and scholars who have subscribed to this argument have emphasized several different mechanisms, including the effect of scale on opportunities for participation, on the ability of citizens to know one another, and on the heterogeneity of a population.[23] In this study I make a more specific claim about the ability of members of a polity to sustain a representative assembly that exerts a degree of constitutional control over the actions of an executive, whether the executive is a ruling magistrate or a monarch. I also emphasize one specific mechanism: prior to the advent of modern technologies for travel and communications, the costs for representatives of attending an assembly in a far-off capital could prove prohibitive. Even if these costs could be overcome, geographic scale posed serious obstacles to the ability of constituents to monitor their representatives.

City-states also differed fundamentally from territorial states in a second way—the types of wealth held by their political elite. Historical work has long emphasized a distinction between city-states, where merchants predominated, and territorial states, which were dominated by a landowning and rural nobility.[24] This same body of work emphasizes that in most of Western Europe, members of the landowning nobility lived outside of the cities, breaking with a pattern set under the Roman Empire.[25] This broad distinction should not be overdone. Political elites in territorial states did not hold only land, and political elites in city-states did not have only liquid forms of wealth. There is evidence that the rich within city-states often had significant landholdings in addition to their financial and commercial investments. However, if we accept that land composed the vast majority of wealth in Europe at this time and that more liquid

---

[23] For examples in Rousseau's thought, see *Considérations sur le Gouvernement de Pologne* (Éditions Pléiade, 1964, *Oeuvres complètes* 3: 970–73) as well as *Du Contrat Social* (Éditions Pléiade, 1964 *Oeuvres complètes* 3: 386–87). For Montesquieu's views on the subject, see *De l'Esprit des Lois* (Éditions Pléiade, 1949, *Oeuvres complètes,* 2: 362–63). See Dahl and Tufte (1973) and Zagarri (1987) for general reviews of debates on size and democracy.

[24] Pirenne (1910, 1925), Guizot (1838), Weber ([1921] 1958), Sidgwick (1903), Van Werveke (1963), and Finer (1995).

[25] For the most recent authoritative discussion of this issue see Wickham (2005). For earlier treatments see Weber ([1921] 1958: 95), Pirenne (1910), Sidgwick (1903), and Van Werveke (1963). The principal exceptions to this pattern were northern Italy and sections of southern France.

forms of wealth were concentrated in cities, then it would seem difficult to dispute the idea that members of the elite within city-states were more likely to have wealth that could easily be invested in an asset like public debt. The composition of elite wealth had direct implications for the politics of public debt in city-states and territorial states. Within city-states there was a pool of potential investors in public debt, and the small size of these states meant that active representative institutions could be sustained that allowed creditors to exert a degree of control over public finances. Territorial states also had numerous individuals with liquid wealth, but given the overwhelming presence of landowners, these individuals made up a much smaller section of the political elite than they did in city-states. Even if a representative institution existed in a territorial state, owners of liquid wealth would have difficulty exercising influence within it.

Broad Sample Evidence

I will support my arguments by presenting and analyzing systematic data on public credit and political representation for 31 European states over the five centuries between 1250 and 1750. To collect the evidence on public credit, which is presented in chapter 2, I began by consulting the sources used by Stephan Epstein (2000). In an important study, Epstein constructed a comparative dataset of interest rates for his review of public debt in Europe over the long run. Consulting these sources and comparing them with all available alternative sources allowed me to construct a dataset that extends Epstein's work. This new dataset includes several new states; it covers a broader period of time for others; and it is more precise in several areas of measurement. The dataset distinguishes between different types of debt instruments (such as life versus perpetual annuities) and different methods that individual authors have used to calculate interest rates (such as recording nominal rates versus using a fiscal interest rate proxy).

In chapter 3, I present new systematic evidence on the evolution and prerogatives of representative assemblies in the same set of 31 states, and I will place this evidence in the context of long-standing debates about the emergence of representative institutions in Europe. For each state I use available evidence from secondary sources to assess whether a representative assembly existed, whether its consent was required for new taxes to be implemented, whether the assembly played a direct role in administering taxes, and whether the assembly played a direct role with respect to the issuance and management of public debt. Finally, the chapter also presents evidence on who was represented within these assemblies, in addition to charting the frequency with which assemblies met. There is evidence not only that city-state assemblies met more frequently, but also that within the group of territorial states, there was a negative correlation between the geographic size of the polity and the intensity of representative activity.

Chapter 4 presents the results of my core statistical tests combining the evidence on the evolution of public credit with evidence on political representation. The goal here is to test three alternative hypotheses: (1) that access to credit depended on commercial and economic development, (2) that access to credit depended on the presence of active representative institutions; and finally (3) that access to credit depended on the differing underlying conditions in city-states and territorial states. I first consider the conditions under which a state was more likely to create a long-term public debt. This is followed by a consideration of the determinants of the cost of government borrowing. As one would expect, the data show a strong correlation between commercial and economic development and access to credit. Beyond this effect, there is also clear evidence from these regressions that the presence of a representative assembly, and in particular one that had a control-right over debt and expenditures, was associated with earlier creation of a long-term debt. However, once one controls for the difference between city-states and territorial states, this correlation between assemblies and credit disappears. One finds a very similar pattern with respect to the cost of borrowing. These results do not automatically imply that representative institutions did not matter. What they do mean is that if representation did matter, then it was, above all, the type of political representation found within city-states that favored access to credit.

The tests in chapter 4 identify a clear and consistent difference between city-states and territorial states. Based on these estimates, in any half-century period, a city-state that had not already created a public debt would be expected to have a 43% chance of doing so. A territorial state would have only a 5% chance of doing so. Comparing states that actually did borrow, I find that a city-state would be estimated to borrow at an interest rate two percentage points lower than a territorial state. The fact that a dummy variable for city-states is statistically significant in these regressions may be capturing the effect of the two factors I emphasize, small geographic scale and merchant political power, but it may also of course simply reflect other differences between these two types of states. One way I guard against this possibility is to use an extensive set of controls for different levels of economic and commercial development, as proxied by urbanization rates.

Chapter 4 also presents a further analysis that examines variation within city-states, in particular between those with more closed institutions of selection where rules stipulated that merchant groups would dominate a representative body, versus those with more open constitutions that allowed significant participation for members of craft guilds. As explained earlier, we would expect these two groups to have potentially different views on debt servicing given that merchants tended to own public debt and members of the craft guilds tended to bear a significant share of the tax burden necessary to service debt. In a set of fixed effects estimates that focus on change within states over time, I show that the greater the percentage of city council seats formally reserved for merchants, the lower the cost of borrowing. Likewise, selection of representatives by cooptation was associated with significantly lower borrowing costs than was selection by election. Both of these findings are consistent with the case study evidence that I present in later chapters.

Origins of City-States

So far, while my story has emphasized the differences between city-states and territorial states, I have not considered why some European cities enjoyed a high degree of political independence while others were subject to control by territorial rulers. Nor have I broached the question of why city-states emerged in only some European regions. These questions are intrinsically interesting. Addressing them is also critical because of the potential implications for my core causal claims. It might be that initial economic, political, or social conditions allowed some cities to establish their political independence while simultaneously favoring the development of public credit. If I did not control for these initial conditions in my statistical analysis, it could lead me to overestimate the effect of representative institutions, and perhaps also the effect of geographic scale and merchant political power. Two main types of initial conditions come to mind. The first involves the possibility that, for idiosyncratic reasons, some cities had attributes that facilitated attempts by their populations to act collectively to establish autonomy. Such attributes may well also have facilitated attempts to establish a public debt. The second possibility involves the initial level of economic development. Scholars have long observed that Europe's city-states emerged in a longitudinal band running roughly from northern Italy to the Low Countries. In recent decades Charles Tilly (1990) and Stein Rokkan (1975, 1973) have provided the leading explanation for this pattern of state development.[26] According to them, this region of Europe had a higher initial level of development (ca. 1000 A.D.) allowing cities to form, to establish their autonomy, and to resist efforts of territorial princes (or of other cities) to absorb them into larger states.

Rokkan and Tilly focus on prior economic events, but there were also prior political events in Europe that had a major impact on the subsequent pattern of state development. Historians have for many years emphasized that the lines of partition decided upon during the partition of the Carolingian Empire in the middle of the ninth century A.D. had long-lasting consequences for the political map of Europe.[27] By the signing of the Treaty of Verdun in 843, the Carolingian Empire was divided among three brothers into three kingdoms, each of which covered a longitudinal strip of Europe. The western kingdom covered much of modern-day France. The eastern kingdom covered much of modern-day Germany. The central kingdom, Lotharingia, covered a narrow longitudinal strip running between the other two. While the heart of the Carolingian Empire lay within Lotharingia, this central kingdom collapsed soon after its creation as a result of a series of idiosyncratic dynastic incidents; this collapse left Europe's central longitudinal band as a fragmented border region. I will use the division line laid out at the Treaty of Meersen in 870, which brought about the end of the middle kingdom, as a measure of location in this region. I will argue that the collapse of Lotharingia facilitated attempts several centuries later by cities within this zone to establish political autonomy. It should be emphasized that, I am certainly not claiming that the pattern of Carolingian collapse was the sole determinant of future city-state development in Europe, but it was an important determinant of this phenomenon and one that has not been sufficiently emphasized.

In chapter 5, I test the above two hypotheses about city-state origins while also considering several additional factors that may have favored

---

[26] See also Tilly's introductory chapter in Tilly and Blockmans (1994).

[27] See Pirenne (1936: 86–91) for an early example.

city-state development. The tests are based on the sample of 31 states used throughout this book, as well as on a much larger sample of 158 European cities. To my knowledge this is the first systematic test of the correlates of city-state development. The evidence does indeed suggest that city-states were more likely to emerge in areas with a high initial level of urbanization. But proximity to the Meersen dividing line appears to have had an even larger effect on the likelihood that a city would establish political autonomy. Proximity to the Meersen line continues to be a statistically significant predictor of city-state development even when multiple controls for initial urbanization are included in the specification. The reverse is not true. I conclude the chapter by presenting a set of instrumental variables estimates that use distance from the Meersen partition line as an instrumental variable for city-state development. This estimation strategy should be most effective at ascertaining whether my conclusions regarding the financial advantage of city-states are biased by the failure to control for idiosyncratic factors that lowered barriers to collective action in some cities. We should be considerably more cautious in suggesting that this estimation strategy also controls for the second endogeneity problem referred to earlier—that city-states simply emerged in areas that were more economically developed to begin with. This book presents a wealth of additional evidence that can be used to form a judgment on this latter issue. Finally, I should emphasize again that the primary goal of chapter 5 is not to develop an instrumental variable even more exotic than those that have gone before it. It is instead to launch an empirical investigation of why city-states emerged in some places but not others and to propose a new explanation that, while certainly preliminary, has clear empirical support.

CASE STUDY EVIDENCE

The case study evidence in chapters 6 and 7 complements the statistical evidence of the previous chapters by providing a much closer look at the mechanisms at play in individual polities. While I make no claim to expanding dramatically the knowledge of any of the individual cases considered in these chapters, I do also believe that the breadth of the comparisons presented here is novel in form. Chapter 6 considers three city-states: Cologne, Genoa, and Siena. All three of these cities had the sort of representative political institutions that could serve as an effective mechanism for creditors to exercise a degree of control over state finances.

All three cities also established public debt at an early date. The question is whether there was actually any causal link between these developments. Chapter 7 investigates the obstacles to public credit in three territorial states: France, Castile, and the Dutch Republic.

The city-state cases in chapter 6 provide further evidence that the city-state advantage in borrowing was dependent not only on the presence of merchants; it was also dependent on them having political control. In fact, it was those city-states with the most closed and oligarchical political institutions, dominated by merchants, that enjoyed the best access to credit. City-states with more open, democratic institutions with broad participation often found access to credit more difficult. In Cologne, Genoa, and Siena public debt, and in particular the taxes required to service debt, were a subject of frequent and sometimes violent political contestation. With some risk of simplification, we can speak of an underlying conflict between mercantile groups who held public annuities, and who sought to ensure that taxes would be levied to service these obligations, and other social groups who protested against heavy indirect taxes on common consumption goods. Disputes about public finances were often coupled with conflict over the structure of representative institutions in each city and with the question of which social groups should be represented on city councils. Should these bodies retain an oligarchical form with a small number of individuals in control, or should they instead be opened to other groups and in particular craft guild representatives? When uprisings were successful in at least temporarily overthrowing existing regimes, this had direct negative consequences for public credit. Such shifts in government triggered unilateral interest rate reductions, partial defaults, or adverse swings in market prices for government debt.

Cologne presents a prototypical example where a political elite with a significant engagement in commerce invested heavily in public annuities while simultaneously retaining an oligarchic control of the city's political institutions. Cologne was also a particularly long-lasting city-state. It retained a high degree of political independence through the end of the eighteenth century. The case of Cologne provides particularly fascinating evidence about the importance of creditor interests controlling the city council, because creditors did temporarily lose political power as a consequence of a revolt in 1513, and one policy consequence of this change in regime was a partial default on public debt.

Genoa was atypical among the city-states considered in this study in that after 1407 management of both its debt and revenues was delegated to an independent corporation, the Casa di San Giorgio. I will argue that while the establishment of the Casa di San Giorgio may have been crucial for Genoa's subsequent financial success, the Casa was not an institution that somehow insulated Genoese public finances from Genoese politics. As emphasized by Jacques Heers (1961), the success of the Casa was instead ultimately dependent on the fact that mercantile interests held prominence both within the Casa and within the institutions of the Genoese Republic itself. In other words, the Casa di San Giorgio existed and prospered because Genoa had a dominant mercantile elite that controlled Genoese political institutions.

Siena, as the third city-state to be considered, provides a contrast to the examples of financial success presented by Cologne and Genoa. During the years between 1287 and 1355, Siena was ruled by a merchant oligarchical regime that bore many resemblances to the regimes in the other states considered here. Siena also provides an example of how a popular uprising could result in an enduring change of regime with negative consequences for public finances. After a revolution in 1355, a series of regimes ruled the city, many of which had a significant element of popular control, and none of which was characterized by the dominance of a merchant oligarchy. After 1355 Siena experienced a period of unstable public finances to match its political turmoil. Siena attests to the significance of merchant political control for public credit, precisely because this is an instance where a merchant elite lost power.

Among the three territorial states considered in chapter 7, France and Castile have traditionally been referred to as lacking creditworthiness while the Dutch Republic has been seen as a model in the development of public credit. One common way to explain this variance in outcomes is to refer to institutional differences; the Dutch Republic succeeded because it was a republic with a strong representative assembly, whereas the rulers of France and Castile were "absolute" monarchs facing few institutional constraints. I will argue that there were more institutional similarities between these three cases than is commonly realized. Executives in all three states were subject to significant institutional constraints on their authority. The difference was that in the Dutch Republic, small geographic scale made it possible for representatives of an assembly to monitor executive actions intensively. In France and Castile, by contrast, geographical scale was much more of an obstacle.

My investigation of France will focus on an interesting aspect of the French monarchy's attempts to create a long-term public debt. France's national representative institution, the Estates General, met very infrequently, and there is little evidence that its members demonstrated sympathies for state creditors when it convened. Though France lacked an active national assembly, at the municipal level in Paris a system for issuing public annuities developed from a very early date, and it was by making use of this system that the French monarchy first established a long-term debt in 1522.[28] As remarked by Cauwès (1895) this system of issuing *rentes sur l'Hôtel de Ville* bore a very close resemblance to the practice in states where active representative assemblies controlled public debt. The problem was that the system of rentes sur l'Hôtel de Ville failed once an attempt was made to expand its scale so that the magistrates of Paris were expected to monitor revenue collection in more distant locations. The problem was not that France lacked the right institutions; it was that France was simply too big.

For consistency, in my broad sample statistical analysis I have classified the Dutch Republic as a territorial state, but whether one decided to call it a city-state, a territorial state, a league of cities, or some other hybrid form, the more fundamental point is that the experience of the Dutch Republic strongly supports the core argument of this book. As numerous scholars have emphasized, the Dutch Republic during the sixteenth century was essentially a confederation in which individual cities remained politically predominant, and the governing bodies of these municipalities were run by merchant oligarchies who themselves invested heavily in public credit. The Dutch Republic was also characterized by a high intensity of representative activity, but there was nothing revolutionary about this development. There is evidence that from a very early date, well before the Dutch revolt against Habsburg rule, representative activity at the regional level in the Low Countries was favored by the geographic proximity of major cities.

As a final case, I consider developments in Castile during the sixteenth century in light of events in the Dutch Republic. Recent historical work undermines the existing argument about absolutism and the Spanish monarchy's difficulties in obtaining credit. First, the Spanish monarchy's debt behavior prior to 1598 was less disastrous than received wisdom suggests, although for the period after 1598 this was not the case.[29] Second, in formal terms, representative political institutions in Castile actually had striking similarities with those in Holland. Much like

---

[28] This episode has also been considered recently in a fascinating study by vam Malle-Sabouret (2008).

[29] Drelichman and Voth (2008 a, b).

the States of Holland (the most prominent provincial assembly in the Dutch Republic) by the sixteenth century, the Cortes of Castile was dominated by urban representatives chosen from a fixed set of towns. It also had very significant prerogatives with regard to the approval of taxation and the administration of revenue collection. Unlike the States of Holland, however, the Cortes never succeeded in establishing itself as an effective monitor of public spending, despite efforts to the contrary. One prominent reason for this failure may have involved the fact that the Spanish crown had another source of revenge—imports of precious metals from the New World—there by reducing its dependence on Cortes.[30] I will suggest that geographic scale presented a further fundamental obstacle to the establishment of a more intensive form of political representation in Spain.

PLAN OF THE BOOK

In this chapter I have presented the questions I address, my core argument, and the evidence used to support it. The remaining chapters proceed in the following fashion. Chapters 2 and 3 discuss the importance and evolution of public credit, and consider the emergence of representative institutions in Europe. In these chapters I present the data I have collected covering a sample of 31 states. Chapter 4 then presents an econometric analysis using this data, and it tests my argument about geographic scale and merchant political power against the alternatives. Chapter 5 pursues the next logical step by considering the origins of city-states. Chapters 6 and 7 then present the case study evidence. Chapter 8 concludes by discussing the implications of this study for debates about state formation, institutions, and development.

---

[30] This effect has been emphasized by Drelichman and Voth (2007).

CHAPTER TWO

The Evolution and Importance of Public Credit

This chapter reviews reasons why access to credit was important for European states, and it provides extensive new evidence on the evolution of public credit across five centuries, from 1250 to 1750. In this analysis there is a clear difference between city-states and territorial states, with city-states enjoying an apparent financial advantage that allowed them to begin borrowing earlier and to obtain access to lower-cost finance. This raises the possibility that the financial advantage of city-states depended on features of their representative institutions—the subject that I will take up in subsequent chapters.

WHY CREDIT WAS IMPORTANT

The ability to borrow was critical in medieval and early modern Europe because it allowed states to participate in wars, either defensive or offensive. For a better understanding of this fact, it is useful first to understand the movement that took place from compulsory to paid service for soldiers, and then to consider opportunities to finance wars through current taxation.

Financing a war through some form of obligatory service limits the extent to which a government must raise finance either through taxation or borrowing. At the outset of the Middle Ages, elites in many large monarchies were bound together by obligations of feudal service, a valuable asset for kings during a period in which armed knights were critical to military success. Other types of polities also could rely on forms of obligatory service. Many towns and cities had defensive militias in which residents were required to serve.

While obligatory service was important at an initial stage, from a very early date these forms of service withered away. In their place rulers turned increasingly to the use of paid soldiers. The study by J. F. Verbruggen (1997) on warfare in medieval Europe lists examples of the extensive use of mercenaries as early as the reign of Phillip Augustus in France

(1180–1223) and of Henry II (1154–1189) in England.[1] An authoritative study by Philippe Contamine (1984) provides a more systematic account of the evolution of feudal obligations and paid military service in these two states.[2] He suggests that feudal military obligations were gradually abandoned because, in practice, they produced far fewer knights than desired. Monarchs adopted two strategies in response: pay those who were obliged to serve so that they would turn up, or in lieu of this, hire mercenaries. As a result of these developments, which occurred at the very outset of the period studied in this book, Contamine suggests that "money was the almost obligatory link between authority and soldiers (1984: 90)."

Within autonomous cities there appears to have been a parallel evolution from unpaid obligatory service to paid service. The Italian communes initially organized their defense through obligatory service in militias. According to the study by Phillip Jones (1997), by the early thirteenth century the communes began paying citizens for such service. Over the course of this century the communes also began to make heavy use of mercenaries. Jones attributes much of this transition to technical developments and the consequent specialization of functions.

If, by the beginning of the period that I consider in this book, money had become "the obligatory link between authority and soldiers," this conclusion alone does not tell us how important war expenditures were as a share of overall spending by territorial monarchies and autonomous cities. Here almost all indications suggest that the demands of military spending placed great stress on budgets. For France and England, W. M. Ormrod (1995) dates this change to the beginning of the Hundred Years War. For autonomous cities we have direct and extensive evidence that military spending constituted the most important item in budgets and that the shift to paid military service placed an increasing strain on cities' finances. Cities also needed to maintain defensive walls, which entailed considerable expense. William Bowsky's (1970) study of the finances of the commune of Siena shows that there were important communal expenditures on public works to improve the city's water supply and on purchases of grain in times of famine, but in his words, "These burdensome necessities might have been taken in stride were it not for the greatest expense incurred by Siena, and, I suspect, other communes as well: military expenditures. Throughout her history as an independent city-state Siena was oppressed

---

[1]Verbruggen (1997: 127–144).
[2]For other accounts see Mallett (1994) and Allmand (1998).

by the weight of her military budget."[3] In the study by Espinas (1902) on the finances of the French commune of Douai, we see a similar conclusion. Autonomous cities in the Low Countries and in Germany were also no exceptions to this pattern.[4]

How did states finance the increased expenditures necessary for their defense? For both territorial states and autonomous cities, the shift to paid military service led to fiscal changes designed to increase the funds available to public authorities. Autonomous cities developed a wide variety of taxes to finance their military spending, and while they sometimes did so by imposing direct taxes on their citizens, a common view is that indirect taxation of trade and common consumption goods was the most prominent source of revenue. For this reason it is often suggested that the fiscal system of Europe's city-states was regressive in form. Larger territorial states also modified their tax systems in response to demands of war, raising a mix of direct and indirect taxes (Ormrod 1995). Large territorial states had a tax base different from that of autonomous cities, and it was certainly one that could not provide the same level of revenue on a per capita basis; but we should also remember that the large monarchies also had cities within their territories that could serve as large-scale sources of finance. In Castile, the monarchy with the cooperation of the Castilian towns drew revenue from a sales tax known as the *alcabala*. In France the monarchy benefited from the presence of Paris, a major commercial center that provided a sizeable tax base.[5]

Increased taxation was part of the solution to the problem of financing defense, but the need for military expenditures could often increase suddenly and in unanticipated fashion. It was difficult or impossible for authorities to increase tax revenues immediately to meet these needs. One particularly vivid illustration of this problem is provided by the efforts of Philippe VI of France (1328–50) to raise a series of extraordinary taxes at the outset of the Hundred Years War. An assessment by

[3] Bowsky (1970: 42–43). The comparative study on Italian city-states by Jones (1997) also emphasizes this point.

[4] Blockmans (1987) provides statistics on military spending for the communal militia as a share of total spending for the city of Ghent, suggesting that in years of war this ratio ranged from 25% in 1353–54 to 77% in 1345–46. In years of peace, military expenditures reverted to much lower levels (between 3 and 8% of total spending). Finally, Eltis (1989) suggests that military expenditure accounted for 82% of Cologne's civic spending in 1379.

[5] For a fascinating example of this, see the evidence on Paris during the commercial revolution presented by Slivinski and Sussman (2009).

John Hennemann (1967) shows that despite extensive efforts, the strategy had little impact on overall royal revenues. This result can be attributed to both administrative obstacles and the simple reluctance of subjects to see a sharp and immediate increase in taxation. In city-states the administrative obstacles to levying extraordinary war taxes were certainly less daunting than in a polity the size of France, but we must not think that citizens held any less dislike for sharp, immediate, and unforeseen increases in tax rates. Given the difficulties in meeting extraordinary war needs with extraordinary taxation, all states had a very clear incentive to seek access to credit. Successful borrowing could raise large sums rapidly. Assuming loans would actually be repaid, war expenditures would ultimately need to be financed by taxation in the long run, but this could be achieved with less of a sharp, immediate, and painful increase in taxation for citizens than would otherwise be the case, and in a time frame that was administratively feasible.[6]

Ultimately, because borrowing was crucial in meeting the financial demands of war, it also had implications for the ability of different states to survive. There are clear indications here that borrowing was particularly important for city-states. Richard Ehrenberg (1928: 44–45) notes the following:

> Towards the end of the Middle Ages an increasing indebtedness descended on the cities as well as on the princes. The independent cities had not only to carry on many wars as they had done before, but had to put forth all their strength to resist the attacks of the princes on their liberty. The citizens had long ceased to take the field themselves, and the mercenary system was nowhere more fully developed than in the cities. The growth of the use of fire-arms had forced them to surround themselves with stronger fortifications, and their regular revenues, often very large, were never sufficient to produce the enormous sums needed. The credit of the cities therefore was accordingly their most powerful weapon in the struggle for their freedom.

The above comments are paralleled by Michael Toch (1995) and David Eltis (1989), who consider how many German cities were able to survive as independent entities. Looking elsewhere, we see similar support for the proposition. If during the early fourteenth century the access of Siena's

---

[6]This view that borrowing emerged as a means of meeting extraordinary expenditure needs is emphasized by a range of scholars including Bowsky (1970) in his study of Siena, Jones (1997) in his general discussion of Italian city-states, and Fryde and Fryde (1963) in their general survey of public credit.

rulers to credit allowed the city to protect itself from external threats, such as incursions by mercenary bands, by the second half of the same century, the city's difficulties in obtaining access to credit would leave it open to this type of attack.[7]

The goal of this brief review has been to demonstrate the broad significance of public credit for European state development. Faced with the need to raise finance quickly to respond to military challenges (or opportunities), states found that access to public credit was a critical ingredient for survival and success. There is ample reason to believe that the ability to borrow at low cost was particularly important in allowing the city-state to survive as a form of political organization in Europe. In what follows I will take a closer look at the evidence on whether city-states did in fact have a financial advantage over territorial states.

WHEN DID STATES FIRST BORROW LONG-TERM?

The ability to raise funds by borrowing clearly had enormous advantages for European states in an era of incessant warfare. If this were so, it raises an important puzzle—why were some European states able to establish long-term debts so much earlier than others? In what follows I present information on the date at which we first observe interest rates on long-term loans for 31 European states. To construct this database I began by reviewing each of the secondary sources cited by Stephan Epstein (2000: ch.2) in his fascinating study of the evolution of public debt. I then compared this evidence with alternative sources, when such sources existed. This effort also involved extending the dataset by including new sources covering additional states or additional time periods for existing states. All sources used to construct the debt data are listed in the following pages. In building the dataset I have also distinguished, where possible, between different types of debt instruments (such as life versus perpetual annuities) and different methods individual authors used to calculate interest rates.

It will not be a surprise to those familiar with the history of public debt to learn, based on this data, that self-governing cities, on average, created long-term public debts earlier than territorial states. What may be less frequently recognized is how general this phenomenon was, and how large the time lag was between the many city-states that began to issue annuities

---

[7]As described in detail by Caferro (1998).

in the thirteenth century and the creation of long-term debts by territorial states, the first of which did not take this action until the beginning of the sixteenth century. For some European states there is fairly unanimous agreement on the date at which a long-term debt was created. The French monarchy's decision in 1522 to issue rentes via the municipality of Paris is traditionally seen as the founding date for France's national debt.[8] For most other European states there is less consensus on an exact starting date, particularly for early political entities that in some cases did not keep systematic public accounts.[9] One simple if imperfect indicator useful for addressing this question is to classify states according to the first year in which there is observable information on the interest rate associated with a long-term loan.

Table 2.1 presents this information for 31 different autonomous cities and territorial states in Europe ranging from Arras in 1241 to Denmark in 1725. The sources for this data as well as the subsequent data on costs of borrowing are as follows.[10] Most of the polities in the sample were also included in the data reported by Epstein (2000). However, I have substantially augmented the sample by adding several new polities and by using a number of additional sources for existing polities.[11] I also excluded

---

[8] Hamilton (1947) cites this as the first national debt, though Castile actually established a long-term debt slightly earlier.

[9] This was the case, for example, in Douai prior to 1297, according to Espinas (1902), or reportedly in the German principalities (Carsten 1959).

[10] Sources consulted included: Arras (Bougard 1988: 61), Austria (Dickson 1987: 404), Barcelona (Usher 1943: 171), Basel (Usher 1943: 171; and Gilomen 2003), Bologna (Carboni 1995: 131), Bremen (Albers 1930: 109–152), Bruges (van der Burg, Derycke and van der Heijden 2006: 9), Castile (Ruiz-Martin 1975: 14; Mauro and Parker 1977: 49), Cologne (Schneider 1954: 491; Usher 1943: 171; Fryde and Fryde 1963: 547; Knipping 1894, 1898), Denmark (Korner 1995: 536), Dortmund (Fryde and Fryde 1963: 532), Douai (Espinas 1902; Usher 1943: 158), England (Homer and Sylla 1996: 126; Dickson 1967), Florence (Pezzolo 2001, 2006), France (Forbonnais 1758; Velde and Weir 1992), Geneva (Bergier 1962: 119), Genoa (Day 1963; Pezzolo 2001; Homer and Sylla 1996), Ghent (Munro 2003: 36 citing van Werveke 1934), Hamburg (Reincke 1953: 500), Holland (Tracy 1985 and Fritschy European State Finance Database), Mainz (Fryde and Fryde 1963: 552), Milan (de Luca 2006), Naples (Calabria 1991: 143–45), Nuremberg (Fryde and Fryde 1963: 549; Homer and Sylla 1996: 117), Piedmont (de Luca 2006; Felloni 1977: 22), Papal States (Partner 1980: 26; Felloni 1977: 22), Siena (Bowsky 1970: 193), Tuscany (Felloni 1977: 22), Venice (Lane and Mueller 1985: 474–475), Württemberg (Tracy 1985: 19), Zurich (Fryde and Fryde 1963: 551).

[11] In restricting my focus to long-term borrowing, I have also reclassified several long-term loans that Epstein (2000) refers to as short-term (or vice versa). For Siena, Epstein

TABLE 2.1
Dates of First and Last Observed Long-term Loans

Autonomous cities	Territorial states
Arras (1241)	Castile (1489–1598)
Venice (1262–1785)	Kingdom of Naples (1520–1785)
Siena (1290–1354)	France (1522–1793)
Bremen (1295–1798)	Holland (1522–1794)
Douai (1295–1399)	Papal States (1526–1785)
Hamburg (1308–1560)	Duchy of Milan (1543–1785)
Genoa (1340–1785)	Württemberg (1550)
Florence (1347–1493)	Austria (1555–1779)
Barcelona (1360–1630)	Piedmont (1684–1785)
Cologne (1375–1472)	Great Britain (1693–1798)
Dortmund (1375)	Tuscany (1700–1726)
Ghent (1375)	Denmark (1725)
Nuremberg (1381–1565)	
Basel (1383–1479)	
Zurich (1386–1404)	
Mainz (1415–1444)	
Bruges (1489)	
Geneva (1538–1681)	
Bologna (1555–1655)	

rates reported by Epstein (2000) for Vicenza, Saxony, and Liege because they did not satisfy the requirements for inclusion in my sample.[12] To aid in interpretation, figure 2.1 presents a histogram showing the number of states creating a long-term debt by date, distinguishing between city-states and territorial states. This helps establish that for the majority

---

reports several interest rates from Bowsky (1970) as short-term, but it is not certain that they should properly be considered as such. As a result, I have included these rates in my dataset. I have also classified all life annuities as being "long-term loans" which is not always the case in Epstein (2000).

[12] In the case of Vicenza the rates reported by Carlotto (1993) are for short-term loans. In the case of Saxony, Epstein (2000) reports a rate for 1496–97, based on information in Fryde and Fryde (1963) concerning a loan from the Bishop of Meissen to the prince of Saxony. It is not clear, however, what the term or characteristics of this loan were. Finally, for rates reported by Epstein for the city of Verviers within the province of Liege there is similarly insufficient information.

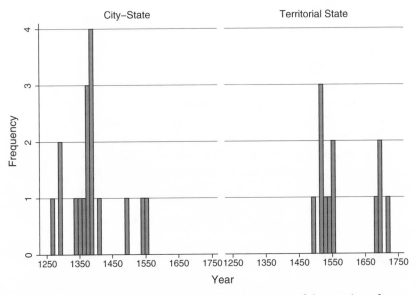

Figure 2.1. Establishment of long-term debts; histogram of the number of states creating a long-term debt by period and by polity type.

of city-states, there is a record of long-term borrowing prior to 1400. For territorial states, we see that only Castile created a long-term debt before 1500, but after this point territorial states moved to create debts in rapid succession. The evidence on city-states amplifies the conclusions of existing historical surveys.[13] It demonstrates how the creation of long-term public debts by cities in the 13th and 14th centuries was a widespread phenomenon, focused especially in Northern Italy and the Low Countries but also involving cities in northern France, Germany, as well as towns in Switzerland and Catalonia.

The list of "city-states" in table 2.1 may provoke immediate interrogations from some quarters. Few would disagree with the idea that cities like Venice and Florence were at one time independent states, but can we say the same of a city like Ghent that, while at times enjoying very substantial autonomy, was also subject to a significant degree of princely control? What about the French communes of Douai and Arras, which, even as early as the thirteenth century, had strong constraints on their autonomy, and finally how can Barcelona possibly be called a city-state

---

[13] Such as Tracy (2003) and Munro (2003).

during this period when it was ruled by kings who were present in the same city? As I emphasized in the introduction, I have adopted an expansive definition of a city-state in this book. This avoids a potential bias whereby only cities that had the highest degree of political and financial success would be included in the sample. This definition has classified as city-states those entities that had a high degree of control of their own legal and financial affairs as well as their own defense. Under this definition even a city under princely control like Barcelona might be classified as a city-state.[14] However, while I adopt an expansive definition of a city-state, I will also discuss how the results of my key statistical tests are altered if I restrict the sample to include only those cities enjoying the greatest degree of autonomy. This restricted sample will exclude Arras, Barcelona, Bologna, Bruges, Douai, and Ghent. As I will discuss in more detail, if we exclude these six questionable cases the results in favor of the core argument of this book are only strengthened.

While Italian city-states like Genoa, Venice, and Florence are commonly seen as forerunners with regard to public debt, it was actually the system of municipal debt developed in northern Europe that would set the model for long-term government borrowing in Europe until the end of the nineteenth century.[15]

Though they initially raised debt finance through several mechanisms, during the thirteenth century Italian city-states converged on the use of forced loans as their primary financing instrument. To the extent that contributions, often referred to as *prestanza,* were obligatory for wealth holders, one might see them as more of a tax than a loan. For this among other reasons Julius Kirshner (2006) has questioned the extent to which one can speak of Italian city-states as having public debts.[16] But unlike

---

[14]Barcelona had a complex institutional history whereby the city's degree of autonomy from princely overlords varied over time. It should be noted, however, that even under periods of stronger princely control (such as after 1472), the city retained very important legal privileges in the area of governance.

[15]The contribution by Tracy (2003) has been influential in demonstrating how politically independent cities in Northern France and Flanders began selling annuities during the thirteenth century as a means of raising finance. Munro (2003) has charted this development in greater detail, emphasizing early debates on whether annuities sales violated the prohibition on usury.

[16]He also suggests that these were not public debts because interest payments were on some occasions not made. But this is, of course, a property also observable in public debts that are purely voluntarily subscribed.

the forced loans one might usually think of as occurring in medieval Europe, the *prestanza* paid interest, even if there was not a provision for repayment of principal (this was, of course, also the case for the perpetual annuities sold by Northern European cities). In addition, in the large Italian city-states an active secondary market developed for these obligations. Because the forced loans used by fourteenth-century Italian city-states were remunerated, and because we also know that the nominal interest rates paid on these loans often bore a close correlation with their yield on the secondary market, it is reasonable to suggest that the ability of states to establish them at an early date and to obtain finance at relatively low cost depended on the perceived creditworthiness of these city-state governments.[17]

Prior to 1500, when territorial states sought debt finance, they did so through short-term loans from merchants with repayment due in no more than one or two years, rather than long-term financing via sales of annuities. Some authors have argued that monarchs in territorial states did this because they sought to avoid the constraints that long-term borrowing would imply in terms of commitment to dedicating a specific revenue stream to debt servicing.[18] But from a very early date, rulers in many territorial states had developed the practice of paying an annuity or rent to certain individuals or entities. So the technology that would later be used by these states to borrow long term was hardly unknown. Another weakness of this argument is that short-term borrowing actually posed much greater financial constraints than did finance based on annuities. Short-term loans in territorial states during this period were inevitably contracted at much higher interest rates than were the long-term loans of city-states.[19] Features such as short maturities for a loan are commonly described as innovations necessary when a borrower's creditworthiness is in doubt. Fryde (1955) suggests that the effective interest rate on loans by the Bardi family to Edward III of England between 1328 and 1331

---

[17]Throughout the first half of the fourteenth century, the *prestiti* in Venice traded at an average of 85% of par, and interest payments were regularly respected. A subsequent fiscal crisis during the War of the Chioggia with Genoa led to a sharp drop in prestiti prices. In Genoa one sees a closer correlation between nominal interest rates on forced loans and their secondary market yields over a longer period.

[18]This view has been expressed by Fryde and Fryde (1963) and by Ormrod (1995).

[19]This would appear to have also been the case for short-term loans contracted from other groups, such as Jewish lenders. See Roth (1987) for the English case; Fryde and Fryde (1963) and Barzel and Kiser (1992) provide a more general discussion.

was 26 percent.[20] Two centuries later, English monarchs were able to borrow short term on the Antwerp money market at roughly half this rate (12–14 percent per annum), but this rate remained significantly higher than that paid by states financing themselves through long-term borrowing, as will be seen later. Equally important, the quantity of finance that could be raised by short-term borrowing was ultimately limited compared to long-term borrowing. [21]

A second possible explanation for the later development of long-term borrowing by territorial states is that they simply had less need. This could have been either because they found their survival less threatened than did city-states, or because territorial states had ample means of raising armies without paying them, such as relying on feudal levies. But the evidence presented earlier has already demonstrated that from a very early date, territorial states moved from mobilization via feudal levies to paying their soldiers, too early a date for the availability of feudal levies to explain why territorial states delayed creating long-term debts. The argument that territorial states may have had less need to create long-term debts because they were less at risk also seems based on incomplete logic. First, many territorial states were threatened by their neighbors. Second, territorial states engaging in offensive wars could have had just as much use for borrowing. Certainly, when territorial states did have means of credit available, albeit short-term ones, they chose to use them.

A final alternative explanation for why European territorial states prior to 1500 did not establish long-term debts, and the one that I will emphasize in this book, is that they were less credible as borrowers than were Europe's city-states.

The speed with which territorial states moved to create long-term debts after 1500 suggests that rather than being produced by isolated changes in individual states, such borrowing was a general phenomenon. Several factors could have contributed to this development. Economic development may have lowered the risk-free return to capital, making it less costly even for very risky borrowers to contract debts. Improvements

---

[20]This figure is based on a sum of 11,000 pounds sterling in "gifts" conceded to the Bardi on a total debt of 42,000 pounds (Fryde 1955: 209).

[21]Outhwaite (1966: 290) suggests that in 1560 during a period of heavy borrowing, the English crown had 279,000 pounds sterling in loans outstanding on the Antwerp money market, "an amount greater than the Crown's ordinary revenue." During this same time period, states financing themselves through long-term borrowing were able to accumulate significantly larger debt stocks.

in revenue collection may also have facilitated access to credit for territorial states. On the political side, the sixteenth century was a period of intensified warfare associated with the Habsburg attempt to establish supremacy in Europe. Governments therefore had an increased need for debt finance. The Habsburgs themselves established a public debt that, at least in absolute terms, was unprecedented in size, and Habsburg demand for war finance also stimulated innovation in public borrowing in dependent territories as far afield as the Kingdom of Naples and the Low Countries. It is recognized that the size of armies fielded by territorial states increased dramatically during this period. For two dramatic examples, Geoffrey Parker (1988: 206) reports estimates suggesting that between the 1470s and the 1630s, Spain increased the number of men it fielded from 20,000 to 300,000, and France increased the size of its army from 40,000 to 150,000. If it is acknowledged that the size of European armies grew substantially after 1500, there is nonetheless considerable debate whether this "military revolution" was a development attributable primarily to exogenous technological changes, such as the introduction of firearms, new infantry tactics, and new styles of fortification, or, alternatively, whether the military revolution depended above all on an exogenous increase in the intensity of inter-state competition within Europe.[22] The presentation of my core arguments in this book does not depend on which of these two interpretations of the military revolution is the more accurate. They both involve forces that, from the standpoint of any individual state, were essentially exogenous. What this does suggest is that in Chapter 4, when I conduct a more systematic examination of the factors that prompted states to create long-term debts, it will be important to take account of this structural change after 1500.

One further feature apparent from table 2.1 involves the changing fortunes of city-states over time. Much historical work has described the period after 1500 as the age of the territorial state in Europe. A number of city-states continued to borrow long-term after 1500, and for the cases of Hamburg, Geneva, Barcelona, Venice, Genoa, and Bremen, we have data available from the seventeenth century, and in the latter three

---

[22] An example here is the debate whether the technological development of the *trace italienne* style of fortification produced an increase in army sizes. Parker (1988) emphasizes this idea, but Lynn (1991) shows that in the case of the French army there is little correspondence between the timing of the adoption of the *trace* and the observed increase in the number of forces. Kingra (1993) also criticizes Parker's interpretation, suggesting that the *trace italienne* was more of an effect produced by underlying trends.

cases the eighteenth century. But a number of city-states also exited the sample at an early date, and it is worth considering why this was the case. This phenomenon may be partly attributable to the pattern of historical research. The period during which a city-state first established a long-term debt may have attracted more attention than later centuries. In a larger number of cases, however, city-states drop out of the sample because they ceased to be independent. In some cases the loss of independence was brought about by internal conflict and fiscal crisis. This is the context in which Mainz lost its status in 1462 as a free imperial city.[23] In other cases a city lost its autonomy upon being forcibly absorbed by a territorial state, as was the city of Ghent during the periods of Burgundian and subsequent Habsburg control.[24] In chapter 4's statistical analysis I will ask explicitly whether my overall conclusions may be influenced by the pattern whereby a number of city-states dropped out of the debt sample over time.

The foregoing discussion has focused on the demand for credit by states. Ultimately, however, the ability of governments to borrow also depended on supply considerations involving the presence of a pool of potential investors seeking the sort of fixed income stream provided by a perpetual or life annuity. Existing evidence suggests that in medieval and early modern Europe, individuals whose wealth was engaged in commerce could profit more directly from this type of savings instrument than did those whose wealth was primarily engaged in agricultural production. The fact that merchants held wealth that tended to be more liquid than that of landowners meant that when a government sought to borrow, merchants could shift wealth into an asset like public annuities more quickly.[25] It has also been observed that in medieval Europe, merchants who made their initial fortunes in risky activities like long-distance trade had an incentive, once established, to become *rentiers*—shifting part of their wealth into assets like public or private annuities that would provide a more regular source of income. In many cases merchants also diversified their wealth by purchasing land, an action that could arguably serve an economic purpose while also conferring social status. These points have been emphasized by Michael Postan (1952: 216–18), and they can be illustrated by specific examples, as in the case of the city of Lübeck, where older mercantile families tended to have a larger section of their wealth held in the form

---

[23] See the discussion in Fryde and Fryde (1963: 551–52) and Dollinger (1954: 458–60).

[24] See Blockmans (1994) and Boone (1990).

[25] See Grassby (1970) for an emphasis on the significance of mercantile wealth being held in liquid form in seventeenth-century England.

of annuities than did more recently established merchants.[26] One should certainly not suggest that only merchants purchased public annuities. There is evidence from France and the Kingdom of Naples in the sixteenth century that certain members of the nobility invested in public debt, but overall, there is little indication of a general movement by landowners in Europe to invest this way. Even as late as the middle of the eighteenth century, the evidence provided by P. G. M. Dickson (1967) and by Ann Carlos and Larry Neal (2006) shows that in Great Britain, ownership of both government debt and Bank of England shares remained heavily concentrated in the London area.

THE COST OF BORROWING

Ideally, to measure the cost of borrowing, one would have a common measure of the interest rate for all states considered. This is unfortunately not feasible when considering a broad sample of states over such a long time period. For a select few states there is information on the yields for government debt on secondary markets. This can provide the closest evaluation of whether investors perceive a state as creditworthy. For a much larger set of states there is information on nominal interest rates at issue (or the effective rate of return in the case of annuities). Finally, in a number of instances, existing historical work provides no direct indication of an interest rate on debt issues, but fiscal data exist that can be used to construct a proxy measure for the interest rate. The latter can be constructed by taking the ratio between annual debt service and the total stock of debt. While it is often not made explicit, this proxy method for reporting interest rates has actually been used by a large number of authors, including a number of the sources reported in Epstein (2000).[27] In what follows, I report interest rates based on nominal rates at issue when these are available, and based on the fiscal proxy when they are not.[28] The subsequent statistical analysis in chapter 4 will control for the type of interest rate measure used, while also

[26] See also the discussion of this idea by Kohn (1999). For the example of Lübeck, see the discussion in Rotz (1977).

[27] One contribution that proposes this method explicitly is Sussman and Yafeh (2006).

[28] It is worth noting that across the sample, we do not observe that fiscal interest rates are significantly lower (or higher) than the nominal rates.

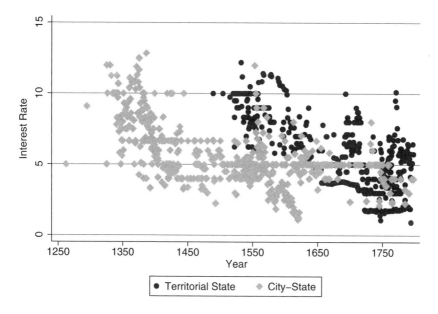

Figure 2.2. Interest rates on debts of city-states and territorial states. Graph shows all annual interest-rate observations for the sample of thirty-one polities.

taking account of the type of debt instrument.[29] In order to smooth out the effect of temporary economic, political, or market events that may in the short run have altered the interest rate at which a state could borrow, in my statistical analysis in chapter 4 (although not in the figures reported in this chapter) I use average interest rates over half-century periods. Ideally, we would be able to complement the interest data with full information on the quantity that states borrowed, but evidence on total borrowing quantities is considerably more scarce.

Figure 2.2 provides an initial look at the interest-rate data by graphing all annual interest-rate observations by year, with observations from city-states indicated in grey and observations from territorial states indicated in black. There is clear evidence of a decline in interest rates over time. But it is also immediately apparent that within any given time period, we observe very considerable variation. In some cases differences in interest rates can be explained by the type of debt instrument, such as life annuities

[29]We would expect there to be a higher interest rate on life annuities in particular, as opposed to perpetual annuities, since life annuities paid an income stream for a shorter time period, while neither life nor perpetual annuities involved repayment of principal.

versus perpetual annuities. But there also remains important variation that cannot be easily explained by this difference. Figure 2.2 also reinforces the point that city-states in Europe began borrowing well before territorial states, and in addition city-states may have paid lower interest rates on their debts. The latter phenomenon can be seen by directly comparing rates in city-states and territorial states beginning in 1500. Prior to 1500, we cannot directly compare city-states and territorial states, because no territorial states had yet created long-term debts. The implications of this sample selection issue are considered in chapter 4.

Beyond drawing a simple comparison of the interest rates on public debt in city-states and territorial states, we can also attempt to compare costs of borrowing after controlling for the level of returns on investment in private markets. One potential source of long-run data on private interest rates in medieval and early modern Europe comes from returns on land rents. Land rent contracts involved a creditor granting a specific sum to a borrower in exchange for the right to a fixed future income stream from the borrower's land. Like the perpetual and life annuities issued by city-states, and later by territorial states, land rent contracts bore a strong resemblance to loans, but they made no provision for repayment of the "principal" and thus were less likely to fall afoul of usury restrictions. The similarity between land rent contracts and those for government annuities makes them a useful source of comparison. Clark (1988) collected data for returns on land rent contracts in England between the 13th and the 18th centuries. He also reports data from earlier sources covering several other European regions. The most salient feature of each of these series (as can be seen in figure 2.3) is the large secular decline that occurred in land rent returns over time. The exception is England, for which Clark's own research suggests a spectacular drop in the return on land rents following the Black Death. While the data on land rents is useful for providing a view of trends in private interest rates, it should be emphasized that these data exist only for broad regions like France, England, Germany, and Italy, and not for the multiple political entities that might have existed within such regions. As a result, these data are best thought of as a proxy for broad changes in private interest rates over time, rather than as a control for differences between two states within a given time period.

As a next step in the analysis, figure 2.4 plots the difference between the interest rate at which a state borrowed and an estimate of the return on land rents. Taking the difference between the interest rates on government debt and land rents provides a closer estimate of whether a particular state paid a premium to obtain finance. Once we control for the return on land

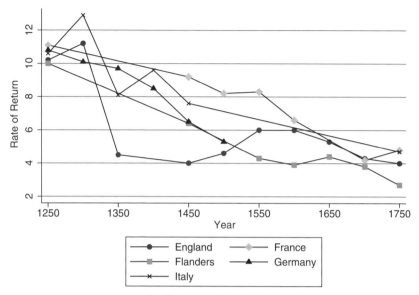

Figure 2.3. Returns on land rents in five European regions (Clark 1988).

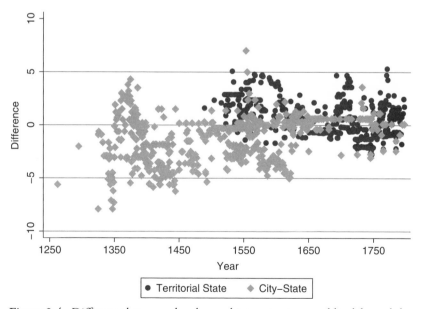

Figure 2.4. Difference between the observed interest rate on public debt and the return on land rents.

rents, it becomes even more apparent that for much of their existence city-states had advantageous access to credit when compared with territorial states.[30]

There are three further issues to consider when asking whether the interest rates reported here reflect the costliness of finance for different states at different times.

First, it is known that some governments, and especially those experiencing financial distress, sold debt below its par value. The interest rates reported here will not always capture this phenomenon, so in some cases they will be underestimated.[31] In the absence of a technique that could eliminate the bias created by not observing whether debt was sold below par, it is still possible to consider whether this bias would be likely to lead to an overestimation of the interest rate differential between city-states and territorial states. For this to be true, city-states would have had to sell debt below par more frequently than did territorial states. The problem with this statement is that while there are known instances where city-states sold debt below par, there appear, if anything, to have been more instances of this taking place in territorial states.[32]

A second issue to consider is whether the interest rates reported here reflect the return investors on an open market would require in order to lend. They might alternatively reflect a degree of moral suasion or compulsion. There is plenty of evidence that such factors may have played a role in decisions to purchase government annuities, but this appears to have been a phenomenon in both city-states and territorial states. We would expect it only to lead to an inaccurate conclusion that city-states had access to lower-cost finance if this practice were somehow more prevalent in city-states than elsewhere. In the case of annuities issued by self-governing cities, it has frequently been suggested that given the extent to which those who managed government also often directly invested in a city's debt, in difficult times town officials served as a lender of last resort. For a city like Bruges in the late fifteenth century, Derycke

[30] Figure 2.4 does not distinguish between perpetual annuities and the life annuities initially sold by many city-states, for which we would naturally expect a higher interest rate. This accounts for a number of the relatively high interest rates for city-states prior to 1400. The statistical analysis in chapter 4 will take account of this factor.

[31] This problem would not affect the fiscal proxy for the interest rate. It may be useful in this regard to note again that for the overall sample, interest rates measured using the fiscal proxy method were not significantly different than those based on nominal yields at issue.

[32] France is a very prominent example of this phenomenon. See Forbonnais (1758).

(2003) has argued that purchasing public annuities may also have helped cement one's position within the city's political elite. But a review of the development of government annuities in a territorial state like France shows that such incentives were also present. They involved the pressures placed by the monarchy on venal office-holders to purchase rentes when it proved difficult to find sufficient purchasers on the open market.[33] Overall, while compulsion or moral suasion may have had an important impact on the observed interest rate for a given state in a given year, there is little evidence that these factors can explain the interest rate differentials between city-states and territorial states observed over the five-hundred-year period considered here.

A third issue to consider involves the fact that in a number of cases, cities that were largely self-governing borrowed at the behest of princely overlords. This was particularly common in the Low Countries after the middle of the fourteenth century, as Burgundian (and subsequently Habsburg) princes pressured cities like Ghent and Bruges to sell annuities to fund princely military expenditures.[34] We would not necessarily expect to observe a different interest rate on this type of loan as long as the city that had contracted it retained control of the taxes that would be used to repay the loan. As such, repayment would depend on the ability and willingness of the municipality to repay. If a municipality was forced into excessive borrowing, or a princely overlord directly interfered with its tax policies, this would of course be a different story.

ECONOMIC EXPLANATIONS FOR THE CITY-STATE ADVANTAGE

I have emphasized that city-states began to borrow significantly earlier than territorial states, and that city-states also enjoyed a persistent advantage over territorial states in paying lower interest rates on their debts. Even if territorial states became more dominant in Europe after 1500, once they did establish long-term debts they often paid a premium on their debt. So far, however, I have not presented any evidence to suggest why city-states enjoyed this financial advantage. The core argument of this book is that the financial advantage of city-states depended on the structure of their representative institutions, but more fundamentally on the fact that these polities were small, and they tended to be dominated by merchants. Before

---

[33] See in particular Doyle (1996) and Bien (1987) for a description of this phenomenon.
[34] See Boone (1990, 1991) and van Nieuwenhuysen (1984).

using the subsequent chapters to present the more detailed statistical evidence, several observations can be made about the alternative argument that city-states simply enjoyed a borrowing advantage because they were more economically developed.

First, if it is known that many economic innovations occurred in areas of Europe where cities held a high degree of autonomy, this same body of work also emphasizes that individual regions remained leaders in terms of technological innovation for only a brief period of time, "as if technological creativity was like a torch too hot to hold for long; each individual society carried it for a short time."[35] But while city-states were innovators for only a relatively brief span of time, all the evidence suggests that they retained their advantage with regard to public credit long after they ceased to be important sites for innovation in early industrial production. So, Venice continued to borrow at very low interest rates into the eighteenth century, long after its period as an innovator in industrial production, or as a principal hub of commerce, had ended. One can make similar observations with regard to cities in the Netherlands or in Germany. What this evidence suggests then is that there were other features of city-states that contributed to their ability to borrow.

If the financial advantages enjoyed by city-states cannot be explained simply by the fact that they existed in more developed areas, or that they were early sites for innovation, another possibility is that city-states could borrow more easily because they found it less costly to raise tax revenues, and they may also have benefited from a greater stability in their sources of revenue. It has been observed that many of the "revolutions" in public borrowing that occurred in European territorial states like Great Britain and the Netherlands were preceded by reforms and improvements in revenue collection.[36] Less has been written about the importance of revenue collection in city-states, but a number of authors have made the plausible argument that city-states benefited financially from their ability to tax trade and consumption easily within their boundaries.

The problem with this argument is that it is also the case that a number of the largest territorial states in the sample—including Castile, France, and England—had at least one large city that was a center of trade from an early date and that would eventually also become a financial center. Even if

---

[35] See Mokyr (1994: 563–564).

[36] See 't Hart (1993), Tracy (1985), and Fritschy (2003) on Holland; and O'Brien (2001) and Brewer (1989) on Great Britain.

TABLE 2.2
Revenue Volatility for Different States

State (cities in bold)	Standard deviation revenues
Basel (1501–1611)	0.12
Holland (1599–1797)	0.13
Florence (1402–1430)	0.13
Denmark (1731–1771)	0.14
Douai (1392–1493)	0.20
Castile (1369–1396)	0.21
France (1322–1344)	0.22
France (1600–1754)	0.23
England (1600–1789)	0.31
Siena (1286–1349)	0.34
England (1485–1599)	0.42
Ghent (1336–1347)	0.37
England (1327–1345)	0.62

these territorial states found it costly to extract revenues across their entire territory, it is not clear why they could not have created long-term public debts at an earlier stage, based on taxes collected in their capital city or in a select number of large cities. Relying on large cities as sources of debt finance was, in fact, the strategy that France and Castile did eventually adopt, but not until the beginning of the sixteenth century.

One might also consider the possibility that the revenue sources upon which cities relied were inherently less volatile than the revenues of territorial states that derived to a lesser degree from commerce. Revenue volatility should also logically have depended on the extent to which a state had a diversified set of revenue sources. Merchants in city-states often had trading partners in a variety of locations, which would imply lower volatility. But it is also known that some city-state economies were highly dependent on trade with a single partner for their economic well-being. This was the case with the Flemish cities of Bruges and Ghent, which during the fourteenth century depended heavily on the wool trade with England.

One way to consider the above issue is to investigate the relative volatility of revenues in different types of European states. Table 2.2 gives a summary measure of revenue volatility in ten European states, two of which (England and France) can be considered for separate time periods.[37] The table reports the standard deviation of revenues after first regressing the level of revenue on a time trend and standardizing the means of the different series to zero.[38] Within this sample (an admittedly very small one) city-states experienced slightly less revenue volatility, but this difference is not statistically significant.

SUMMARY

In this chapter I have suggested that city-states had a significant financial advantage when compared to territorial states. City-states established long-term debts during the thirteenth and fourteenth centuries, whereas it was not until a new period of intensified warfare after 1500 that territorial states moved to establish long-term debts. When territorial states did begin to borrow, they faced higher costs of borrowing than did city-states, and there is little evidence of a swift convergence in interest rates between these two types of states. An initial look at economic factors involving private interest rates and revenue developments suggests that these alone cannot explain the observed difference between city-states and territorial states, a subject that will be considered more formally in what follows.

---

[37] Sources (ESFDB refers to European State Finance Database): Basel (Korner 1995), Holland (Fritschy neth1 file in ESFDB), Florence (Mohlo 1971: 61), Denmark (Poulsen ESFDB), Douai (Espinas 1902: 327), Castile (Ormrod ESFDB), France (Ormrod ESFDB, Malet ESFDB, François Velde 2004, and Riley 1987), England (Ormrod ESFDB, O'Brien ESFDB, and Mitchell 1988) Siena (Bowsky 1970: 298) Ghent (van Werveke 1934).

[38] De-trending here is a simple way of distinguishing between the effect of anticipated trends and unexpected changes. Ideally one would be able to find a measure of exogenous sources of revenue volatility, since part of the volatilily may have depended on state policies.

CHAPTER THREE

Representative Assemblies in Europe, 1250–1750

So far I have suggested that city-states enjoyed an advantage over territorial states when it came to public credit, and it seems difficult to explain this advantage by referring exclusively to economic factors like levels of private interest rates or sources of revenue. I have not yet considered in detail the alternative possibility that access to credit depended on the structure of representative institutions. To address this question adequately we first need to establish a broad picture of the representative phenomenon in Europe during these centuries. Numerous historical sources provide evidence of a sharp distinction between the financial roles played by representative bodies in city-states and by those in territorial states. Within city-states, representative bodies met frequently, they played a direct role in controlling government finance, and, crucially, they were often controlled by individuals who themselves invested in government annuities. Within territorial states, representative assemblies at times had significant prerogatives, particularly with regard to taxation. But it was rare for assemblies in territorial states to meet frequently, and when they did meet, there is little evidence that state creditors enjoyed a prominent position within them. In some cases, representative assemblies were even an obstacle to a government's efforts to obtain credit.

In order to provide more systematic evidence for these suggested trends, I have collected data on the presence and prerogatives of representative bodies in each of the 31 European states considered in the previous chapter. This includes information on whether a representative assembly existed, whether it had veto power over taxes, whether the assembly played a role in administering taxes, and finally whether it also had direct control of government debt issues. I also report information on the frequency with which representative bodies met. The results of this effort support the initial contentions of the chapter about differences between city-states and territorial states, but they also point to significant variation within the group of territorial states. I will present evidence to show that part of this variation within the group of territorial states can be explained by differences in geographic scale.

ORIGINS OF REPRESENTATIVE ASSEMBLIES

Historical accounts of representative assemblies in medieval Europe emphasize two causal mechanisms that led to the emergence of these bodies, both of which may have operated within a given state at a given time. The first involved spontaneous action by social groups seeking recognition from a prince. The second involved efforts by princes to establish assemblies as a means of securing finance and obtaining support for foreign policy.[1]

The first mechanism involved spontaneous efforts by groups to organize and obtain recognition from princes, thereby breaking with the feudal system that was based on individual ties between lord and vassal. According to the "corporatist" interpretation of medieval representation, the emergence of assemblies depended on a weakness of princely authority in the period between 1200 and 1400.[2] Princes found themselves faced with cities that had spontaneously organized, a clergy that had organized, and pressures from organized groups of feudal barons. The best-known example of the latter phenomenon involves the Magna Carta of 1215 in England, but very similar events took place elsewhere in Europe at this time. In a number of German principalities, nobles and leaders of towns formed confederations, or *einungen*, to protest against princely abuses of power. This led subsequently to the development of more regularized assemblies.[3] Émile Lousse (1943) suggests that representative assemblies in territorial states had their origins in the curia, a body composed of all the vassals of the prince. During the twelfth and thirteenth centuries cities were given representation in these bodies, followed subsequently by councils of bishops.[4] It has been suggested that the mechanism through which these different groups established assemblies was similar to that used by trade unions in the early twentieth century: Groups first established a de facto existence by overcoming barriers to collective action and to holding assemblies. They then obtained formal legal recognition by princes. It was as a part of this movement that a wide set of European cities obtained status as legal entities unto themselves.

---

[1] The distinction between these two mechanisms has been emphasized by Blockmans (1998).

[2] de Lagarde (1937, 1939).

[3] See the description in Folz (1965).

[4] See Lousse (1943: 242–45). He cites dates for the introduction of cities into assemblies as 1136 for the Diet of the Kingdom of Italy, 1188 for the Castilian Cortes, 1207 for the Papal States, 1263 in the French *concilia*, and 1265 in the English Parliament.

The representative phenomenon was no less important within city-states. Actions by groups seeking princely recognition for the autonomy of their cities presupposed some sort of regularized institution for conducting meetings at the municipal level. Representation within city-states was often characterized by the presence of multiple bodies. In many cases a city council with broad membership existed, but this council would itself delegate considerable authority to a smaller group of magistrates, who played the most important role in monitoring public affairs. There was also very significant variation in the form of city-state constitutions. In some cases representation was explicitly reserved for mercantile groups at the expense of members of craft guilds, and representatives were selected by a system of cooptation that tended to preserve mercantile dominance. In other cases, particularly after a series of popular revolts beginning in the fourteenth century, institutions were opened so that members of craft guilds could gain representation, and allowing for representatives to be elected by citizens.

The second mechanism through which representative assemblies emerged was through the deliberate efforts of princes seeking both finance and support for foreign policy initiatives. It is widely argued in both recent and earlier scholarship that princes consented to have representative assemblies, and to hold them more frequently, when they were in a weak financial position, because they could best obtain new tax revenues with the support of a representative assembly.[5] Though this motivation is less frequently cited, in some instances princes also convened assemblies in a direct effort to strengthen their hand in external conflicts, as was the case with Phillip the Fair's decision to convene an Estates General in France in 1302 in anticipation of a conflict with the Papacy.[6] Finally, some of the earliest assemblies in European territorial states were often military meetings convened by rulers, a practice that led ultimately to the more permanent establishment of representative assemblies.[7]

---

[5] One finds this argument in the writings of authors like Schumpeter (1918), Beard and Lewis (1932), and Lousse (1943), as well as in the more recent work of Rosenthal (1998), Hoffman and Rosenthal (1997), Bates and Lien (1985), Levi (1988), and Finer (1995 2: ch.8), to mention but a few examples. See also Barzel and Kiser (2002) on this issue.

[6] While this is often presented as the date for the first meeting of France's national representative body, it was not actually formally referred to as the "Estates General" until considerably later. See the interesting discussion of the political context for the 1302 meeting in Decoster (2002).

[7] This point has been made forcefully by Bisson (1966).

While there is not general agreement as to why this was the case, it is very widely argued that what Georges de Lagarde (1937) calls the "age of the territorial state" (beginning in 1500) is often said to have witnessed a marked waning in the powers of representative assemblies across Europe. One interpretation points to a gradual and exogenous increase in the rise of absolutism. A variation on this argument, advocated by Brian Downing (1992), is that the post-1500 revolution in military technology increased imperatives for states to obtain financing, and representative assemblies actually presented obstacles to satisfying this objective. As a consequence, European territorial states, and particularly those in the most geographically exposed positions, established new bureaucratic mechanisms for raising revenue that bypassed existing assemblies.[8]

The foregoing accounts of the development of representative institutions focus on the temporal variation between an early age (pre-1500) where assemblies were widespread and influential, and a second era after 1500 where princes increasingly asserted control. Another theme in historical work on the origins of representative government focuses specifically on the role of city-states as pioneers. Authors as diverse as Henri Pirenne (1910), M. Guizot (1838), Max Weber ([1921] 1958), Henry Sidgwick (1903), Susan Reynolds (1984), Hans Van Werveke (1963), and Samuel Finer (1995) all emphasize the extensive development of representative institutions within medieval city-states. These same authors also emphasize the important role played by merchants within city-states. The relatively closed group of merchants who controlled politics in many medieval city-states has often been referred as a "patriciate" by historians.[9] However, these authors do not necessarily share the same interpretation of this phenomenon. Guizot (1838) emphasized that the bourgeois within city-states were the forefathers of the French revolutionaries of 1789. In contrast, Pirenne (1910) and the numerous historians inspired by him have emphasized how representative government under the patriciate often involved an oligarchic form of rule, coupled with very high levels of inequality.

While a large number of authors acknowledge the early and extensive development of a representative style of government within city-states, there remains the question why city-states would be so different from

---

[8]Ertman (1997) also emphasizes the effect of geographic proximity to conflict zones.

[9]For an extended discussion of this term and its meaning as applied in the medieval context (as opposed to the original Roman context) see Van Werveke (1963).

territorial states in this regard. One simple but powerful explanation can be drawn from the work of Wim Blockmans (1978, 1998).[10] He stresses, among other factors, the importance of geographic scale as an obstacle to frequent meetings of representative bodies in premodern Europe. Given premodern costs of travel, gathering for meetings was arguably easier to achieve on a sustainable basis in smaller polities. Peter Spufford (2002: ch.4) suggests that following the collapse of the Roman Empire, the European road network continued to deteriorate and reached its nadir during the twelfth century.[11] From this point a series of improvements occurred during the thirteenth and fourteenth centuries, but it was not until the eighteenth century—the end of the period considered in this study—that major road improvements involving paved roads took place in many countries. As one striking example, Spufford notes that there was no bridge across the Rhine at Cologne after the collapse of the Roman bridge until a railway bridge was built during the nineteenth century. In this context of difficult transport and communication there was an obvious difference in the challenges posed by size between self-governing cities on one hand and territorial states on the other. In France during medieval times it regularly took travelers two weeks to travel from the Mediterranean coast to Paris.[12] In Holland in contrast, none of the cities that had voting rights in the Estates of Holland during the sixteenth century lay more than a day's travel time from the Hague, a situation that was brought about not just by small size but also by navigable rivers.[13] In small city-states the barriers of geographic scale were even lower. Within city-states meetings could often be convened by the simple sounding of a bell or by town crier. Likewise, groups that sought to assemble for a protest could coordinate their actions by banging on objects like metal bowls or pots.[14] At the regional level, authors have argued that in geographically compact areas where cities were clustered closely together it was possible to sustain intensive representative activity among groups of cities, as has

[10]The idea that geographic scale could help determine possibilities for political representation has also been emphasized for the Early Republic in the United States by Zagarri (1987).

[11]See also Reyerson (1998) for another survey on medieval transport and communications.

[12]Reyerson (1998).

[13]See the discussion in Tracy (1990: ch.2) on the Estates of Holland.

[14]One such episode from 1301 is recounted in the *Annals of Ghent* a contemporary chronicle translated from Latin by Johnstone (1951).

been emphasized by Blockmans (1976) for the case of Flanders and by Tracy (1990) for the case of Holland.

In strong contrast, references to distance in territorial states often refer to the obstacles it posed for sustaining an active representative assembly. Because of both its geographic size and its historical prominence, one sees this argument applied most frequently to the case of France.[15] The Hanseatic League provides another instructive example, because it was actually a league of independent cities rather than a conventional territorial state. It was a polity that was dominated by merchants, but it was also a far-flung entity that, because of its geographic dispersion, faced difficulties in maintaining a central representative assembly that would be regularly attended. Philippe Dollinger (1971: 94) notes that the League's general assembly, the Hansetag, suffered from chronic absenteeism caused in part by "the desire to avoid the cost of sending a representative." This is particularly interesting given that trade routes were, of course, well established between the major Hanseatic cities. In another example, Goran Rystad (1987: 94–95) presents evidence of complaints aired by Swedish towns involving the high costs of sending representatives to the Swedish Estates. We can also gain insight into the effect of distance on representation in territorial states by comparing representative assemblies in Castile and those in the Low Countries, two areas where representative assemblies were dominated by a group of towns. Both assemblies maintained a practice where representatives were bound by strict mandates from their constituents. In Holland this proved to be no obstacle to the functioning of the Estates, because representatives could continuously refer back to their home cities. In a polity the size of Castile, such frequent contact was simply not feasible. James Tracy (2002) has argued that "the parliaments of the separate Low Countries provinces met more frequently than in any other part of Europe; this is certainly because of the fact that distances were not so great as in large kingdoms like Naples and Castile."[16]

The problem of geographic scale was arguably crucial not only because it raised costs for representatives, but also because it raised costs for citizens

---

[15]See Fawtier (1953), Reynolds (1984: 312), Ertman (1997: 93), Levi (1988: 97) and Blockmans (1998). The idea that distance was a fundamental obstacle to maintenance of an active representative assembly in France has been questioned by Lewis (1962) and Boucoyannis (2006) who argues that French towns regularly sent delegations to Paris, and French nobles often held residences in the city.

[16]See also the comparable comments of Koenigsberger (1992) on geography and its effect on representative assembly behavior in Castile and Holland.

of monitoring the actions of their representatives when and if they did attend an assembly. The historical evidence I have cited so far supports the notion that there could be significant costs to attending a representative assembly. For an individual town that needed to send a representative to an assembly meeting, funding costs of travel could prove prohibitive. But if this was the only obstacle to sustaining an assembly, then it could have been overcome in several ways. First, the size of constituencies could have been enlarged to reduce per capita costs of sending a representative. Second, an assembly could have been structured so that it met for longer periods at more infrequent intervals so as to minimize travel costs. Finally, an assembly could also have delegated authority to a standing committee of a limited number of representatives, or perhaps rely on individuals who, for other reasons, divided their time between a provincial home and the capital city. Some European polities did adopt these solutions. In Castile during the seventeenth century monarchs argued for having the Cortes meet for increasingly long periods of time so as to be able to transact business.[17] In far-flung polities like Austria, much of the financial work of the Estates was delegated to a standing committee.[18] But in each of these two instances, as well in others, there is evidence that such arrangements led to assemblies being effectively "captured" by executives either through direct corruption or through other means. Individual towns or constituencies found it increasingly difficult to monitor the actions of their representatives.[19] The end result then was that geographic scale still posed an important constraint on the ability to sustain constitutional control of an executive.

The importance of geographic scale in conditioning possibilities for representative activity may also help explain two other important differences between assemblies in city-states and those in territorial states. Attendance at territorial state assemblies was initially seen as a duty rather than a privilege. Consider the medieval English Parliament for which Hanna Pitkin (1967: 3) suggests that "far from being a privilege or right, attendance at Parliament was a chore and a duty, reluctantly performed."[20] One plausible reason for making parliamentary attendance a duty (and the same pattern occurred in other medieval assemblies) is that representatives would otherwise have chosen not to attend. In city-states,

[17] Thompson (1982, 1994a, b).

[18] See Dickson (1987) and MacHardy (2003).

[19] This point is emphasized by Blockmans (1978).

[20] On the context for knights' attendance in medieval English parliaments see Wood-Legh (1932).

in strong contrast, one sees constant reference to battles over who would be awarded the privilege of representing his group, and there is no indication of reluctance to participate. Another feature of representative assemblies in territorial states, which is absent in city-states, is that representatives were often paid to attend and in some cases this payment was indexed according to the distance they had to travel. These costs were certainly not negligible, as Major (1955) reports that the French crown spent 50,000 livres tournois indemnifying the deputies to the Estates General of 1484.

PREROGATIVES OF REPRESENTATIVE ASSEMBLIES

In the attempt to provide a systematic overview of the development of representative assemblies, I have collected data on the existence and prerogatives of representative bodies in the same set of 31 European states for which I have data on the development of public credit. The assemblies of the largest European states, such as France, Castile, and England, have been well documented, as have the assemblies of a number of the most prominent city-states. In other cases a much more limited number of sources is available. For compiling this work the different studies published by the Société Jean Bodin, a historical society based in Belgium that since 1935 has promoted work on the study of law and institutions provide an invaluable set of sources. In 1954 and 1955 the Société published two volumes on the administrative, economic, and social institutions of cities, with a heavy emphasis on the experience of self-governing cities in premodern Europe.[21] In 1965, 1966, and 1969 the it published collected volumes on the theme of "Governors and Governed."[22] These include

---

[21] *La Ville: Première Partie, Institutions administratives et judiciaires, Recueils de la Société Jean Bodin*, vol.6. Bruxelles: Éditions de la Librairie Encyclopédique, 1954.*La Ville: Deuxième Partie, Institutions économiques et sociales, Recueils de la Société Jean Bodin*, vol.7. Bruxelles: Éditions de la Librairie Encyclopédique, 1955.

[22] *Gouvernés et gouvernants: Quatrième Partie, Bas moyen age et temps modernes (II), Recueils de la Société Jean Bodin pour l'Histoire Comparative des Institutions*, vol.25. Bruxelles: Editions de la Librairie Encyclopédique, 1965. *Gouvernés et gouvernants: Troisième Partie, Bas moyen age et temps modernes (I), Recueils de la Société Jean Bodin pour l'Histoire Comparative des Institutions*, vol.24. Bruxelles: Editions de la Librairie Encyclopédique, 1966. *Gouvernés et gouvernants: Première Partie, Synthèse générale, civilisations archaïques, islamiques, et orientales, Recueils de la Société Jean Bodin pour l'Histoire Comparative des Instituitions*. Bruxelles: Editions de la Librairie Encyclopédique, 1969.

a wealth of individual studies focusing on the representative institutions of different states. In addition to relying on the studies published by the Société Jean Bodin, I have also consulted a large number of additional studies, including those published under the auspices of the International Commission for the History of Representative and Parliamentary Institutions. The goal of this exercise in quantification is not by any means to imply a degree of exactness; it is instead to attempt to provide an overview that will be useful for establishing broad patterns in the evolution of representation across countries and over time. In consulting these works (please see table 3.1 for a full list), I have focused on four specific questions involving the presence and prerogatives of a representative body. The response to each question is coded as a dummy variable with 1 for "yes" and 0 for "no," based on the best available information.[23]

1. *Is there a representative assembly?* This condition is satisfied if there is a collective body at the level of the state that had at least a consultative role in decision-making. In addition, the assembly or body must have met at least once during the fifty-year period in question. As noted before, city-states often had multiple assemblies, with a more restricted representative body that managed day-to-day affairs, as well as a larger assembly that met less frequently but with larger membership. I have coded as "yes" all cases where there was such a smaller representative body that was selected from a broader constituency or assembly. In coding states according to this first criterion, I also attempted to distinguish between assemblies that were purely isolated events, such as a one-off meeting called to sanction a royal succession, as opposed to bodies that had some regular aspect, even if they did not meet frequently.

2. *Is there a representative assembly the consent of which is sought in order to levy taxes?* This is a more restrictive classification for representative institutions. We might expect that an assembly with veto power over taxes could use this power to sanction a ruler who defaulted on a debt. In many cases assemblies had the right to veto

---

[23]In coding information on representative assemblies in territorial states I have not attempted to distinguish between the two ideal-types of the two-chamber assembly and a tricurial assembly of estates. This distinction is emphasized by Hintze ([1931] 1975) and forms a key part of the account in Ertman (1997). However, Blockmans (1978) argues that the diversity of forms of representation in medieval and early modern Europe makes this dichotomization, even as an ideal-type, far less useful than Hintze had believed.

TABLE 3.1
Sources on Representative Institutions

State	Sources
Arras	Dumont and Timbal (1966), Bougard (1988)
Austria	Dickson (1987), MacHardy (2003)
Barcelona	Font y Rius (1954), Corteguera (2002)
Basel	Gilliard (1965), Gilomen (2003), Schib (1954), Liebeskind (1939)
Bologna	Carboni (1995), Carniello (2002), Jones (1997)
Bremen	Schwartzwalder (1965), Albers (1930)
Bruges	Van Houtte (1967), Murray (2005)
Castile	Marongiu (1968), Thompson (1982, 1994a, b), Beneyto (1966), Ucendo (2006)
Cologne	Dollinger (1954, 1955), Schneider (1954), Knipping (1894, 1898)
Denmark	Lönnroth (1966), Jespersen (2000), Graves (2001)
Dortmund	Dollinger (1954, 1955), Schneider (1954)
Douai	Espinas (1902), Dumont and Timbal (1966), Gilissen (1954)
England	Keir (1938), Hayton (2002), Marongiu (1968)
Florence	Finer (1995), Rubinstein (1966)
France	Major (1960), Dumont and Timbal (1966), Mousnier (1966), Soule (1965)
Geneva	Gilliard (1965), Liebeskind (1939)
Genoa	Epstein (1996b), Fratiannni (2006), Heers (1961)
Ghent	Van Werveke (1946), Pirenne (1910)
Hamburg	Klessman (2002), Reincke (1953)
Holland	Gilissen (1966), Grever (1982), Tracy (1990), Israel (1995)
Mainz	Dollinger (1954, 1955), Schneider (1954)
Milan	Epstein (1993), Belfanti (2001)
Naples	Marongiu (1968), Koenigsberger (1977)
Nuremberg	Dollinger (1954, 1955), Schneider (1954)
Papal States	Partner (1980), Marongiu (1968), Caselli (2003)
Piedmont	Marongiu (1968), Koenigsberger (1971)
Siena	Bowsky (1970, 1981)
Tuscany	Koenigsberger (1977)
Venice	Lane (1973)
Württemberg	Folz (1965), Carsten (1965), Wilson (1992)
Zurich	Gilliard (1965), Schib (1954)

certain taxes but not others. For reasons of simplicity the above question is coded "yes" for those cases where an assembly appears to control a large share of a country's taxation.[24]

---

[24]As such, I am overlooking the important issue raised by Rosenthal (1998) and Dincecco (2009) whereby fragmentation between a crown with decision-making power over levying some taxes and an assembly with power over others could create serious problems of free-riding when it came to collective goods provision.

3. *Is there a representative assembly that has a prominent role in administering taxes?* This distinguishes between cases where the consent of a representative assembly was required to raise taxes but where taxes were collected by agents of a prince or executive, as opposed to cases where a representative assembly decided whether to approve taxes and also played a direct role in administering and monitoring tax collection. It was common in premodern Europe for representative assemblies to play this latter of role, given the relative weakness or absence of state bureaucracies to which the task of collection could be delegated. Granting a control right of this type might be expected to increase the willingness of creditors to lend to a government, provided, of course, that those exercising the control right sought to act in the interest of state creditors.

4. *Is there a representative assembly that directly controls decisions regarding spending?* Representative assemblies with the most extensive financial privileges played a direct role in spending decisions, as well as in decisions regarding public credit, with the assembly's approval necessary for a new loan to be issued or annuity to be sold. This is a further type of control right, the granting of which we would expect might improve a state's access to credit.

I begin the presentation of the data on representative assemblies by considering their evolution over time. The data are presented in terms of individual countries over separate fifty-year periods from 1250 to 1750. For each of the four above questions, figure 3.1 plots the percentage of states with a "yes" response for each of the fifty-year time periods from 1250 to 1750. One can see in figure 3.1 that for each of the four criteria, there is evidence of a greater role for assemblies in the "corporatist age" between 1250 and 1500 than in the period after 1500. This trend is apparent irrespective of whether one asks the simple question of whether an assembly existed or whether it had more significant prerogatives. It should be noted, though, that the observed time trend in figure 3.1 is also influenced by the fact that there are more city-states in the sample for earlier centuries, and city-states tended to have assemblies with strong prerogatives.

Independent of trends over time, the data also point to striking differences between the prerogatives of representative assemblies in city-states and territorial states, as well as to sizeable variation within the group of territorial states. Figure 3.2 presents summary statistics for the four characteristics, pooling together all time periods but differentiating

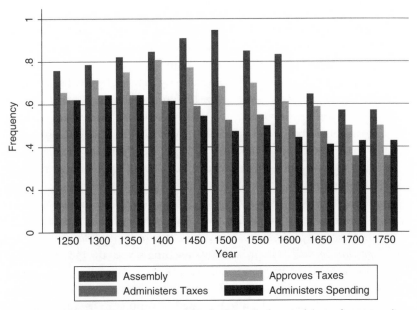

Figure 3.1. Representative assemblies by historical period (sample averages).

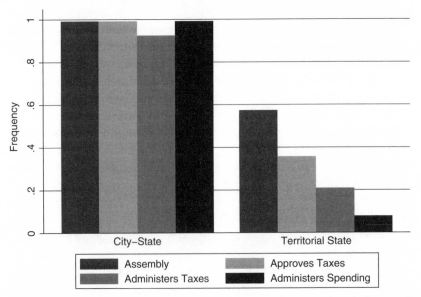

Figure 3.2. Representative assemblies in city-states and territorial states (averaged over periods).

between city-states and territorial states. A sizeable portion of territorial states had assemblies, but many of these assemblies had a relatively weak role with regard to finance. In contrast, all city-states in the sample had an assembly, and almost all assemblies in city-states had very significant control of state finances. The only two real exceptions to this pattern are Arras and Genoa.[25] A second source of variation is also apparent. When we examine data for territorial states in figure 3.2, it is clear that there is very significant variation within this category. While the fraction of territorial states with assemblies that directly administered debt was small (the only states in the sample to which this applied were Holland, Great Britain after 1688, and Württemberg), in roughly half of the territorial state cases (again considered in terms of country half-centuries) there was at least some regularized assembly, and in a significant fraction of these cases the consent of the assemblies was sought to create new taxes.

Though the responses to the four above questions about prerogatives are helpful in producing a broad classification of representative assemblies in Europe, it is also important to ask whether they are consistent with more detailed evidence regarding the existence and functioning of representative bodies in specific European states. This is a subject that will be considered at length in the case studies in chapters 6 and 7 of this book, but it is also worth presenting supporting evidence at this stage. This evidence will also be helpful in pointing to common features of the assemblies that go beyond the criteria already discussed.

A first observation regarding city-state assemblies such as Cologne and Siena is that they developed quite intricate systems for managing public debt. This obviously would have been critical if representative bodies in these states were to exert a control right on behalf of creditors. Richard Knipping (1894, 1898) and Jean Schneider (1954) refer to the system developed in Cologne, where ruling magistrates used three separate treasuries and an elaborate system of revenue collection. This system

---

[25] In the Genoese republic after 1407, revenue collection was controlled by an independent and nonlegislative body, the Casa di San Giorgio, an institution that will be discussed at length in chapter 6. In the case of Arras, a French city that issued long-term annuities in the thirteenth century and that enjoyed some autonomy from the French crown, political representation existed in the form of a group of aldermen (échevins) drawn from the city's mercantile class, but because of the incomplete control of this body over municipal finances, I have not coded it as having a control right over taxation or spending. One might also legitimately question whether Arras should be included as an autonomous city in this sample. Dropping it from the sample results in essentially no change in the statistical estimates that I report in later chapters.

will be described at greater length in chapter 6. The Sienese financial system under the rule of the Nine (1287–1355) provides another prime example of a sophisticated system for the collection and management of revenues and expenditures, as has been demonstrated most clearly by Bowsky (1970), and which will be considered in chapter 6. Though city-states certainly varied in the sophistication of their financial procedures, there is no reason to think that Cologne and Siena were exceptions. One reason why city-states were able to develop sophisticated systems for the management of public credit is that they could imitate and adopt techniques developed by merchants for private transactions.[26] It should be remembered, however, that territorial states with large commercial cities should also logically have been able to take advantage of the same opportunity.

If representative bodies in city-states had extensive control rights, it should not be automatically assumed that information about the state of public finances was transmitted to a broader segment of the population. More commonly than not, it appears that the small groups who exercised power within city-states, and who also often owned public annuities, sought to keep information about public finances hidden from public view. One obvious motivation for this is that while those who owned public annuities benefited from knowing the state of public finances, information about levels of indebtedness (and the future tax burdens that it implied) could raise protests from broader social groups. These groups paid the taxes on common consumption goods, which were often the primary basis for servicing annuity obligations. When members of the broader population within city-states sought to acquire greater representation in municipal government, they often also demanded greater publicity regarding the state of municipal finances.[27]

Though some assemblies in territorial states had control rights over public expenditures, in most territorial states public debt and public spending were managed through other means. In Castile, spending and borrowing were managed by a royal Council of Finance, rather than the Cortes, despite the fact that this assembly (or more precisely its constituent cities) played a prominent role in administering taxes within the realm. Toward the end of the sixteenth century, the Cortes attempted to gain a degree of direct control over royal expenditure, but ultimately it had

---

[26]This is suggested by Schneider (1954) for the case of Cologne.

[27]One example here is provided by the city of Douai at the end of the thirteenth century, as described by Espinas (1902).

only limited success in this enterprise.[28] In France, while the monarchy often borrowed through intermediaries such as the municipality of Paris, overall management of the kingdom's finances was, from the sixteenth century onward, the responsibility of the Conseil des Finances (later the Conseil d'État et des Finances and subsequently the Conseil Royal des Finances). The members of this council were appointed by the king. After the sixteenth century, finances were also managed by the *secrétaires des finances*.[29] What was distinct about this system was that representatives drawn from mercantile groups played a much less direct role in managing state finances than would have been the case in a typical city-state.

WHO WAS REPRESENTED?

There is a long-standing historical argument that city-states tended to be dominated by mercantile interests while territorial states tended to be dominated by landed interests. Not surprisingly, we lack a general measure that could give us a full comparative picture of the wealth composition of the political elite across the 31 European states in my sample. However, since European assemblies during this era tended to have rules explicitly dividing representation among different social groups, it is possible to consider this issue indirectly. The constitutions of city-states often gave a fixed number of seats on the city council to merchants or patricians with remaining seats granted to representatives of craft guilds. Within city-states, in areas like Germany, the Low Countries, and Catalonia this was a subject of frequent contestation, as representatives of the craft guilds demanded greater representation on city councils that had previously been dominated by patrician elites. This "democratic revolution" took place in the Low Countries in the early 14th century and in Germany roughly a century later.[30] Assemblies in territorial states also generally had fixed representation for different social groups, including members of the clergy, representatives of the towns, members of the nobility, and, in a few cases, representatives from the peasantry.

---

[28] See Gelabert (1999: 215–216) and the discussion in chapter 7 of this book.

[29] See the description of the evolution of these institutions in Dumont and Timbal (1966) as well as the extensive work of Hamon (1994, 1999), who focuses on French finances during the sixteenth century.

[30] For a concise description of this movement see van Werveke (1963: 34–37).

In addition to deriving from different social groups, representatives in premodern assemblies were also selected using a variety of different methods. Broadly speaking, it appears from the sources listed in table 3.1 that in territorial states, representatives were either directly nominated by a monarch, or they were elected by a group of constituents. One should not draw the conclusion from this that assemblies where representatives were nominated in the former manner were necessarily weak. Established protocols often placed significant constraints on the ability of a ruler to refuse to extend invitations to specific individuals.[31] Within city-states one also sees an important distinction in how representatives were selected, in particular for the executive councils charged with day-to-day administration in towns. In many cities, particularly before the democratic revolution of the fourteenth century, these executive councils were selected by a system of cooptation, as a sitting council chose new members. In other cases, the executive was elected by a wider body of citizens, and after the democratic revolution this became the norm in many regions (though interestingly not in the cities of Holland). In some cases this constitutional shift appears to have produced a significant change in membership of representatives, while in other cases this was less true.[32] Finally, in a number of cases selection to the council was by lot.[33]

I have used all available information from the sources listed in table 3.1 to estimate the extent of merchant representation in the assemblies of each of the 31 states in my sample for each time period. For city-states "merchant participation" is characterized by the existence of rules that exclusively reserved representation for merchants, or by a certain number of seats being reserved on a ruling council area for individuals described as patricians or high bourgeois. For territorial states, I have measured merchant representation according to the presence of members of towns, as opposed to clergy, nobility, or other groups. In a few cases, such as France, I have also been able to distinguish between bourgeois engaged in commercial activities and those who were royal administrators.

---

[31] See Major (1960) on this point with regard to the French Estate General.

[32] The former phenomenon is illustrated by the case of Douai in the fourteenth century (Espinas 1902; Gilissen 1954; Dumont and Timbal 1966). Ghent provides a contrasting example (Blockmans 1999).

[33] This involves the extensive use of lot in Italian city-states (as has been emphasized by Manin 1995) and in the city of Barcelona (Corteguera 2002). Selection by lot was also the system used by a number of Castilian towns to select their representative to the Cortes.

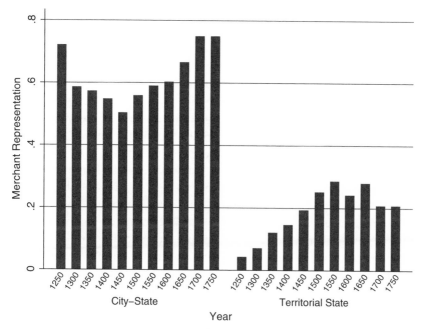

Figure 3.3. Merchant representation in city-states and territorial states (averages).

Figure 3.3 shows the evolution of merchant representation over time, while also distinguishing between city-states and territorial states. The variable "merchant representation" has a minimum of zero and a maximum of one. For city-states one can see a decline in average representation for merchants that corresponds to the period of the "democratic revolution." However, the most salient feature here is the very large and persistent difference between the extent of merchant representation in city-states as opposed to that in territorial states.

It is possible to supplement the systematic evidence on representation of mercantile interests with more specific information on the identity of government creditors in different European states. There are a number of important investigations into the identity of government creditors, particularly in city-states. With great frequency one finds reference to the fact that members of representative assemblies were themselves prominent investors in public debt. There are at least three recent prosopographic studies that provide evidence of a link between ownership of public debt and government office-holding in the Low Countries and that support the earlier evidence in this regard identified by Tracy (1985). Laurence Derycke (2003) provides detailed evidence on the identity of annuity purchasers in fifteenth-century Bruges, and she emphasizes the extent to which those who were representatives in the Bruges city government themselves invested in public debt. Her evidence also points to a very high degree of concentration of annuities ownership, which went hand in hand with the very high degree of wealth inequality observed in the city. The study by Manon van der Heijden (2003) of annuities ownership in the city of Dordrecht at the time of the Dutch revolt makes a similar point, finding that 34% of town magistrates and their family members were registered as public annuity purchasers. Finally, the work by Martijn van der Burg and Marjolein 't Hart (2003) on annuity purchasers in the city of Amsterdam at the end of the sixteenth century, emphasizes the fact that urban magistrates were often prominent merchants and that these same magistrates were often prominent purchasers of public annuities.

There is less extensive evidence on the identity of annuity purchasers in German and Swiss city-states, but the evidence that does exist suggests a very similar relationship between political representation and debt ownership. So, for example, Schneider (1955: 491) refers to the development of annuities sales in German city-states by suggesting that "the control of financial operations was exercised by men of the same condition and sometimes those directly interested [the annuity owners] acting as magistrates." Close investigations of representative politics and public credit in Lübeck and Cologne provide direct evidence to support this assertion.[34]

The city-states of Northern Italy may have had a pattern of debt ownership different from those of other city-states. Those who governed owned debt, but ownership was also spread more widely among wealth holders, presumably due to the heavy reliance on a system of forced loans. Pezzolo (2003b) cites evidence suggesting that in 1427, almost a quarter of Florentine households held debt, while by 1500 this was true of 14 percent of Genoese households.[35]

A question one might ask about the membership of representative assemblies is how critical was this for public credit. For example, Merchants might dominate politics within a city-state through informal social networks or by lobbying a city council even if they were not actually

---

[34] For Lübeck, see the discussion in Rotz (1977) and for Cologne see Knipping (1898).

[35] Macdonald (2006: 94–96) also comments on the extensiveness of ownership of Casa di San Giorgio shares among Genoese citizens.

members of this body. There is evidence for specific city-states showing that merchants were frequently consulted by town councils even when they were not members. It is also known that mercantile elites in city-states often participated in social organizations with restricted membership that had significant political influence.[36] Ultimately, however, the clearest indication that membership on representative bodies mattered is that the number of seats on city councils reserved for different groups within a community was a subject of active political contestation. Those who led revolts and uprisings in city-states often focused on the objective of reforming town constitutions so as to broaden participation on councils while also making the selection of representatives more democratic. This was the case in Cologne in 1396, Ghent in 1302, Lübeck in 1408, and Siena in 1355. In the next chapter I will present statistical results showing that on average, shifts in the degree of formal merchant control had important implications for public credit.

The Intensity of Representation

With the origins, prerogatives, and membership of representative assemblies considered, the final question I address in this chapter is how frequently these assemblies actually met. In order for a representative body to exercise a control right over spending, the body will have to meet frequently. I have already referred to the argument by Blockmans (1998) that in premodern Europe intensive forms of representation could occur only in relatively small polities. City-states were small compared to territorial states. There was also significant variation in size within the group of territorial states. In this subsection I report systematic evidence on the frequency with which representative bodies met. As with the data on prerogatives and membership in assemblies, my data on meeting frequency is drawn from a wide variety of secondary sources that are listed in table 3.1. The quality of this information varies from state to state. In some cases, such as France or England, we have an essentially complete record of meetings by national representative institutions. In other cases the evidence is much more approximate, and I have been forced to infer meeting frequency from much less precise sources. The

---

[36]The Circle Society in Lübeck and the Richerzeche of Cologne provide good examples of this phenomenon. See Rotz (1977) on Lübeck and Dollinger (1955) on Cologne.

data should nonetheless be helpful in addressing qualitative differences in the intensity of representative activity.

I have coded a measure of the frequency of assembly meetings that ranges from 0 (no meetings) to 1, which represents a meeting taking place at least once a year.[37] I also made use of information on assemblies in several territorial states for which no information on costs of borrowing was available.[38] Based on this exercise, I found no evidence of a city-state with an assembly or collective representative body that did not meet at least once a year. In contrast, in over half of the territorial state cases, an assembly met less than once every two years, and in roughly a quarter of cases less than once every four years. The disparity between frequent meetings of city-state assemblies and infrequent meetings of territorial states assemblies is strongly suggestive of an effect of geographic scale. But of course there may also have been other reasons why city-state assemblies tended to meet more frequently. For example, it may have been the case that the highly commercialized economies of city-states required greater regulation, and an assembly is one actor that could have played such a role.

We can also investigate the relationship between geographic scale and political representation in a more systematic way. To do so I will report results using geographic scale data collected for a related project.[39] I will use two measures of geographic scale, constructed from a historical GIS data set, that provide feasible proxies for the cost that societies would incur in sending their representatives to an assembly and in monitoring their actions. The first is the natural log of the number of square kilometers (in thousands). This measure is available for all of the territorial states in my sample, in addition to a limited number of the city-states.[40] Area in square

---

[37] Since some representative assemblies actually met more frequently than once a year, this measure is "censored." I have opted for this approach because of the difficulty of measuring activity at intra-annual frequencies. Results of regression estimates that take explicit account of this censoring (a tobit model) are substantively similar to those reported in table 3.2.

[38] These cases include Hungary (Bonis 1965), Saxony (Carsten 1959), Prussia (Brandenburg), or Brandenburg (Carsten 1954), Sweden (Schuck 1987; Rystad 1987), Poland (Bardach 1977; Jedruch 1982), Portugal (Payne 1973), and Burgundy (Flanders), or Flanders (Dhondt 1950, 1966).

[39] See Stasavage (2011) for full details.

[40] The source is the Euratlas GIS dataset produced by Nussl: (2003). The city-states included in these estimates are Cologne, Siena, Florence, Genoa, and Venice. These estimates also use data from several territorial states for which I was able to identify

TABLE 3.2
Geographic Scale as a Determinant of Meeting Frequency

estimation in	levels (1)	differences (2)	levels (3)	differences (4)
ln(Area)	−.087 (.019)	−.042 (.025)		
Polity Scale			−.082 (.033)	−.048 (.019)
R²	.25	.06	.13	.07
N=	229	205	229	205
period dummies?	yes	yes	yes	yes

OLS estimates, standard errors in parentheses clustered to allow for arbitrary with in polity correlation.

kilometers will be a better proxy the more uniformly a polity's population is distributed across its territory. I also employ a second proxy measure, which is the log distance that the average urban inhabitant in a country would need to travel to reach a country's capital (the most common site for an assembly). This measure, which I will refer to as the *polity scale*, will be a better proxy the greater the extent to which the distribution of the urban population in a polity reflects the distribution of the total population.[41]

Table 3.2 reports the results of estimates of the following equation where meeting frequency is estimated as a function of a geographic scale measure S and a set of controls:

$$Frequency_{it} = \alpha + \beta S_{it} + u_i + z_t + \varepsilon_{it} \qquad (1)$$

I report results using the two alternative geographic scale measures: (1) the natural log of a polity's *log area* in thousand square kilometers, and (2) the *polity scale* measure. In addition, I also estimate the equation in both levels and in first differences. First differencing the data is one way of removing unobserved factors specific to each polity u_i that might be biasing my inference that there is a causal relationship between geographic scale and meeting frequency. As such, this is a very strong test of the hypothesis.

---

information on representative institutions but not information on long-term public debt. States in this category include Burgundy, Saxony, Portugal, Prussia, Sweden, Hungary, Poland, and Russia.

[41] Using existing data sources it is not possible to provide a measure for the geographic dispersion of the total population within each polity.

However, first differencing also means throwing out much of the usable information in the data, making it more difficult to obtain statistically significant results even in the absence of bias. As a result, I also report results of an estimation in levels.

The results of the regressions in table 3.2 point to a clear effect of geographic scale on the intensity of political representation. A much more complete set of tests can be found in Stasavage (2010). When estimating in levels there is a highly statistically significant correlation between area and meeting frequency, and the implied effect is large. A square-shaped polity 50 kilometers across would be estimated to have an assembly that met in about three out of every four years. In a similar polity 250 kilometers across, the predicted frequency would drop to a little less than once every two years. When estimating in first differences, *log area* is no longer statistically significant, but this is not surprising given that polity square area is highly persistent within this dataset.[42] When using *polity scale* as a measure of geographic scale, we observe a statistically significant coefficient on this variable both when estimating in levels and when estimating in first differences. This is particularly strong evidence of a causal effect of geographic scale on the intensity of political representation. In work elsewhere I have demonstrated that this result is robust to a number of further potential endogeneity and robustness concerns.[43]

Summary

In this chapter I have presented an overview of the evolution of representative institutions in Europe. In so doing I have emphasized how my evidence relates to long-standing historical arguments about the emergence and evolution of political representation. Though my classifications are certainly far from exact, several trends are apparent, and these are of such a magnitude that it seems difficult to argue that they could be purely the result of statistical coding choices. First and foremost, there is a dramatic difference in the activities of representative assemblies in city-states and territorial states. The fact that there is such a stark difference in the financial prerogatives of these two groups of states, and that this difference persisted over several centuries, suggests

---

[42] A regression of the log area measure on a set of polity dummies resulted in an R^2 of 0.93.

[43] See Stasavage (2010).

that strong representative institutions did not evolve by accident. Once the pattern of division was set between city-states on one hand and territorial states on the other, and this happened before the middle of the thirteenth century, then the subsequent evolution of representative institutions was heavily conditioned by the fact that city-states were small. Small size made it easier to sustain frequent meetings of an assembly. The fact that city-states were dominated by merchants had further clear implications for the development and evolution of their institutions. This assessment is supported by the evidence I have presented on the correlation between polity size and the intensity of representative activity, as well as by information on the heavy representation of merchants in city-states when compared to territorial states. In territorial states, underlying factors were less favorable to the evolution of active representative institutions. However, there was also significant variation in representative institutions within the group of territorial states (both across states and over time). In the next chapter I will explore whether this variation in representative institutions had implications for the evolution of public credit.

CHAPTER FOUR

Assessing the City-State Advantage

The previous two chapters have painted a broad picture of the emergence of representative assemblies and the development of public credit in Europe. I have emphasized the strong contrast between city-states and territorial states and suggested that strictly economic factors may not suffice to account for this difference. City-states created a long-term debt earlier than their territorial neighbors, and on average they borrowed at significantly lower rates of interest. City-states also had more active representative assemblies that played a more direct role in managing and monitoring spending, taxation, and debt. The goal of this chapter is to bring the evidence on the evolution of public credit and of representative institutions together to present a more complete set of empirical tests. I first develop a basic game theoretic model that illustrates how both representative institutions and public credit might emerge as an equilibrium outcome dependent on an underlying cost for representatives of monitoring public finances. I then use the model to develop an empirical specification that can help test the core argument of this book.

In the empirical tests I first examine what factors were correlated with the initial creation of a long-term public debt. I test three separate hypotheses: (1) that access to credit depended on commercial and economic development (2) that access to credit depended on the presence of representative institutions; and (3) that access to credit depended on the differing underlying conditions in city-states and territorial states. There is clear evidence from the regressions that greater commercial and economic development favored access to public credit. This is not surprising. The big question is whether anything else mattered. The regression results also provide a strong indication that the presence of a representative assembly, and in particular an assembly that met frequently and enjoyed the prerogative to monitor spending, was associated with earlier creation of a long-term debt. However, once we control for the difference between city-states and territorial states this apparent effect of representative institutions disappears. This result does not automatically imply that representative institutions did not matter. What it does mean is that if representation did matter, the form of representation associated with early creation of a public debt was above all present in city-states. Because these regression estimates include extensive controls for commercial and economic development, we can have some confidence that this empirical finding supports my core argument about the underlying factors of small size and an elite class of citizens holding liquid wealth. However, there certainly remain possibilities that other underlying conditions present in city-states were responsible for this result, and it will be the goal of subsequent sections and chapters to explore this possibility.

I next examine the correlates of borrowing costs, again considering the potential role of economic and commercial development, representative institutions, and underlying conditions within city-states and territorial states. Here we see a clear picture. As we would expect, costs of borrowing were correlated with private interest rates and were decreasing in the level of commercial and economic development (as proxied by measures of urbanization). When controlling for these factors, but not for underlying differences between city-states and territorial states, we observe that the presence of an intensive form of political representation is associated with significantly lower borrowing costs for states. However, once we control for the difference between city-states and territorial states, the measures of representative institutions are no longer statistically significant, whereas there is a consistent statistically significant difference between borrowing costs in city-states and territorial states. The interest rate advantage enjoyed by city-states is estimated to have been two percentage points, though this estimate is likely to be biased downward because in initial periods territorial states were unable to borrow long-term at any rate.

As a final step in the analysis, I provide a more direct test of the proposition that it was political control by merchants, and not simply their presence, that was critical for access to credit. In the previous chapter I highlighted a stark difference between the degree of merchant representation in the assemblies of city-states as opposed to that territorial in the assemblies of states. If this was the most salient feature of merchant representation in Europe during these five centuries, it is also true that rules governing the degree of merchant representation varied over time within the group of city-states. That they varied not only across cities but also over time allows us to construct a more powerful test of the proposition that merchant representation mattered. Using a specification that includes polity fixed effects, I identify a negative correlation between the degree of merchant representation on city councils and costs of borrowing. I also observe that those city-states that selected their representatives by a system of cooptation borrowed at significantly lower rates than did those in which representatives were elected. Both of these findings support the idea that the best thing for ensuring access to credit was to have a merchant oligarchy.

REPRESENTATION AND CREDIT AS AN EQUILIBRIUM

The core argument of this book is that small geographic scale and the presence of a political elite holding liquid wealth favored the emergence of an intensive form of political representation, which in turn gave states better access to credit. Before proceeding with an econometric test, it may first be useful to illustrate this argument more formally and to use this exercise to develop several explicit hypotheses. To do so I consider a scenario where an executive (either a monarch or ruling magistrate) seeks to raise finance by borrowing from a group of lenders. Rather than focus exclusively on the possibility that an executive might choose to default even if he has the money to repay, I focus instead on another possibility—prior to knowing whether he has sufficient funds to repay a loan, an executive might prefer to take a risky course of action that increases the possibility that a default will be triggered by exogenous circumstances. Under these circumstances an executive may then have greater access to credit if lenders are able to engage in monitoring that involves frequent verification of the state of public finances and implementation of corrective actions when necessary. In the literature on corporate finance such prerogatives are referred to as control rights.

The model is built on several assumptions. For one, there is an exogenous risk that the enterprise engaged in by the executive fails to result in sufficient revenues to repay the loan. In the model it is also possible for lenders to select a representative who monitors the financial situation, thereby reducing this exogenous risk. However, engaging in monitoring is costly for the representative. Finally, it is assumed that outside monitoring is necessary because the executive himself is unwilling to take actions that reduce the exogenous risk of default. This could be the case if such actions involve choices like scaling back military adventures that have important political costs. In equilibrium any exogenous factor that lowers the cost of monitoring will have three effects. First, the representative will choose to monitor more intensively. Second, and as a consequence, there will be lower costs of government borrowing. Finally, and following from the previous two predictions, there will be a greater likelihood that the executive decides to enter the debt market in the first place. This illustrates the key theoretical points that I have been making throughout this book.

Setup of the model

Consider a scenario with three types of players: (1) an executive who has the option of borrowing a sum L from (2) a set of n risk-neutral lenders with unlimited resources, and (3) a representative who is selected by the lenders and who can monitor the executive. If the executive chooses to borrow, he produces output with the loan amount according to a function $F(L, \omega)$, where ω is a binary state variable. If the level of the state variable is high, production is equal to βL, where β is an exogenous parameter and $\beta > 1$. If the level of the state is low, then $\beta = 0$ triggering an automatic default.

In this model lenders select a representative who can engage in monitoring that reduces the risk that $\omega = 0$. In practice this would involve taking regular actions to verify the state of public finances, anticipating the future situation, and, if needed, taking corrective actions to restrict spending or raise taxes so as to ensure that debt can be repaid. I will model these different possibilities in a very stylized fashion by suggesting simply that the representative can choose a level of monitoring $m \in [0, 1]$ that determines the probability that the state is high $\Pr(\omega = 1) = m$.[1]

The foregoing specification follows existing models of corporate finance.[2] Following this literature, I also allow for the possibility that the representative finds it costly to monitor. The representative incurs a monitoring cost $cm^2 L$, where c is an exogenous parameter and $0 < c < 1$. In practice, for the historical context that I am considering, the parameter c could reflect two polity features that I have emphasized. First, in larger polities it will be more costly to attend assembly meetings regularly. Second, in polities where lenders are prominently represented within an assembly, it will be less difficult to obtain sufficient political support to take corrective measures.

I also assume that when the representative monitors the executive, this imposes a cost on the executive equal to hm where h is an exogenous

---

[1] This can be thought of as a reduced form for a more realistic, but more elaborate, specification where the representative must choose between two discrete actions, and the optimal action depends upon the realization of an unobserved state variable. In this alternative specification, the representative can choose the degree of monitoring, and a higher level of monitoring implies a more accurate signal about the state.

[2] In particular Tirole (2006, 1999).

parameter and $h > 0$. If such a cost did not exist, the executive would have no reason not to choose $m = 1$ on his own so as to exclude the possibility of an exogenously triggered default. In practice, the cost for the executive could involve a loss of prestige, reputation, or "ego rents" from having to scale back military engagements, or other political costs of curtailing spending. If such costs exist, then an executive might be more willing to run the risk of a default than would government creditors. This is a plausible assumption, in particular for the countries and time period I am considering.[3]

Finally, in addition to each of the previously mentioned assumptions, I also assume that if the executive decides to default at the end of the game, he suffers an exogenous cost d. This would include costs from loss of reputation and any political or economic sanctions that might be incurred.[4]

The order of play of the game is as follows:

1. The executive chooses the quantity of debt to issue L. If he chooses not to issue any debt he receives a default payoff v.

2. Lenders allocate their capital between government debt and a safe asset that yields return r. The interest rate is determined by perfect price competition between lenders.

3. A monitor is chosen by lot from the set of individuals who purchase government debt. The monitor chooses $m \in [0, 1]$, which determines the probability that the state of the world is high p. The monitor incurs a cost equal to cm^2L.

4. The state of the world ω is realized. With probability p the state is $\omega = 1$. If $\omega = 0$ a default occurs automatically. If $\omega = 1$ the executive must decide whether to repay or default on the debt. In any case of default, the executive incurs an exogenous cost d.

---

[3] Previous game theoretic work since at least Downs and Rocke (1994) has emphasized that executives might have a greater appetite for risk than their citizens for fighting wars. Rosenthal (1998) develops a model that incorporates this assumption and which is specifically tailored to the early modern European context.

[4] It has been suggested previously that the magnitude of this cost will be higher in countries with representative assemblies that could take actions such as withholding revenues. See North and Weingast (1989) and Robinson (1998). In the context of international debt, Tomz (2007) has made an important critique of the idea that repayment in practice is ever ensured by the threat of sanctions. Mitchener and Weidenmier (2010) have presented empirical evidence of the use of sanctions in cases of default on international loans.

Equilibrium

I focus on establishing how much an executive will borrow, at what cost, and with what level of monitoring in a symmetric equilibrium where each lender purchases an identical quantity of government debt.

Proceeding by backward induction, at the final stage of the game the executive will know the state of the world, the loan quantity, the interest rate, and the exogenous cost d. If $\omega = 1$, it is possible to have an equilibrium in which he repays the loan as long as the following incentive compatibility condition is satisfied.

$$L(1 + i) \leq d \tag{2}$$

Consider the case where the incentive compatibility constraint is just satisfied. In the prior stage of the game, the representative will face a trade-off whereby greater monitoring reduces the likelihood of an involuntary default, preserving the return on whatever he has lent to the executive. However, monitoring also comes at a cost. Given this, the representative will maximize the following expression with respect to m (after substituting in for $p = m$). In this expression l is the amount loaned by an individual lender.

$$p(1 + i)l - c m^2 L \tag{3}$$

The solution to this problem is given by the following expression. In it we can see the intuitive result that the higher the exogenous cost of monitoring c, the less intensively the representative will monitor.

$$m = \frac{1 + i}{2cn} \tag{4}$$

Now consider the determination of the interest rate. Provided the executive's incentive compatibility condition is satisfied, competition between lenders will drive the interest rate on government debt down to the point where the expected return from investing in government debt is equal to the return from the safe asset. For an individual lender the expected return from investing in government debt depends on the interest rate i, the probability that $\omega = 1$, the likelihood that they will be selected as representative $\frac{1}{n}$, and the cost of monitoring $c m^2 L$.

$$p(1 + i)l - \frac{1}{n} c m^2 L = (1 + r)l \tag{5}$$

Lenders will anticipate the level of monitoring chosen by the representative. Dividing both sides of the expression by l and then substituting in for $p = \frac{1+i}{2cn}$ allows us, after several algebraic steps, to obtain the following equation. Here the interest rate is expressed purely as a function of three exogenous parameters of the model:

$$i = \sqrt{\frac{2cn(1+r)}{1-c}} \tag{6}$$

We can see from equation 6 that the equilibrium interest rate will be strictly increasing in the cost of monitoring c. The intuition behind this result is that a higher cost will prompt the representative to choose a lower level of monitoring, making investing in government debt more risky, and consequently lenders will need to be offered a higher interest rate in order to purchase the asset.

As a final step, consider incentives for the executive in the first stage. The executive will need to decide whether to issue debt or instead to receive utility v. If he does issue debt, then he will need to decide in what quantity. In deciding whether to issue debt, the executive will take into account the expected likelihood that revenues will be sufficient to repay, the level of the interest rate (which depends on the exogenous parameters c, r, and n), the cost he suffers in case of default, and the anticipated cost of being monitored. He will thus decide to issue debt if the following participation constraint is satisfied.

$$p(\beta L - (1 + i)L) - (1 - p)d - hm \geq v \tag{7}$$

Given the linear relationship here between production and repayment, an executive that issues any debt will do so up to the point where the incentive compatibility constraint is just satisfied. Taking this into account, we can simplify equation 7 based on the fact that $L = \frac{d}{1+i}$. We can then substitute in for the equilibrium values of p and i to express the participation constraint in terms of the exogenous parameters of the model.

$$\frac{1}{2cn}\left[d\beta - h\left(1 + \sqrt{\frac{2cn(1+r)}{1-c}}\right)\right] - d \geq v \tag{8}$$

Here we see that the likelihood of the participation constraint being satisfied is greater the lower the level of the exogenous cost of monitoring for the representative.

One clear prediction of the theoretical model is that there will be less intensive monitoring the higher the exogenous costs of engaging in this activity. I have already tested this prediction empirically in the previous chapter with the examination of geographic scale and the intensity of political representation. In the remainder of the current chapter I will focus on two further predictions of the theoretical model.

First, the model predicts that the observed interest rate on government debt should be increasing in c, the cost for representatives of monitoring the executive. I have suggested that monitoring costs should be lower in city-states. But the interest rate should also be increasing in r, the risk-free return to capital, and there are several reasons why the risk-free return of capital might be significantly lower in city-states than territorial states. As a result, much of my effort in this chapter will be devoted to examining whether the city-state financial advantage observed in chapter 3 continues to be observed even after we attempt, as best possible, to control for the different economic conditions in city-states and territorial states.

A second key prediction of the model is that an executive will be more likely to create a public debt when the cost for representatives of monitoring the executive is low. As such, city-states can be expected to have created public debts earlier than territorial states.[5] But since we should also expect an executive to be more likely to create a public debt when the risk-free return on capital is low, this again raises the possibility that any observed advantage of city-states may be attributable to this alternative causal channel.

REPRESENTATIVE INSTITUTIONS AND THE CREATION
OF A PUBLIC DEBT

The theoretical model presented in the previous section suggests that a sovereign will be more likely to take the decision to borrow when the cost for a representative of monitoring is low, when the return on alternative assets is low, and when the sovereign's outside option is less attractive. To test these implications fully one would need direct measures for each of

---

[5]More specifically, we might justify this prediction as follows. If the risk-free return to capital r was higher during earlier periods in my sample, which is known to have been the case, then we would expect a polity with lower monitoring costs to be more likely to create a long-term debt at an earlier date, because the state would pay a lower premium relative to the risk-free rate.

these parameters. Though this is clearly not possible, we can nonetheless use the predictions of the theoretical model to aid in a choice of empirical specification. In what follows I use a probit regression to estimate the probability that a state will create a long-term public debt. The goal here is to attempt to test three alternative hypotheses: (1) that access to credit depended on commercial and economic development, which should be the primary determinant of the risk-free return on capital r; (2) that access to credit depended on having strong representative institutions (independent of underlying conditions); and (3) that access to credit depended on the different underlying political conditions in city-states and territorial states.

$$\Pr(\text{debt}_{it}) = \Phi(\alpha + \beta \text{city}_i + \gamma \text{represent}_{it} + \delta \ln(r_{it}^{\text{lr}}) + \zeta \mathbf{X}_{it} + \eta 1500 + u_{it})$$

$$(9)$$

In equation 9 the variable *debt* takes a value of 0 for all time periods where a state has not yet created a long-term public debt, and a value of 1 for the period where a state first established a long-term debt. The notation i here refers to an individual state, and t refers to time. The data are grouped into fifty-year time periods. Once a state creates a public debt, it is dropped from the estimation for subsequent periods. This method allows for focusing on the factors associated with the initial move to create a long-term public debt.[6]

The core variables in the regression are those that distinguish between city-states and territorial states and that capture the structure of representative institutions.

The variable *city-state* is a dummy indicator taking a value of 1 for city-states and 0 for territorial states, based on the classification proposed in chapter 2. The core argument of this book is that underlying conditions involving geographic scale and the composition of elite wealth drove outcomes with regard to both representative institutions and public debt. In using the city-state dummy variable to test my argument, I am in effect suggesting that this variable can serve as a proxy for these two underlying conditions.

---

[6]If I did not drop observations for states that had already created a public debt, then the estimation would have a different interpretation, because it would involve a comparison between economic and political conditions when a public debt had not yet been created with conditions during or subsequent to the establishment of a debt. See Beck, Katz, and Tucker (1998) on this point.

In equation (9) the variable *represent* is designed to capture the extent to which there is a representative body that has prerogatives in the area of taxation and/or finance. Five alternative measures are proposed, following the distinctions in chapter 3. These are (1) the presence of an assembly, (2) an assembly that could refuse tax increases, (3) an assembly that administered taxes, and (4) an assembly that exerts control over spending, in addition to (5) a measure based on the frequency with which an assembly met.

Since either the representative institutions variables or the city-state dummy variable may be proxying for different economic conditions, it is critical that the regression also include as extensive a set of controls as possible to capture potential economic differences between city-states and territorial states.

As a first control, I proxy for r the risk-free return on capital by using the data on returns for land rents compiled by Gregory Clark (1988). Were this a perfect, or close to perfect, measure, it might suffice as a control, and we could then be more confident that the β coefficient on the city-state dummy is capturing the effect of the underlying political conditions I have emphasized. But this is not likely to be the case. In practice, as already noted, the measure for the return on land rents r_{it}^{lr} varies almost exclusively over time rather than across states. So it is best thought of as a control for the broad decline in interest rates that is known to have occurred in Europe over the five centuries that I consider.

It is generally acknowledged that in the absence of more direct measures, data on urbanization presents one of the best available proxy measures for economic and commercial development in medieval and early modern Europe. I will make use of three separate urbanization measures. These controls are denoted by the matrix $\mathbf{X}_{it}$. These three measures are each certainly highly correlated with one another, and so we should be cautious in interpreting individual urbanization coefficients. Collectively, however, they should serve as a more effective set of controls than if only one of them were included.

For one, I include the natural log of the urbanization rate ln(urbanization) for each major European region as measured by Bairoch, Batou, and Chèvre (1988). This is based on the data constructed by these authors for populations of all individual cities in a territory that by 1800 had reached a size of at least 5000 inhabitants. The urbanization rate is then measured as the overall urban population for a territory divided by the territory's total population. Territories are defined according to modern European country boundaries, as opposed to the historical boundaries of polities in my data. This is a significant shortcoming that provides an important reason for supplementing the Bairoch urbanization rate with other urbanization measures.

There does exist an alternative database of historical European city populations that was constructed by Jan de Vries (1984), which is often considered to have a lower degree of measurement error than the Bairoch database, but it has the other shortcoming of beginning only in the year 1500. Like Bairoch, de Vries reports urbanization rates based on modern European country boundaries. In practice the urbanization rates in my sample reported by Bairoch and de Vries turned out to be extremely similar, with a pairwise correlation coefficient of 0.95. As a result, I will use the Bairoch data in my regressions.[7]

As a second urbanization measure, I also include the natural log of capital city population (in thousands) denoted $\ln(\text{population}_{it})$ in the regression tables to follow. For city-states this variable measures the population of the core city, excluding population in any subject areas. For territorial states this variable measures the population of the capital city. Unlike the land rent return and urbanization variables, we have access to an estimate of capital city population that is specific to each state, and not just to a region.

A third urbanization measure, the *urban potential*, is specific to each capital city. It is designed to measure whether a capital city is located in a region where there is a significant concentration of urban population. First proposed by de Vries (1984), this measure has the great advantage of not requiring the prior specification by the researcher of regional boundaries. For each capital city the urban potential measure is simply a weighted sum of all city populations, where the weights are defined by the distance of each city from the city in question.[8]

As a final step in the specification, I also include a crude control for structural change. As has been emphasized in previous chapters, the

[7]I did consider an alternative urbanization measure constructed as follows. First, I regressed the de Vries urbanization rate on the Bairoch rate and computed fitted values, including for those out-of-sample observations where there was no rate reported by de Vries (observations prior to 1500). I then constructed a variable in which I used the de Vries rate when it existed and the fitted value from the regression for all other observations. Regression estimates using this alternative urbanization variable turned out to be almost identical to those reported in this chapter.

[8]Following de Vries (1984), all cities lying at a distance of less than 20 kilometers from the city in question are counted as if they were at a distance of 20 kilometers. Without a restriction of this sort, the urban potential measure would tend to infinity as an adjacent city's distance was shrunk to zero.

conditions that favored creation of a public debt in the three centuries between 1200 and 1500 were significantly different from those favoring this institutional innovation after 1500. I include a dummy variable *1500* that takes a value of 1 for all periods beginning in this year and a value of zero for all previous periods.

Regression Results

In table 4.1 the first regression includes only the economic controls, the dummy variable for years after 1500, and the city-state dummy variable. (The reported standard errors are clustered by polity to allow for arbitrary intra-polity correlation.) The two clear results from this regression are the marked increase after 1500 in the likelihood of a state creating a public debt (the coefficient on the post-1500 dummy is positive and highly significant) and the clear difference between city-states and territorial states, with the former group being much more likely to create a public debt at an early date. This constitutes strong evidence that the observed difference between city-states and territorial states is not simply attributable to the fact that city-states emerged in more developed regions of Europe. Based on regression (1), if we consider the economic control variables at their means, in any given period where it had not already done so, a city-state would have an estimated 43% probability of creating a long-term debt. Under the same conditions, a territorial state would have only a 5% likelihood of doing so. Among the urbanization variables, in some specifications we observe a statistically significant effect of urban potential. This fits with what we would expect. States in more urbanized regions may have found it easier to establish a public debt at an early date for strictly economic reasons. The coefficient on the land rent return is never statistically significant, but it should be remembered that almost all of the observed variation in land rent returns involves the secular decline in these returns over time, as opposed to variation between regions, and change over time in this estimation is partly controlled for by the inclusion of a dummy variable for periods after 1500.[9]

The regressions in columns 2 through 6 extend the specification by adding, alternatively, one of the five different representative institutions variables. These involve whether an assembly existed, whether its approval

---

[9]Very similar results are obtained in the table 4.1 regressions if we include a linear time trend instead of the land rent return variable, or if we include a full set of period dummies as a substitute for both the land rent return variable and post-1500 dummy.

TABLE 4.1
Probability of Creating a Long-Term Debt (Probit Estimates)

	(1)	(2)	(3)	(4)	(5)	(6)	(7)	(8)	(9)	(10)	(11)
land rent return	-.116 (.144)	.069 (.128)	.100 (.141)	-.028 (.156)	-.044 (.147)	.019 (.125)	-.113 (.139)	-.117 (.140)	-.101 (.153)	-.101 (.142)	-.096 (.148)
ln(urbanization)	.067 (.054)	.066 (.049)	.061 (.049)	.046 (.044)	.051 (.050)	.050 (.054)	.069 (.052)	.067 (.053)	.056 (.047)	.062 (.054)	.062 (.053)
ln(capital population)	-.010 (.038)	-.018 (.047)	.001 (.048)	.002 (.037)	.001 (.039)	.007 (.043)	-.012 (.037)	-.010 (.038)	-.003 (.035)	-.006 (.040)	-.003 (.036)
urban potential	.137 (.108)	.204 (.124)	.130 (.123)	.250 (.120)	.151 (.121)	.179 (.100)	.151 (.097)	.137 (.111)	.191 (.106)	.138 (.109)	.142 (.101)
post-1500 dummy	.424 (.174)	.338 (.136)	.371 (.160)	.365 (.171)	.394 (.165)	.366 (.154)	.423 (.164)	.423 (.174)	.417 (.183)	.420 (.175)	.417 (.166)
city-state	.374 (.104)						.329 (.110)	.375 (.132)	.221 (.119)	.278 (.283)	.275 (.148)
assembly existed		.202 (.057)									
assembly approves taxes			.182 (.069)				.088 (.070)				
assembly admin. taxes				.332 (.084)				-.002 (.100)	.183 (.100)		
assembly admin. spending					.335 (.090)					.090 (.246)	
frequency of meetings						.335 (.092)					.120 (.128)
Prob > Chi²	<.001	<.001	<.001	<.001	<.001	<.001	<.001	<.001	<.001	<.001	<.001
Mcfadden R²	.220	.145	.138	.217	.211	.196	.226	.220	.240	.222	.226

Marginal Effects from probit estimates of the probability of creating a long-term debt. Dummy variables' marginal effect is for discrete change from 0 to 1. Standard errors are clustered to allow for arbitrary within polity correlation. N = 133. Each observation represents a fifty- year period. Polities that created a long-term debt are subsequently dropped from the sample.

was required for taxes, whether an assembly existed that administered taxes, whether an assembly existed that administered spending and debt, and finally a variable coding the frequency with which an assembly met. In all five cases we observe that the coefficient on the representative institutions variable is positive and highly statistically significant. States with representative institutions are estimated to be more likely to have created a public debt at an early date. The substantive magnitude of this estimated effect is largest when we dichotomize between states that had representative institutions that engaged in direct control of expenditures, and those states that either did not have assemblies or that had assemblies that lacked this prerogative.

Regressions 7 through 11 consider the effect of representative assemblies while simultaneously adding a dummy variable to control for the differences between city-states and territorial states. We now observe significantly less evidence of an effect of representative institutions independent of the underlying differences between city-states and territorial states. Among the five representative institutions variables, the only one that approaches statistical significance (p = .078) is that for an assembly that administers taxes. These results do not automatically imply that representative institutions did not matter. What they do suggest is that if representative institutions did matter, it was only those representative institutions that existed primarily in city-states that had this property. Given that city-states almost universally had representative bodies that met frequently and that engaged in active monitoring of public finances, the coefficients on the representative institutions variables in regressions 7 to 11 are now capturing differences exclusively within the group of territorial states.

In contrast to the finding for the representative institutions coefficients, there continues to be a strong and statistically significant difference between the group of territorial states and the group of city-states in all but one of these regressions. The exception is the case where representative institutions are measured based on a dichotomy between states with an assembly that controls spending and states without such an assembly. This is not surprising, given that this variable is extremely highly correlated with the city-state dummy.

The results discussed in this section can be interpreted as follows. The creation of a long-term public debt was indeed associated with the presence of an intensive form of political representation, but these two features were themselves correlated with the fundamental difference between city-states and territorial states. This is consistent with my argument that it was the small size of city-states and political dominance of merchants (as opposed to just their presence) that accounts for this difference, but of course it does not necessarily prove the case.

One might ask how the results reported here are altered if we adopted a more restricted specification that does not include all three urbanization proxies. When I ran separate regressions using each of the urbanization variables alternatively, the size and statistical significance of the city-state coefficient remained virtually unchanged. Among the three urbanization variables, the *urban potential* measure had the highest level of statistical significance, and the coefficient in this variable was larger in magnitude than that reported in table 4.1, column 1. Even so, the results of this regression implied a much larger effect of polity type (city or territorial) on debt when compared to the effect of urbanization. Holding other variables at their means, one finds that in any given period a city-state would have a 43% chance of creating a long-term debt, whereas a territorial state would have only a 6% chance of doing so. In contrast, the effect of an increase in the *urban potential* measure from the 25th to the 75th percentile of the sample would be to increase this probability from 14 to 25% (holding other variables at their means).

Finally, we can consider how the results are altered if we exclude "questionable" city-states from the sample, in particular Arras, Barcelona, Bologna, Bruges, Douai, and Ghent. In a more restricted sample that excludes these cities, the magnitude of the city-state effect is even larger than in the estimations reported in table 4.1. This is primarily due to the effect of excluding Bologna. If we exclude each of the questionable states but retain Bologna in the sample, then the conclusions regarding the magnitude and statistical significance of the city-state effect remain very close to that reported in table 4.1.

Representative Institutions and the Cost of Borrowing

In addition to finding that city-states established long-term debts before their territorial neighbors, in chapter 2 I also presented summary evidence showing an apparent interest rate differential between city-states and territorial states. I now ask whether this interest rate differential appears attributable primarily to the different economic conditions that prevailed in city-states, or alternatively, to the political conditions that prevailed within these entities. I also consider whether, when it came to costs of borrowing, city-states were similar to other states that had strong representative institutions.

In equation (10) the variable $\ln(i_{it})$ represents the observed interest rate on public debt in state i at time t, based on the interest rate data discussed in depth in chapter 2.

$$\ln(i_{it}) = \alpha + \beta\,\text{city}_i + \gamma\,\text{represent}_{it} + \delta \ln(r_{it}^{\text{lr}}) + \zeta \mathbf{X}_{it} + \eta\,\text{life}_{it} + u_{it} \quad (10)$$

The core variables concerning my political hypotheses remain the same as in the previous set of regressions. A dummy variable is included to distinguish between city-states and territorial states, together with a variable measuring the presence of a representative assembly. Five measures are again considered for representative institutions.

The regression includes the same set of economic controls as used in the previous estimates involving the creation of a public debt. In addition, I include a dummy variable *life*, which takes a value of 1 for interest rates associated with annuities on a single life, and a value of 0 for interest rates on perpetual annuities, annuities on multiple lives, and all other forms of long-term debt observed here. Since the income stream from a life annuity was extinguished upon the death of the holder or a nominee, we would expect lenders to require a relatively higher return in order to purchase this type of debt.[10]

Regression Results

The first column in table 4.2 reports results of a baseline model that includes the city-state dummy and the control variables but no representative institutions variables. The coefficient on the city-state dummy is negative and highly significant. If we consider other variables at their mean values, there is an estimated difference of 2.0 percentage points between the interest rate at which a city-state could borrow and the interest rate at which a territorial state could borrow. This estimate does not take into account the potential bias introduced by the possibility that territorial states did not establish long-term debts prior to 1500 because they would have faced a very high cost of borrowing, an issue that I will consider next.

The next five columns consider each of the five representative institutions variables sequentially and without controlling for underlying

[10]I also considered a final control for structural change in the regression by including a dummy variable for periods beginning with the year 1500. In contrast to the previous estimates on the likelihood of a debt being created, this structural change dummy was never significant in any of the interest rate regressions, and as a consequence it was excluded from the final reported results.

TABLE 4.2
OLS Estimates of the Cost of Borrowing

	(1)	(2)	(3)	(4)	(5)	(6)	(7)	(8)	(9)	(10)	(11)
land rent return	.807 (.168)	.626 (.161)	.645 (.165)	.629 (.154)	.688 (.166)	.638 (.164)	.813 (.170)	.813 (.175)	.811 (.170)	.808 (.184)	.831 (.183)
ln(urbanization)	-.183 (.068)	-.168 (.086)	-.166 (.091)	-.172 (.089)	-.133 (.083)	-.169 (.090)	-.185 (.063)	-.184 (.067)	-.181 (.065)	-.184 (.077)	-.185 (.066)
ln(capital population)	-.086 (.069)	-.055 (.080)	-.090 (.087)	-.071 (.094)	-.130 (.084)	-.070 (.081)	-.092 (.068)	-.083 (.073)	-.079 (.081)	-.086 (.081)	-.085 (.070)
urban potential	.044 (.107)	.077 (.108)	.093 (.113)	.085 (.114)	.140 (.113)	.068 (.114)	.066 (.104)	.041 (.110)	.044 (.108)	.043 (.132)	.046 (.110)
life annuities (dummy)	.289 (.174)	.320 (.178)	.254 (.169)	.292 (.173)	.231 (.162)	.324 (.175)	.280 (.175)	.298 (.178)	.303 (.179)	.290 (.177)	.281 (.177)
city-state (dummy)	-.334 (.105)						-.373 (.109)	-.352 (.112)	-.352 (.113)	-.338 (.188)	-.393 (.130)
assembly existed		-.059 (.088)					.120 (.080)				
assembly approves taxes			-.189 (.102)					.030 (.080)			
assembly admin, taxes				-.080 (.175)					.047 (.135)		
assembly admin. spending					-.264 (.088)					.005 (.138)	
frequency of meetings						-.197 (.108)					.095 (.094)
constant	1.19 (0.38)	1.17 (0.42)	1.35 (0.44)	1.23 (0.54)	1.32 (0.40)	1.32 (0.44)	1.10 (.394)	1.16 (0.43)	1.13 (0.51)	1.19 (0.41)	1.11 (0.43)
R²	.443	.358	.383	.361	.418	.382	.451	.444	.445	.444	.447

OLS estimates of the cost of borrowing. Clustered standard errors-allow for arbitrary within polity correlation. N = 115 with each observation representing a half-century time period.

differences between city-states and territorial states. Here we observe that certain types of representative institutions were associated with lower borrowing costs. States with assemblies that played a role in providing consent to taxation faced lower borrowing costs than those without this institutional feature. The same result is observed for states with assemblies that enjoyed a degree of control over spending. Finally, the coefficient on meeting frequency in column (6) is also negative, and it is borderline significant (p = .078).

The final five regressions in table 4.2 consider the correlation between interest rates on public debt and representative institutions while simultaneously controlling for underlying differences between city-states and territorial states. Irrespective of the measure included, there is a statistically significant interest rate differential between the group of territorial states and the group of city-states. The estimated magnitude of this differential also remains close to that observed when omitting a variable for representative institutions from the specification. The one partial exception here is the regression in column (10) where the city-state dummy variable and the *spending* variable are very highly correlated. These results provide strong evidence of an underlying difference between city-states and territorial states. In regressions 7 through 11 in table 4.2 none of the coefficients for the measures of representative institutions is statistically significant.

I also repeated the regression in column (1) while including each of the three urbanization variables, while dropping the two others. The magnitude and significance of the city-state coefficient remained virtually identical across these three alternative specifications. From these three specifications we can also gain some idea of the relative importance of urbanization versus polity type in determining borrowing costs. Focusing on a regression that includes the Bairoch urbanization rate but excludes the other two urbanization variables, we observe that the difference in borrowing costs between a city-state and a territorial state is roughly equivalent to a shift in borrowing costs produced by an increase in the urbanization rate from 8% (the 25th percentile of the sample distribution) to 22% (the 75th percentile of the distribution).

Since the regressions reported in table 4.2 pool countries over a very long time span, it is important to examine whether the observed difference between city-states and territorial states was the product of one specific time period. In his important work on this subject, Epstein (2000) argued that city-states initially were able to borrow at lower rates of interest than monarchies, but this difference diminished over time as large monarchies adopted better financial techniques. One logical way to address this question is to consider the difference between city-states and territorial states only for later centuries, and in particular for the period after 1500 when territorial states first began to create long-term public debts. When I performed this test, the results were remarkably similar to those observed when considering the entire sample. A second way to address Epstein's argument is to interact the city-state dummy with a time trend in the estimation of equation (10) while also adding a linear time trend to the specification. When I did this I observed, as Epstein suggested, that the city-state financial advantage declined over time (the coefficient on the interaction terms was positive and statistically significant). However, it was also the case in this estimation result that the overall magnitude of the city-state advantage continued to be very sizeable through the seventeenth century. According to this regression estimate, even as late as the first half of the seventeenth century, a city-state would have been able to borrow at a rate of interest two percentage points lower than a territorial state.

Instead of splitting the results by time period, we can also consider whether the city-state advantage remains consistent when looking at individual regions within Europe. One promising opportunity here is to compare city-states and territorial states within Italy. Ten of the 31 sample states are located in Italy, with an even balance of five city-states and five territorial states. When repeating the regression specification in (10) using only Italian data, we continue to observe very similar results. The coefficient on the city-state dummy is consistently negative and statistically significant. The magnitude of the coefficient on the city-state dummy is actually slightly larger than in the table 4.2 regression results.

The estimates of equation (10) may be influenced by problems of selection, as well as by problems of attrition. With regard to the first problem, my theoretical model suggests a natural-selection effect whereby states in which costs of monitoring are high may choose not to borrow at all because they could have access to credit only at very high interest rates. In any observed sample of borrowers, we might underestimate the city-state advantage if territorial states initially chose not to borrow on account of being able to do so at only extremely high interest rates, and if territorial states chose to create long-term debts only once they could borrow at lower cost.

It is possible in principle to control for selection in the estimates of equation (10) using the method developed by Heckman (1979), but doing so in a convincing manner requires identification of a variable that influences selection into the sample (creation of a long-term debt) but that has no effect on the interest rate. This is not an easy task. In the theoretical model that I presented earlier most variables affect both the likelihood that the executive's participation constraint will be satisfied and the equilibrium interest rate. The one exception is v, the value of the executive's outside option. One possibility might be to use the dummy variable for years after 1500 as a proxy for v. I estimated equations (10) and (9) jointly in a sample selection model while also adding a time trend to each equation to ensure that the dummy variable for years after 1500 was not proxying simply for general change over time. The results were consistent with the idea that there is selection bias that results in an underestimation of the interest rate differential between city-states and territorial states. Judging from these estimates, when setting other variables at their means, we would expect a city-state to borrow at 3.0 percentage points less than a territorial state. However, given the significant uncertainty whether the 1500 dummy is proxying only for factors that determine selection, and not the interest rate, we should interpret these results with caution.

A second sample problem that may influence my regression estimates involves attrition—it may be that certain types of states for which we initially observe an interest rate subsequently drop out of the sample because the state ceased to exist. This would not pose a problem for inference about the difference between city-states and territorial states if each state had a similar probability of ceasing to exist, but we know this not to be the case. There are several instances in the sample where city-states failed politically and then were absorbed by larger neighbors. It is also the case that city-states that borrowed at higher interest rates in previous periods, perhaps reflecting some underlying political weakness, were particularly likely to drop out of the sample. There are fewer cases within the sample of territorial states disappearing. If only successful city-states survived while both successful and unsuccessful territorial states survived, this could lead to a biased estimate. Were this the case, over time we would expect, holding other factors constant, to observe a growing interest rate gap between city-states and territorial states. We would also not expect to observe an interest rate advantage for city-states in initial periods. The foregoing results suggest a different story. There was a large interest rate differential between city-states and territorial states in earlier sample periods that included both city-states that would be absorbed at an early date and those that would not. Moreover, we also know that the observed interest rate differential decreased over time, rather than increasing as we would expect if attrition bias were a predominant factor.

As a final robustness check, we can again consider how the results are altered if we exclude the six "questionable" city-states from the sample. In the more restricted sample it was consistently the case that the city-state variable increased in statistical significance, and it was slightly larger in magnitude than when including the broader sample of autonomous cities. This is further strong evidence that while there may be substantial uncertainty about when a city qualifies as a city-state, my core conclusions about a financial advantage of city-states do not depend on the particular classification scheme that I have chosen.

VARIATION WITHIN CITY-STATES

So far in this chapter I have provided evidence that city-states found it easier than territorial states to gain access to credit, and when they did so, they were able to borrow on better terms than their larger neighbors. The regression results can also be interpreted as providing evidence that representative institutions fostered access to credit, but only to the extent that such institutions themselves depended on underlying conditions found in city-states. I have attempted to control for the possibility that city-states had better access to credit simply because they were more economically developed and because they were located in more economically developed regions. In this section I propose a test that allows for further demonstrating the importance of political conditions within city-states, and in particular merchant influence on city councils.

In chapter 3, I presented evidence on merchant representation in the assemblies of territorial states and city-states, noting the dramatically higher level of merchant representation in city-states. While emphasizing this difference, I also pointed to several notable cases where the fraction of an assembly's seats reserved for merchants was either reduced or augmented. Significant reductions in the formal political power of merchants took place in city-states like Siena (in 1355) and Cologne (in 1396), as well as in Douai and in Bruges during the course of the fourteenth century. These institutional changes were associated with revolts by artisans and other groups demanding increased representation. In Genoa in 1528 the opposite development took place as institutional changes strengthened the formal control of mercantile groups over the state. Within the assemblies of city-states, changes in the formal representation of merchant groups often coincided with changes in the process used to select members of a ruling council. The same popular groups that demanded reserved seats on councils also often called for a shift from selection based on cooptation to selection based on open election, a process that, it was thought, would further weaken the position of ruling patriciates. It should be emphasized that not all cases of constitutional change within city-states resulted in a fundamental reordering of power among different groups, as the case of Cologne discussed in chapter 6 will show. However, we can nonetheless expect that in a number of instances constitutional change did bring about a real shift in influence.

Within my sample of city-states, there are a small number of recorded cases of such significant changes in formal representation for merchants. The small number can be explained by the imperfect nature of my data collection, the fact that many city councils were not fundamentally reordered, and finally the fact that revolts producing a change in city council representation were often associated with an interruption in access to credit, and thus disappearance from my sample. This, for example, was the case with Siena after 1355.

While we should be cautious about drawing broad conclusions based on changes in a small number of cases, the existence of the just mentioned changes involving merchant representation and council selection nonetheless provides us with an important opportunity to examine whether it was in fact the political control of merchants, and not just their presence, that mattered for credit. Using the same core specifications from equation (10), I substitute the city-state dummy with a continuous variable measuring the fraction of seats in an assembly reserved for mercantile groups. In some specifications I also add a binary variable measuring whether an assembly's members were selected by election or by cooptation. Since these measures vary both across states and over time, I am now also able to introduce state fixed effects into the estimation. These control for the likely possibility that there are unobserved features of states that determined the cost at which they were able to borrow.

In the fixed effects estimates in table 4.3, the first column reports a regression using the entire sample of states. We observe a negative and statistically significant correlation between the cost of borrowing and merchant representation. Setting the control variables at their mean values, if we compare a state where merchants held a quarter of the seats in an assembly with a state where merchants held three-quarters of the seats, the estimated interest rate differential between these two states would be 2.6 percentage points. This is roughly equivalent to the estimated difference between the cost of borrowing in a territorial state and the cost of borrowing in a city-state.

TABLE 4.3
Fixed Effects Estimates of the Cost of Borrowing

	All polities (1)	City-states (2)	Territorial (3)	All (4)	City-states (5)
land rent return	.691	.670	1.43	.683	.656
	(.158)	(.122)	(1.00)	(.161)	(.121)
ln(urbanization)	−.495	−.837	.521	−.528	−.913
	(.199)	(.229)	(.431)	(.211)	(.237)
ln(capital population)	−.028	.208	−.237	−.034	.212
	(.149)	(.181)	(.206)	(.152)	(.190)
urban potential	−.274	−.276	−.044	−.265	−.295
	(.314)	(.319)	(.485)	(.318)	(.332)
life annuities (dummy)	.425	.360		.493	.424
	(.231)	(.218)		(.196)	(.163)
merchant representation	−.935	−1.18	−.207	−.900	−1.07
	(.353)	(0.42)	(.280)	(.352)	(0.39)
recruitment by cooptation (dummy)				−.154	−.212
				(.135)	(.089)
R² (within)	.568	.663	.664	.571	.673
N =	115	73	42	115	73

Fixed Effects estimates of the cost of borrowing with standard errors clustered by polity. Each observation represents a fifty-year time period between 1250 and 1800.

Since my core argument involves the simultaneous presence of merchant wealth and small size facilitating an intensive form of representation, we can also push further in the analysis. If my argument is accurate, we should expect that a change in merchant representation would have a much bigger impact within a city-state than within a territorial state where geographical obstacles would have been more likely to impede strong representation irrespective of who was selected. The second and third columns in table 4.3 report results for separate sub-samples of city-states and territorial states. As can be seen, within the group of city-states there is evidence of a negative and highly significant correlation between merchant representation and the cost of borrowing. Within the territorial state sub-sample there is no evidence of such a correlation. The final two columns in table 4.3 report results of the same procedure adding a dummy variable to the regression that takes a value of 1 if the members of a state's assembly were selected by a process of cooptation, as opposed to open election.[11] The results regarding merchant representation remain consistent with my argument. We also see here in the city-state sample that when city councils were selected in a more closed fashion this was associated with lower borrowing costs. Since no territorial state assembly selected its members by cooptation, it is not possible to run the same test on a sample limited to territorial states.

The evidence in table 4.3 provides further strong evidence that the preferential access to credit enjoyed by city-states stemmed not only from their economic characteristics but also from the presence of merchant political control. We also see clear evidence here that within the group of city-states, greater closure in the system of representation was actually associated with lower costs of borrowing. Overall, the best thing for access to credit appears to have been a merchant oligarchy.

Summary

In this chapter I have combined my statistical evidence on the evolution of public credit and on the emergence of representative institutions, in order to draw conclusions about the link between debt and representation. The results suggest that the development of public credit did indeed tend to accompany the development of representative institutions, but this phenomenon happened almost exclusively within city-states. This supports the idea that the development and evolution of both debt and representation were dependent on underlying conditions. I have argued that small size and the wealth composition of the political elite were particularly important in this regard. My arguments about political representation of merchants have been further supported by evidence showing that changes in the degree of merchant representation were associated with changes in borrowing conditions.

---

[11] Since the cooptation procedure is observed only within the group of city-states, it is not possible to estimate this specification for the territorial state sample.

CHAPTER FIVE

Origins of City-States

City-states had better access to credit than territorial states, and there are reasons to believe that this can be attributed to their small size and to the strong representation of merchants within their political assemblies. But why did city-states emerge in some European regions in the first place, whereas elsewhere the territorial state became the dominant mode of state organization? In this study I have so far been silent on this important issue. It has long been observed that within Europe, autonomous cities tended to emerge in a relatively narrow belt stretching from the Low Countries to northern Italy, and this empirical observation has invited several different explanations. Answering this question is critical to our conceptualization of the broad process of state formation in Europe. Understanding where city-states came from is also critical in my effort to demonstrate the significance of the underlying conditions I emphasize—small size and the political predominance of merchants. An alternative possibility is that there were other conditions that simultaneously favored attempts by certain cities to establish their autonomy and to gain access to credit. Were this the case, the statistical estimates from the previous chapter might be misleading.

In what follows I review the principal existing explanation for the pattern of city-state development, which is to refer to initial economic conditions. I argue that we may find a more fundamental explanation by investigating the way in which the Carolingian Empire was partitioned during the middle of the ninth century and focusing on the long-term repercussions of this event. I then present a set of empirical tests to bolster these claims. As a final step, I explore the possibility that the Carolingian partition can be used to produce an instrumental variable for city-state development. I discuss the results while also cautioning that we have little assurance that the necessary exclusion restriction for this instrument is satisfied. The principal goal of this chapter is to examine empirically the correlates of city-state development, not to develop a new instrumental variable even more exotic than those that have preceded it.

THE ROKKAN/TILLY HYPOTHESIS

The leading existing explanation so far for the pattern of city-state formation refers to the role of initial economic conditions. For Tilly (1990) city-states developed in those areas of Europe with the highest prior levels of commercial and economic development. Initial commercial and economic development then set these areas on a "capital intensive" path of state development. As a reference point, Tilly uses the year 1000 A.D. For Rokkan (1975, 1973) the emergence of city-states also depended on prior economic development. He emphasizes the early development of European cities that benefitted from their location on core riverine trade routes running from northern Italy to the Low Countries.[1] Other authors have also emphasized the role played by water transport in this regard.[2] A city could have access to water transport if it was an oceanic port, or if it was situated on a major navigable river. Geography, therefore, may have played an important factor in the pattern of city-state development within Europe, given the relative ease of water transport in the Low Countries, in the plain of Lombardy, and along the Rhine. It is certainly known that the Rhineland corridor was an important medieval trade route.

While plausible, what the above analyses may overlook is that many cities that eventually became part of territorial states were also often oceanic or riverine ports, and many of these territorial state capitals were themselves situated on major trade routes. So, while the Rhineland corridor was a major trade route, Europe also had other major trade routes that did not run through regions where city-states were prominent. Peter Spufford (2002: 390–391) suggests that in the thirteenth century the key land trade routes of Europe were represented by a triangle. The western side of the triangle ran from Flanders to Tuscany, via France. The eastern side ran from Tuscany to Vienna. The northern side ran from Freiburg to Bruges.

THE CAROLINGIAN PARTITION HYPOTHESIS

While Rokkan's and Tilly's analyses are very plausible, in focusing on initial economic conditions, both ignore the possibility that prior patterns

---

[1]The role of trade in European city development has of course been emphasized since Pirenne (1925). See Verhulst (1989, 1999) for important corrections to the idea that trade led to the early development of towns.

[2]See in particular Fox (1971) and his discussion of the Rhineland corridor.

of state development and collapse may have influenced the subsequent distribution of city-states and territorial states across Europe.[3] It is often emphasized that political fragmentation and weakness of princely authority favored efforts by European cities to establish autonomy. Following along these lines, we can investigate the political events that produced this fragmentation. Rather than depending exclusively on initial levels of economic development, I wish to argue that a further explanation for the pattern of city-state development in Europe can be found by examining the history of the Carolingian Empire and the manner in which it collapsed. In the year 800 A.D. the area that would eventually become part of Europe's "city belt" lay at the Carolingian Empire's core. By 900, as a result of a series of events that one might term "historical accidents," what had formerly been the core zone of the empire became a peripheral border zone flanked by larger and more cohesive kingdoms to the East and West.[4] I will suggest that it was this curious and accidental pattern of collapse that helps explain why European city-states emerged predominantly in a central longitudinal band running from the present-day Low Countries to Northern Italy. In so doing, I will be following an established historical tradition that suggests that the partition of the Carolingian Empire had very long-term consequences for the political map of Europe. To construct the following brief account, I have drawn on work by a number of different historians of the period.[5]

In the year 843, as part of the Treaty of Verdun, the Carolingian Empire that covered much of Western Europe was divided into three separate territories. Each of these territories formed a roughly longitudinal band: (1) West Francia covered territory centered around present-day France, (2) East Francia covered territory centered around present-day Germany, and (3) Lotharingia, also referred to as the Middle Kingdom, covered a central portion of territory running from the present-day Netherlands to Northern Italy but never evolved into a single state.[6] This territorial

[3]This is not entirely correct to the extent that Rokkan discusses the effect of Roman heritage. However, neither author considers the effect of the Carolingian partition.

[4]In the words of Maclean (2003: 81), "The political core had become peripheral, and the periphery had become the core".

[5]This includes Airlie (1998), Fried (1995), Ganshof (1971), Goldberg (2006), Innes (2000), Maclean (2003), Mckitterick (1983), Nelson (1995, 1999), Parisot (1898), Riché (1983), and Thompson (1935).

[6]This territory derived its name from its ruler, Lothar, who nominally retained the imperial title. Technically this region, referred to as "Franca Media," comprised both

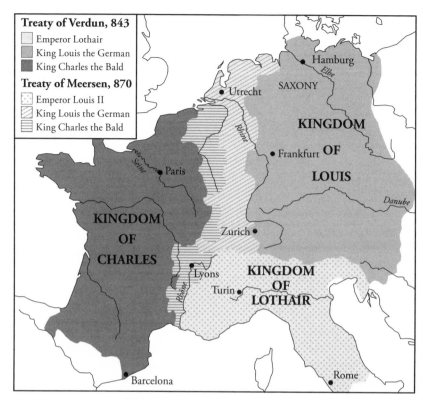

Figure 5.1. The Carolingian Partition. The map shows the division of the Carolingian empire as it occurred in 843 A.D. at the signing of the Treaty of Verdun. Depicted are the territories of West Francia, Lotharingia, and East Francia. Since the original text of the treaty has been lost, the borders here should be treated as approximations. The map also indicates the subsequent division at Meersen.

division is shown in figure 5.1, though it should be emphasized that this map is actually an approximation, because the original text of the Treaty of Verdun has been lost. A range of authors have emphasized the importance of the Treaty of Verdun in shaping the future political development of Europe. For Henri Pirenne (1936: 86), "This was the first of the great treaties of European history and the one with the most enduring consequences." In a preface to his discussion of the Treaty of

Lotharingia and the Kingdom of Italy, but I will follow the usage of referring to the entire region under the control of Lothar as "Lotharingia."

Verdun, Fernand Braudel remarked that "history thus tends to provide frontiers with roots, as if they had been caused by natural accidents; once incorporated into geography, they become difficult to move thereafter.[7] Within this group of authors, most scholars also take pains to emphasize how the location of the dividing lines was determined by temporary political circumstances involving the need to produce a roughly equal division of territory and to reward supporters of each of the three brothers that signed the Treaty of Verdun.[8] The partition divided existing linguistic groups as well as ecclesiastical provinces. It also paid little heed to existing political divisions within the Carolingian Empire, and in particular the regional divisions laid out in the *ordinatio imperii* of 817.

Crucially for the future pattern of European state formation, the Middle Kingdom proved to be short-lived. It was first divided in 855 between the three sons of Lothar I, with one receiving northern Italy, a second receiving Provence, and a third receiving the Lotharingian heartland. In 870 at the Treaty of Meersen, the territory of Lotharingia was itself divided between the rulers of West Francia and East Francia. As had been the case with the division at Verdun, it seems clear that the partition at Meersen was not designed to respect existing linguistic, ethnic, or political boundaries; it was instead determined by the need to produce a roughly equal division of assets.[9] But rather than resulting in the solidification of control over the territory of the former Middle Kingdom by its Eastern and Western neighbors, the pattern over the following century was instead one of increasing fragmentation with frequently shifting political boundaries in this central zone. While power was certainly fragmented everywhere in the ninth century, according to existing accounts it was most fragmented in this central border zone of what had once been the Carolingian heartland.

There are two differing explanations for why the Middle Kingdom collapsed so quickly. According to the first, there was nothing preordained following the Treaty of Verdun in 843 that the kingdom of Lotharingia would quickly collapse in this fashion. Stuart Airlie (1998) makes a convincing argument that one important element helping to lead to the

---

[7]Braudel (1988: 1:312). For a more recent example see Mckitterick (1983: 173), who suggests that "the decisions taken at Verdun largely determined the future shape of Europe." The significance of the Treaty of Verdun has also been emphasized in earlier work by Ganshof (1971), Riché (1983), Thompson (1935), and Parisot (1898).

[8]This view has been most prominently expounded by Ganshof (1971).

[9]See Parisot (1898) and Thompson (1935) for the most detailed accounts of the Meersen division. Northern Italy remained under separate control of the emperor Louis II.

collapse of Lotharingia was the bitter divorce dispute of King Lothar II, who ruled from 855 to 869. Inheritance in the Frankish kingdoms did not yet follow a rule of primogeniture, which made the survival of kingdoms more susceptible to idiosyncratic dynastic succession disputes. Without obstacles like this, Lothar II might have been able to use the considerable resources at his disposal to establish a more lasting kingdom. According to a second interpretation, the collapse of Lotharingia was preordained in 843, given the odd shape of this polity and the geographical obstacles located within it.

The division laid out at Verdun in 843 would have lasting implications, not only because the Middle Kingdom collapsed, but also because stronger kingdoms emerged in the other parts of the former Carolingian Empire. To the west, it would be centuries before there was any consciousness of a French polity, but the 10th and 11th centuries witnessed the solidification of a west Frankish kingdom.[10] To the east, the Ottonian dynasty emerged with its territorial control centered around Bavaria. During the 10th and 11th centuries, Lotharingia, in strong contrast, remained a border zone of fragmented and shifting political control, flanked by larger powers on either side.[11] It was this political fragmentation that facilitated subsequent attempts by cities to establish their autonomy.

If one accepts the idea that the Carolingian partition had "accidental features," it remains to be established empirically to what extent this pattern of partition was correlated with the subsequent pattern of city-state development. Among the records showing the partitions of the Carolingian Empire that took place, the full text of the Treaty of Verdun (843) has not survived, but the full text agreed to at the subsequent Treaty of Meersen (870) remains, enabling James Westfall Thompson (1935) to map out in detail the line of partition established therein. The actual division at Meersen involved a partition of holdings rather than being based on a clear line that firmly demarcated territories. As can be seen from Thompson's work, however, a longitudinal line running through the town of Meersen (5.75 degrees east longitude), which is located near the present-day border between the Netherlands and Germany, provides a very close approximation to the actual division of territory at this second treaty. Given the absence of the complete text of the Treaty of Verdun, in what follows I will use a city's distance from the Meersen partition

[10] See the overview by Dunbabin (1999).
[11] See the historical overview by Parisse (1999).

line as a predictor of future city-state development. The idea here will be that proximity to the Meersen line is proxying both for location in Lotharingia, as well as for the subsequent degree to which a city lay distant from emerging territorial powers.

EMPIRICAL EVIDENCE

While much thought has been devoted to explaining the pattern of city-state development in Europe, to my knowledge no effort has been made to subject it to a systematic empirical test. One obvious reason for this is the very serious data constraints involved. In drawing inferences based on the results in this section, we should keep this in mind. In attempting an empirical evaluation of city-state formation we face an immediate problem: what are the counterfactuals to which we should compare city-states? On one hand, we might want to compare city-states with other types of states. The question would be as follows: given that a city became a capital, either of an independent city-state or of a territorial state, what factors determined the path that it took? On the other hand, we might prefer to consider a broader group of cities, including those that became independent city-states, those that became capital cities of territorial states, and those that were other cities subsumed within territorial states. In what follows I will pursue both approaches. I make use of a narrow sample of cities that includes the 31 capitals of the states I consider throughout this book. I also make use of a broader sample that includes all Western European cities from the database constructed by Bairoch, Batou, and Chèvre (1988) that by the year 1500 had at least ten thousand inhabitants.

To construct indicators for commercial and economic development (see table 5.1), I use three proxy measures derived from the information in the Bairoch, Batou, and Chèvre database, as I have done in the previous tests presented here. Depending on the measure in question, I use either the year 1200 or the year 1300 as the point of measurement for "initial" economic conditions. Since city-states very often became independent prior to 1300, ideally we would use an earlier set of dates. The problem is that in the Bairoch et al. database, the year 1300 is the first date for which there is near-complete coverage of cities. Since we might expect city-states to have grown more quickly than other cities, the implication of this choice of dates is that, if anything, it should lead to overestimating the causal effect of initial economic conditions on city-state formation. The first urbanization measure is the log population of the city in the year

TABLE 5.1
Sample Means For Initial City Conditions

	Narrow sample			Broader sample		
	Total	City-states	Territorial	Total	City-states	Other
Initial size (thousands)	30	26	35	19	20	19
Initial urbanization (percent)	13	13	14	15	13	15
Initial urban potential	1.0	1.05	0.91	1.0	1.11	0.95
Roman heritage (dummy)	.61	.58	.67	.51	.51	.51
Bishop's seat (dummy)	.61	.63	.58	.58	.61	.56
Oceanic port (dummy)	.35	.37	.33	.21	.24	.21
Riverine port (dummy)	.35	.32	.42	.30	.41	.28
Meersen distance (100km)	3.2	2.5	4.3	4.4	2.8	4.8

1200.[12] The second is the rate of urbanization in 1300 within the modern-day region in which the city is located. I have already described calculation of this variable in the previous chapter. Finally, the third variable is the urban potential measure, constructed (as described in chapter 4) following the method proposed by de Vries (1984). I estimate identical specifications for the broad and narrow samples. The one exception is that the larger number of observations in the broader sample makes it feasible to include a set of region fixed effects as additional controls, with regions based on modern state boundaries. Since the "initial urbanization" variable does not vary within these regions, it is excluded from the specifications that include fixed effects.

The regressions in table 5.2 also investigate the correlation between a city's distance from the Meersen partition line and the pattern of city-state development. Once again, the idea here is that the closer to the line a city is located, the greater the likelihood that it lay within the territory of the short-lived kingdom of Lotharingia, and the greater its distance from emergent territorial powers. We can include the Meersen distance variable simultaneously with the urbanization variables because while proximity to the Meersen line is certainly associated with higher levels of urbanization, the correlation is far from perfect.[13]

[12] In this case I use log population in the year 1200 because this is generally available for both the narrow and broad samples.

[13] In the broad sample of cities, when the Meersen distance is regressed on city size in 1200, the regional urbanization rate in 1300, and the urban potential in 1300 (with the former two in log form), the r-squared is 0.32.

TABLE 5.2
The Correlates of City-State Development

	Narrow sample							Broader sample					
	(1)	(2)	(3)	(4)	(5)	(6)	(7)	(8)	(9)	(10)	(11)	(12)	(13)
ln(initial size)	.026					.107	.235	.123				.097	.075
	(.073)					(.132)	(.145)	(.053)				(.057)	(.057)
ln(initial urbanization)		.008				.032	−.003						
		(.109)				(.126)	(.140)						
Initial urban potential			.233		.168	.162	−.455		.341		.146	.077	.077
			(.270)		(.281)	(.437)	(.503)		(.111)		(.142)	(.138)	(.152)
Meersen distance				−.116	−.115	−.147	−.211			−.100	−.095	−.097	−.091
				(.046)	(.046)	(.052)	(.066)			(.024)	(.030)	(.029)	(.028)
Roman heritage							−.311						−.037
							(.239)						(.108)
Bishop's seat							.129						.014
							(.250)						(.110)
Oceanic port							−.189						.305
							(.247)						(.122)
Riverine port							−.313						.109
							(.298)						(.105)
Mcfadden R²	.004	<.001	.025	.143	.155	.170	.246	.191	.200	.259	.254	.269	.300
N=	31	31	31	31	31	31	31	143	139	149	139	139	139
Region effects?	no	no	no	no	no	no	no	yes	yes	yes	yes	yes	yes

Marginal effects from probit estimates of the correlates of city-state development, with heteroskedastic consistent standard errors. Narrow sample includes those polities considered elsewhere in this book. Broader sample includes narrow sample plus all other Western European cities that by 1500 A.D. had at least ten thousand inhabitants. Region fixed effects are included for following modern-day regions: Austria, Belgium, Denmark, England, France, Germany, Italy, Netherlands, Portugal, Spain, Switzerland. Danish, English, Portuguese, and Swiss cities dropped from final estimation because of absence of within-region variation.

In addition to the urbanization measure and the Meersen distance, some regression specifications in table 5.2 also include four further controls. These include dummy variables for cities that were oceanic ports, as well as for cities that lay on navigable rivers.[14] I have also included dummy variables for cities that were significant settlements during the Roman Empire, as well as for cities that were the seat of either a bishop or an archbishop.[15] Under the Roman Empire it was common for individual towns or cities to be granted the status of independent cities, or *civitas*, which had a substantial measure of self-government, particularly with regard to tax collection. These cities were administered by town councils called *curia*. Though this mode of autonomous city governance disappeared centuries before the appearance of medieval city-states, the civitas provided an obvious model for later city-states. It is conceivable that towns that had previously been civitas under the Roman Empire would have been able to draw on this tradition when attempting to (re)establish autonomy. The presence of a dummy variable for cities that were the seat of a bishop or archbishop is justified by the arguments of Guiso, Sapienza, and Zingales (2009), who suggest that within Italy, such figures aided towns in overcoming barriers to collective action necessary to establish their autonomy.[16]

Before discussing the results of the regression estimates, it will first be useful to discuss city characteristics in the two samples. In the narrow sample there are nineteen city-states and twelve territorial states, following the classification in table 2.1. In the broader sample there are 49 city-states and 108 cities that were either capitals of territorial states or other cities within territorial states.[17] In both the narrow and broad samples we

---

[14]Whether a river was navigable was judged by its width, with 50 meters used as a threshold.

[15]The criterion used for being a "significant" Roman site was if the city is listed in the *Princeton Encyclopedia of Classical Sites*. The seats of bishops and archbishops were derived from the website catholichierarchy.org

[16]This factor may have had a much different effect in other regions. In Germany, towns often had to establish their independence from bishops rather than being aided by them in this manner.

[17]The classification here was based on several criteria to identify cities that could be characterized as city-states at least in the initial phase of their development (ca. 1200). For Italian cities, I followed the list of Italian communes produced by Guiso, Sapienza, and Zingales (2008). For Germany, all free imperial cities were classified as city-states. For all other regions, cities were classified as city-states when there was clear evidence that they had a charter, independent judicial powers, independent powers to tax, and, finally,

observe that, on average, city-states emerged in areas that had a higher initial urban potential. This is consistent with the Rokkan and Tilly hypothesis. The other consistent result we see is that in both samples, city-states, on average, lay substantially closer to the Meersen partition line. This is supportive of the hypothesis that the political fragmentation created by the Carolingian collapse favored the development of autonomous cities within Europe's central belt. What a simple glance at this table cannot tell us, of course, is whether proximity to the Meersen partition line is simply proxying for initial urban potential, or vice versa. The next step is to provide a more systematic regression analysis.

The regression results reported in table 5.2 provide further important inferences about the correlates of city-state development in Europe. First, when not controlling for a city's distance from the Meersen line, initial urban potential is a strong predictor of city-state development. In specification (9) in the broader sample the coefficient on initial urban potential is positive and statistically significant. In substantive terms, an increase in the urban potential level from the 25th to the 75th percentile's of the sample is associated with an increase in the probability of being a city-state from 17 to 38%. This is a sizeable effect, but an important caveat is that in any specification that controls for distance from the Meersen line, the coefficient on initial urban potential is substantially smaller, and in addition it is not statistically significant.

Consider next the evidence for the Carolingian partition hypothesis. In both the narrow and broad samples, distance from the Meersen partition line is a statistically significant predictor of city-state development. The coefficient on the Meersen distance variable is very similar across the two samples, and it is statistically significant in all specifications. In addition, adding a control for initial urban potential has essentially no effect on the magnitude of the Meersen coefficient. The substantive magnitude of the Meersen distance is also large. Based on specification (10), a city lying 100 kilometers from the line would have a 59% chance of becoming a city-state. At 250 kilometers from the line, this estimated probability drops to 39%, and at 500 kilometers from the line it is only 13%. This conclusion regarding distance from the Meersen line is robust to inclusion of a range of different control variables. This should mitigate against the

---

independent authority with regard to defense. This information was drawn primarily from the *Dictionary of the Middle Ages*, edited by Joseph Strayer. Differences in the coding method across regions are controlled for by the inclusion of region fixed effects in the regressions.

possibility that distance from the Meersen line is simply proxying for other initial conditions, such as access to water transport, Roman heritage, or other features of urbanization. Since the broad sample regressions include a set of region fixed effects, we can also be confident that distance from the Meersen line is not simply proxying for other unobserved features of individual regions. As a final issue, one might ask whether the above results, particularly for the small sample, are robust when compared to alternative estimation procedures, such as the substitution of a linear probability model for probit. I reestimated all regressions using ordinary least squares and obtained very similar results to those obtained with the probit estimation.

I have offered several reasons for preferring to use distance from the Meersen line to capture the effect of the Carolingian partition, but we can also use available evidence to consider other alternatives. The recent study by Goldberg (2006) provides a map of the division lines drawn at the Treaty of Verdun in 843 A.D. that corresponds closely to those portrayed in figure 5.1. Using this map, I coded a dummy variable that takes a value of 1 for cities lying in Lotharingia, and 0 otherwise. I then reestimated specifications 8 through 13 in table 5.2. Across each of these regressions, there was a large and statistically significant coefficient on the Lotharingia dummy variable. The substantive magnitude of this effect was also large. In the specification including all controls, in addition to region fixed effects, a city outside of Lotharingia would be estimated to have only a 16% chance of becoming a city-state. A city inside Lotharingia would have a 42% chance of becoming a city-state. There was, however, a key difference in these regressions when compared to those using the Meersen distance. When using the Lotharingia dummy variable, the coefficient on the initial urban potential variable remained large and statistically significant, even when the two were included simultaneously. The implied magnitude of the effect of urbanization in this regression was essentially identical to that observed in table 5.2 column (9) estimate.

We can conclude from the foregoing analysis that the two factors most consistently correlated with city-state development are proximity to the Meersen line and the initial urban potential measure. But should we therefore conclude that these were the causes of city-state development? The potential concern with initial urban potential is that because we are measuring this in 1300 A.D., a point at which city-states had already become independent, this "initial" degree of urbanization may have been a consequence and not just a cause of city-state formation. There is no similar question posed by the Carolingian partition. Its division of territories occurred well prior to the development of city-states. The primary issue is whether proximity to the Meersen line is capturing the effect of factors other than the Carolingian partition. I have tried to argue that the "accidental" manner in which the partition was decided mitigates against this. I have also demonstrated that distance from the Meersen line remains a very robust predictor of city-state development even when using multiple controls and region fixed effects. Ultimately, however, we need to acknowledge the possibility that given data constraints and measurement issues, the observed correlation between proximity to the Meersen line and city-state development may not reflect the causal effect I have suggested.[18]

Reassessing the City-State Advantage

The principal objective of this chapter has been to understand better what factors led to the emergence of city-states. The secondary objective has been to judge, based on the discoveries from the first line of inquiry, whether my inferences about the importance of geographic scale and about merchant political power might be biased by a failure to take sufficient account of the factors that allowed certain cities to become politically autonomous in the first place. In the introductory chapter, I laid out two main possibilities. First, it may have been the case that, for idiosyncratic reasons, inhabitants of certain cities found it less costly to overcome barriers to collective action. This would imply greater ease in organizing so as to establish political independence. It might well also have implied greater ability to gain access to credit. A second possibility is that city-states simply existed in more developed, more capital-rich locations, and that despite

---

[18] I also further considered the robustness of my results by examining whether alternative dividing lines drawn to the west or east of the Meersen line could provide a similarly strong prediction about the pattern of city-state development. To evaluate this possibility, I repeated the estimates from table 5.2 while shifting the line of division by increments either to the east or west of the Meersen dividing line. The results of this procedure suggest that alternative longitudinal lines placed more than a small distance to the east or west of the Meersen line had much weaker power in predicting where city-states emerged. We can also provide one final important piece of evidence to support my interpretation that the statistical significance of the Meersen partition line reflects the effect of the Carolingian partition. Instead of drawing a longitudinal dividing line through the city of Meersen, draw a latitudinal dividing line through the same city. When repeating the estimates using this latitudinal dividing line we observe that it is an extremely poor predictor of subsequent autonomous city development.

my extensive use of controls for urbanization, my significant coefficients on the city-state dummy variable are simply capturing this feature.

The fact that proximity to the Meersen partition line is highly correlated with city-state development provides us with an opportunity to use an instrumental variables strategy to deal with the first of the aforementioned two potential endogeneity problems. While idiosyncratic conditions may certainly have favored collective action in certain cities but not in others, there is no strong reason to believe that these idiosyncratic factors would necessarily be correlated with proximity to the Meersen line. However, proximity to the Meersen line is certainly correlated with the initial degree of urbanization in my sample, and more importantly, it may still be correlated with the current level of economic development even after the inclusion of my multiple urbanization controls in a regression. If this (untestable) hypothesis is true, then using distance from the Meersen line as an instrumental variable would not be a useful strategy for dealing with the second of the two forms of bias referred to earlier, and it might actually worsen the problem. It is for this reason that the instrumental variables results that I report next should be considered with much caution. This also points to the particular importance of considering the evidence I provide elsewhere in this book in which I focus on change within city-states over time. This includes both the fixed effects estimates in chapter 4 and the qualitative historical evidence in chapter 6.

The regressions in table 5.3 repeat specifications (1) and (7) through (11) from table 4.2 while instrumenting for city-state development with the linear distance from the Meersen partition line. Across all but one of these specifications we see very similar coefficient results for the city-state variable compared to the OLS specifications in table 4.2. This may mean that the OLS results were not seriously biased because of my use of an extensive set of controls for those factors that may have aided city-states in gaining access to credit for reasons independent of those that I have proposed in this book. Alternatively, we should always acknowledge the possibility that by using the Meersen partition line as an instrumental variable, I have traded one form of bias for another, and these two effects have roughly cancelled each other out.

SUMMARY

In this chapter I have sought to explore the origins of city-states, asking why some cities became independent while others did not and why

TABLE 5.3
Instrumental Variables Estimates of the City-State Advantage

	(1)	(2)	(3)	(4)	(5)	(6)
Land rent return	.847	.821	.840	.830	1.05	.863
	(.228)	(.210)	(.215)	(.200)	(0.94)	(.251)
ln(urbanization)	−.186	−.186	−.187	−.182	−.286	−.188
	(.063)	(.058)	(.061)	(.060)	(.376)	(.061)
ln(capital population)	−.093	−.093	−.082	−.079	.003	−.087
	(.068)	(.066)	(.070)	(.077)	(.333)	(.066)
Urban potential	.035	.066	.033	.041	−.150	.043
	(.104)	(.099)	(.107)	(.102)	(.710)	(.108)
City-state (dummy)	−.404	−.391	−.408	−.389	−1.01	−.459
	(.200)	(.191)	(.212)	(.178)	(2.45)	(.303)
Life annuity	.283	.278	.305	.304	.408	.274
	(.171)	(.173)	(.170)	(.171)	(.442)	(.178)
Assembly existed		.128				
		(.132)				
Assembly approves taxes			.064			
			(.173)			
Assembly administers taxes				.061		
				(.148)		
Assembly administers spending					0.54	
					(2.00)	
Frequency of meetings						.144
						(.269)
Constant	1.21	1.11	1.13	1.12	0.93	1.07
	(0.36)	(0.39)	(0.48)	(0.50)	(1.15)	(0.51)
R^2 (centered)	.440	.450	.443	.445	.340	.445
Partial R^2 (excluded instrument)	.136	.177	.202	.188	.001	.133
F excluded instrument	4.9	5.4	4.7	5.8	0.24	4.5

Instrumental Variables (2SLS) estimates of the cost of borrowing. Clustered standard errors to allow for arbitrary within polity correlation. The excluded instrument in the regression is the linear distance from the Meersen partition line.

city-states clustered in some regions but not others. I have found evidence to support the leading existing explanation for city-state development—that city-states emerged in Europe's central band because this was the most highly urbanized area of Europe at an early date. However, I have also suggested a more fundamentally political explanation for the pattern of city-state development. City-states were able to emerge in Europe's central core because this was where central political control collapsed to the greatest extent after the partition of the Carolingian Empire. As a result of a series of idiosyncratic events, the Middle Kingdom became a border region of constantly shifting loyalties within which it was easier for cities to achieve political autonomy. The evidence in support of this political explanation is strong, even when taking into account the other features of Europe's central core, including its high initial level of urbanization, the presence of rivers, and its Roman legacy. As a final step in the chapter, I have drawn upon these conclusions to provide further estimates of the city-state advantage.

CHAPTER SIX

Three City-State Experiences

Up to this point, my empirical analysis has taken the form of a broad comparison involving a large number of states and a very long time span. I have identified an apparent financial advantage of city-states. I have argued that this financial advantage stemmed from the fact that public creditors were well represented in the governance of city-states, but creditor representation was itself dependent on underlying factors involving small geographic size and the presence of an elite that held liquid forms of wealth. The econometric tests in chapter 4 provide significant support for this argument, but even after considering these results, there remain questions whether the financial advantage of city-states might be attributable to alternative mechanisms. City-states may have had better access to credit for economic reasons that had little or nothing to do with political representation of creditors, and these economic factors may have been incompletely controlled for in my cross-state regressions. I now present a more detailed analysis of credit and representation in three city-states: Cologne, Genoa, and Siena. This analysis will be critical in highlighting the mechanisms at work that determined whether a state had access to credit and at what cost. The contribution of this chapter is threefold.

First, the chapter makes a novel contribution by explicitly comparing outcomes between two Italian city-states and a major Northern European city-state. Too often in discussions of the development of public debt, Italian city-states are seen as precursors without a full examination of similarities between their experiences and those of autonomous cities elsewhere in Europe.[1] The second contribution is to emphasize how public indebtedness was an issue of strong and often violent social conflict within city-states. Given this basic fact, any argument that city-states were more successful in sustaining representative institutions and in accessing credit because they were more homogeneous and consensual is hard to sustain. The third contribution of the chapter is to emphasize the importance of political control by merchants. I give particular emphasis to changes in political control by merchants within states. While the core argument of

[1] An important exception is the contribution by Tracy (2003).

this book emphasizes that merchants controlled city-state affairs much of the time, it should nonetheless be possible to identify periods within individual states when merchant power was less secure. In the previous chapter I have already referred to the existence of these episodes. In this chapter I will elaborate on several such developments in greater detail.

The experience of Cologne, Genoa, and Siena shows that there was nothing more effective in ensuring access to credit than being ruled by a merchant oligarchy. We also have evidence that when merchant control was challenged, this had negative consequences for access to credit. The most dramatic example of this is provided by Siena, where a merchant oligarchy known as the regime of the Nine held power from 1287 to 1355 but then lost power as the result of a popular uprising. The series of regimes that ruled Siena after 1355, and that had substantially more popular participation, found it considerably more difficult to obtain access to credit. In Cologne we see examples where several similar popular uprisings had dramatic effects on public credit, but these proved to be temporary, as a governing oligarchy succeeded in reestablishing control. In Genoa we see that the lowest interest rates on public debt occurred during a period where a merchant oligarchy had most firmly entrenched its power.

MERCHANT OLIGARCHY IN COLOGNE

While the role of Italian city-states as financial innovators is well known, I have argued throughout the previous five chapters that city-states elsewhere in Europe also obtained access to credit at low interest rates. In Northern Europe the experience of the city-state of Cologne presents a particularly interesting example in this regard. Though it did not attain formal status as a Free Imperial City until 1475, Cologne's leading patrician families had established de facto political control by the thirteenth century, the outcome of a dispute with Cologne's archbishop. The city did not lose this independence until it was conquered by French Revolutionary armies in 1794. Cologne is located in a favorable geographic position on the Rhine, and from an early date it became an important European center for long-distance trade. The city's population is estimated to have numbered 54,000 before the Black Death and continued to number between 40,000 and 45,000 through the end of the sixteenth century, making it one of the largest cities in Northern Europe.[2]

---

[2] These figures are drawn from Bairoch, Batou, and Chèvre (1988).

The city of Cologne also developed a long-term debt at a very early stage, during the thirteenth century. In the discussion that follows I will review the development of public credit and political representation in Cologne, demonstrating the intimate link between political control by merchants and access to credit.

Development of Public Credit in Cologne

While the first records of borrowing by the city of Cologne involve short-term loans contracted with merchants from Siena, it is also known that from the thirteenth century the city began borrowing long-term by issuing annuities. The best, albeit brief, English-language account of the evolution of public credit in Cologne is provided by Fryde and Fryde (1963). In producing their summary these two authors drew on the fundamental earlier work of Richard Knipping (1894, 1898), and the following discussion is based heavily on these sources.[3] Long-term borrowing by the city of Cologne went through several successive stages during the fourteenth and fifteenth centuries. After initially relying on the sale of life annuities, between 1350 and 1370, the city shifted in the following decades toward raising money through short-term interest-free loans from rich citizens, as well as from the sale of perpetual but redeemable annuities to citizens of other free towns in Germany, including Augsburg, Lübeck, and Mainz. After an interruption in access to credit following a popular revolt in 1396, the city borrowed during the fifteenth century by selling both life and perpetual annuities to its inhabitants.[4] This was the point at which the institutions of public credit in Cologne became the most sophisticated and at which the city found itself able to borrow at particularly low interest rates. City finances were managed by the city council, which in turn relied on a chief financial official known as the *rentmeister*, as well as managers of three separate annuity chambers (*rentkammern*) or treasuries: the Wednesday Chamber, the Friday Chamber, and the Saturday Chamber.[5] Finally, according to

---

[3] I would like to thank Tolga Sinmazdemir for assistance with Knipping (1894, 1898).

[4] Knipping (1894) suggests that during this period the municipality also began to sell annuities in smaller denominations to a broader segment of the population, a development that appears to have been spurred by the fact that after the revolt in 1396, a number of wealthy individuals were initially reluctant to lend to the municipality.

[5] According to Knipping (1894), these chambers also served as savings banks for the population of Cologne, which provided a further source of finance to the municipality.

Knipping (1894), there is also evidence of the development of a secondary market for public annuities during this period.

The extensive study by Knipping (1898) provides interest rates on both life annuities and perpetual annuities issued by the city of Cologne for a period running from the middle of the fourteenth century to the 1470s. By the end of the fourteenth century the city council of Cologne was able to issue annuities at interest rates as low as 5%. This compared favorably with the lowest interest rates prevailing in Italian city-states. After an interruption in access to credit after the 1396 revolt, during the course of the fifteenth century the 5% level became a ceiling rather than a floor for interest rates on perpetual annuities sold by the city. The evolution with regard to rates on life annuities was similar if somewhat less marked.

After the middle of the fifteenth century, public finances in Cologne appear to have taken a decided turn for the worse. The need to finance a war to defend the city of Neuss against the Duke of Burgundy resulted in the city borrowing more in two years than it had borrowed in the preceding half-century. This represented a turning point when the emergence of larger territorial states on Cologne's borders began to pose a new challenge for the city. That the ruling magistrates of Cologne were actually able to find purchasers for such a large quantity of annuities testifies to the public's perception of the municipal government as creditworthy. Ultimately, however, the choice made by Cologne's ruling magistrates to service a rapidly accumulating stock of debt almost exclusively through indirect taxes on common consumption goods helped to trigger popular revolt. During this period, proposals had been made that would have increased revenues through the creation of a property tax and other taxes that would fall primarily on the wealthy, but these ideas were rejected (Knipping 1894). A first revolt occurred in 1481, followed by another significant revolt in 1513. It is unfortunate that the interest rates provided by Knipping (1898) do not cover this later period of fiscal crisis. We can nonetheless conclude from the foregoing analysis that after an interruption in access to credit following the popular revolt of 1396, the city-state of Cologne during much of the fifteenth century was particularly successful in obtaining access to long-term credit at low cost. The next question is to what extent this might be attributed to the system of political representation in Cologne.

Political Representation in Cologne

Speaking of the political system of German cities, the historian Robert Scribner has suggested that "[i]f any blanket term is applicable to the polity of German towns it is that they were inherently oligarchic."[6] Cologne was no exception. Its governance went through two distinct regimes during the period considered here.

From the time it first established its independence until the late fourteenth century, Cologne was governed by a patrician regime in which a small number of the city's wealthiest families governed the city. From the eleventh century the Cologne patriciate organized itself through the city's merchant guild. Subsequently, the members of the patriciate formed the *Richerzeche*, a social club that included the city's great merchants and property owners. The distinction at this time between patriciate and non-patriciate in Cologne, as in other German cities, did not correspond perfectly to a divide between "merchants" and "artisans."[7] Many members of the patriciate were merchants, but this was not the case for all of its members. Likewise, there were also many successful merchants who were not part of the patriciate. Overall, however, it does not appear unreasonable to suggest that there was clearly a strong correlation between patriciate membership and mercantile capital. The patriciate in other autonomous German cities had similar organizations, a prominent example being the Circle Society of the Hanseatic port of Lübeck.[8] Finally, the role of the patriciate in Cologne, as in other German cities, was also strengthened by intermarriage.

Beginning in 1216 formal authority in Cologne was exercised by the city council. This was a small body of fifteen members that was renewed each year and for which the fifteen new members of the incoming council were chosen by the outgoing council—a system of cooptation. Philippe Dollinger (1954: 461) suggests that in Cologne, as well as in other German cities at this time, this selection mechanism ensured that control of the council remained with a small number of influential families. One final feature of patrician control in Cologne is the extent to which, at least until the late fourteenth century, its governing class was not subject to the sort of factional divisions that would threaten political stability in Italian city-states like Genoa.[9]

The popular revolt in 1396 led to the creation of a new constitution, the *Verbundbrief*, which was designed to ensure broader representation in

[6]Scribner (1996 p. 313).

[7]This would follow the caution suggested by Dollinger (1955).

[8]See Dollinger (1971) and Rotz (1977).

[9]This distinction between German city-states and Italian city-states has been emphasized by Finer (1995) as well as by Sidgwick (1903).

Cologne's governance. As a result of the 1396 reform, the *Richerzeche* club was abolished, and the selection method for the city council was altered. Political organization in the city was now to be based on 22 individual corporations, or *Gaffel*. Five of these were associations of merchants, and the remaining seventeen were designed to represent Cologne's numerous craft guilds. The Gaffel in turn elected 36 of the 49 members of a new city council. The remaining thirteen members were to be selected by the first thirty-six.

What is striking about this new constitution is that the abolition of the patrician regime does not appear to have produced more than a temporary change in the social groups that in practice ran the city. As Robert Scribner (1976: 237) observes, "In theory this structure seemed to provide a government with broad participation of the commune organized in the Gaffel. In practice it provided the basis for a system of tight political control by a merchant oligarchy." If anything, the only real change may have been to strengthen the position of merchants in Cologne with respect to older patrician elements, a number of whose wealth was held primarily in property.

Perhaps the best indication that Cologne's constitutional change of 1396 did not produce a real increase in political participation is that a frequent demand of those who led subsequent revolts in Cologne was to apply the true principals of the 1396 constitution, the *Verbundbrief*. The reasons why the constitutional change of 1396 failed to radically broaden political participation have been considered by Scribner (1976). One problem with the Verbundbrief seems to have been that the devil was in the details. So, for example, while the Gaffel now elected thirty-six of the forty-nine council members, the heads of each Gaffel were not themselves chosen in an open election by all members—they were instead selected by a special committee of more prominent members. The principle of free election of Gaffel representatives was briefly established during a popular uprising in 1481, but it was abolished in 1482 following the overthrow of the rebellion. A second problem seems to have been that, over time, the new rules were simply ignored, as a body of sitting magistrates consulted informally with "friends and capable men." A third problem involved the frequent use of electoral manipulation and fraud. Finally, the Gaffel system also strictly regulated rights of assembly, which served as a further mechanism to control potential opposition. The Gaffel system was not perfect at suppressing revolt. A revolt in 1513 produced a document called the *Transfixbrief*, which called for reasserting the original intentions of the 1396 reform. The revolt led to the arrest and execution of six sitting city councillors, as well as institutional changes, such as the provision that the city's seal, which was necessary to certify annuity letters, would be kept under 23 keys with the head of each of the Gaffel holding a key. In the end, however, this revolt apparently produced little durable change in actual governance.[10]

Distributional Conflict over Debt

So far I have argued that the city of Cologne was able to borrow at low interest rates and that it was ruled by a merchant oligarchy. Formal political influence of merchants was significantly reduced in 1396, but the real effect of this change appears to have been short lived. I have not, however, presented any evidence to suggest that outcomes would have been any different had the merchants not held political power. One way of considering this problem further is to investigate what transpired in instances where the power of Cologne's merchant oligarchy was placed in jeopardy. Political revolts occurred in Cologne in 1371 and 1396, and again in 1481 and 1513. In each of the four instances dissatisfaction with decisions regarding debt and taxation was a prominent factor fueling unrest. This was particularly clear for the latter two revolts, which occurred during a period of rising debt and rising taxation. In 1481 a proposed increase in excise taxation triggered a revolt in which its more radical leaders called for a suspension of payments on annuities. The revolt in 1513 resulted in an actual reduction in payments on annuities as well as new provisions requiring the consent of the whole community before new debt could be issued.

The basic cleavage in Cologne over the issue of public debt was the same one that existed in many European city-states. Public annuities were owned primarily by wealthy individuals who very often tended to be those who had accumulated wealth through commerce. The revenues to service these annuities depended primarily on indirect taxes, many of which were levied on common consumption goods. The structure of the tax system ensured that poorer groups of artisans within the town bore a significant part of this tax burden. It is important not to oversimplify by implying that this idea of a fundamental cleavage between merchants and artisans over public finance can adequately represent what was certainly a more complex picture in Cologne, or in other Hanseatic cities for that

---

[10]Knipping (1898) hints at this fact in the conclusion to his introductory essay on Cologne's finances.

matter. The detailed study by Rhiman Rotz (1977) on events in Lübeck during the early fifteenth century points to divisions within the city's elite between individuals actively engaged in long-distance commerce and individuals who had acquired wealth in long-distance commerce but then adopted more rentier lifestyles by investing in land and in annuities. With this said, it would seem difficult to contest the basic idea that the financial policies pursued by the city-state of Cologne had significant distributional effects, and that we can see evidence of this in the case of demands made by protestors during each of the four popular revolts that I have listed.

Summary

We can conclude that in Cologne merchant control was a critical factor in explaining the municipal government's access to long-term credit. The nature of political conflict within the city strongly suggests that it was not just a strong merchant presence but also merchant political control, facilitated by a particular set of institutions, that sustained the city's ability to borrow. Had one of Cologne's numerous popular revolts produced a more durable change in the system of government, outcomes with regard to public credit would, in all likelihood, have been very different.

GENOA AND THE CASA DI SAN GIORGIO

The Genoese republic is widely recognized to have been a pioneer with regard to public debt and a notable example of a European state that was able to gain access to long-term finance at low cost. Observers since the time of Machiavelli have attributed Genoa's financial success to the presence of the Casa di San Giorgio, a private centralized institution established in 1407 that managed the Republic's debt while also being responsible for collecting much of its revenues.[11] Because of its reliance on delegation to a private company, the ingredients for financial success in Genoa on the surface appear to have been quite different from those in Cologne, or many of the other city-states considered in this study. In

---

[11] The discussion in this section relies primarily on the recent histories of Genoa by Epstein (1996b) and Kirk (2005), as well the classic study of Genoa in the fifteenth century by Jacques Heers (1961). An insightful recent analysis of Genoese public debt and the Casa di San Giorgio is provided by Fratianni (2006). Machiavelli included a brief description of the Casa di San Giorgio in his *History of Florence*.

these states, city councils retained direct control of their finances. In what follows I will reveal a more fundamental similarity between these cases. The Casa di San Giorgio achieved its greatest success as an institution after Genoa's mercantile aristocracy established a lasting political dominance over both popular elements and the landed aristocracy of this particular region of Italy. Moreover, there was an extremely close association on a day-to-day level between the individuals who managed the Casa and the individuals who managed the affairs of the Genoese Republic. The more oligarchic the Genoese Republic became, the better its access to credit.

Development of Public Credit in Genoa

The city of Genoa emerged in an area of Italy (Liguria) that had few natural resources, and it developed an economy based primarily on long-distance commerce. The first record of a self-governing commune in Genoa dates from 1099. Involved in frequent military conflicts, the Genoese state also began borrowing at a very early date to finance its military operations. One of the earliest forced loans in Genoa occurred in 1221, and it involved an assessment of 1% of wealth.[12] As was generally the case in Italian city-states, this loan was not voluntary, but it did pay interest. From a very early date, the Genoese state also developed a practice of borrowing by creating a *compera*, which involved a loan by private individuals to the state in exchange for the right to future revenues from a specific tax. These *compere* were initially also compulsory but would eventually become voluntary. In 1259 a reform was implemented to consolidate Genoa's existing debt. Existing holders of debt were given shares in a new *compera* that paid a nominal rate of 8%. In addition, they also had the right to sell these shares, which created a secondary market.[13] In 1339 under Genoa's first doge, Simone Boccanegra, a new principal was established of paying variable interest on the consolidated debt, depending on the level of customs revenue, which in turn depended on the level of trade.[14] As a result of this change, holding Genoese debt began to resemble holding an equity stake in the state. This type of debt differed from that seen both in Northern European city-states that financed themselves through the sale of annuities and in other Italian city-states where fixed

---

[12] Epstein (1996b: 111).
[13] Epstein (1996b: 146–52).
[14] Day (1963: xxiv).

interest rates were paid on obligatory loans that in many cases could be traded on a secondary market.

The Casa di San Giorgio emerged in 1407 as part of a new attempt to consolidate the Genoese Republic's debt.[15] Holders of existing shares in different *compere* were given shares in the new *compera* of San Giorgio. These paid a nominal rate of 7%, but the actual rate varied depending on the level of receipts on trade duties. It is worth following Jacques Heers (1961: 112) in pointing out that there was nothing fundamentally new or revolutionary about the Casa compared to previous mechanisms for managing government indebtedness in Genoa. The principle that interest rates could be conditioned on tax receipts had already been established in 1339. In terms of its internal management, Jacques Heers (1961: 117–18) suggests that it closely resembled other compere that preceded it. According to the Casa's initial constitution of 1411, its day-to-day affairs were run by a committee of eight "protectors." To be eligible for selection as a Protector of San Giorgio, individuals were required to own at least ten shares in the Casa (a significant sum representing 1000 lire), and Protectors were chosen by a system of cooptation. The Casa also had a larger council of shareholders that appears to have met infrequently and exercised only a relatively limited influence over the Protectors. Where the Casa differed from the institutions that preceded it is that it eventually succeeded in controlling the totality of the republic's debt. The other critical feature of the Casa, which will be described shortly, is that the Protectors of San Giorgio were intimately involved with the governance of the Genoese Republic itself.

Distributional Conflict over Debt

One of the contributions of Avner Greif's important (1994) work on Genoa has been to show that governance in this Republic, or in other Italian communes for that matter, cannot be reduced to a simple scenario of "governments of the merchants, by the merchants, for the merchants."[16] There were instead major distributional struggles and factional conflicts between merchant groups within Genoa. However, inter-merchant factionalism is not to be ignored, it is also important when considering the

[15] For an analysis of the Casa di San Giorgio, see the recent study by Fratianni (2006), as well as the earlier study by Heers (1961).

[16] The original quote is from Lopez (1971).

specific issue of Genoa's public indebtedness not to overlook the presence of very significant distributional conflict among different economic groups within the Republic. Since much of the city's debt was held by those who had originally made fortunes in commerce, popular groups consistently protested against heavy levels of indirect taxation on common consumption goods. It was these taxes that helped service the city's debt. When a popular revolt brought Guglielmo Boccanegra to power in 1259, one of the motivations was popular dissatisfaction with public finances. In the law that Boccanegra passed to consolidate Genoa's existing debt, he made explicit reference to the fact that Genoa's debt was held by the wealthy while the bulk of the tax burden was borne by popular groups.[17] Eighty years later, when a popular revolt brought Simone Boccanegra to power, popular discontent with the costs of servicing Genoa's public debt was again the motivation. One of the new regime's first acts was to burn the official list of the state's creditors. The motivation for this act was undoubtedly fueled by the fact that a very large fraction of the Republic's annual budget was devoted to debt servicing.[18] One further thing to note about popular protest in Genoa is that the city's craft guilds were always weak, and as a result there was no vehicle by which the guilds might demand a place in government. This represents a fundamental difference from Cologne, where craft guilds were much better organized, even if their rank and file ultimately had little impact on the city council's decisions.[19]

Genoese Political Institutions

Medieval Genoa was characterized by an extremely high level of factional conflict. For the 270-year period between the captainship of Guglielmo Boccanegra in 1259, who first consolidated Genoa's long-term debt, and the initiation of the Andrea Doria Republic in 1528, Steven Epstein (1996b) documents no fewer than 54 major revolts, the majority of which were successful in creating a change in control of government. This is a very high level of political instability even by the standards of most Italian city-states. It is certainly indicative of a much higher

---

[17] See Epstein (1996b: 148).

[18] Day (1963: XXXIV) reports annual budgets for two years in the late fourteenth century. In 1377 debt servicing amounted to 61% of revenues. In 1382, a year of higher customs receipts, it amounted to 49% of current revenues.

[19] Epstein (1996b) suggests that this weakness of the Genoese craft guilds was attributable at least in part to Genoa being a port city.

degree of instability than existed in German city-states, such as Cologne, Bremen, and Hamburg. In keeping with this high level of instability, the structure of Genoese political institutions also changed frequently during the medieval period. During the twelfth century, Genoa was governed by a committee of between four and eight consuls. In 1190 the commune attempted for the first time to resort to rule by a podesta, an official originating from outside the city who would serve a period of one year. The role of the podesta has been examined extensively by Greif (1994, 2006), who argues that this institution initially helped to limit open conflict between warring factions in Genoa, but that it failed to provide an enduring solution to the problem. From 1339 Genoa's supreme magistrate was an elected doge, but the selection process was often a source of violent conflict.

When we turn to considering the structure of Genoese representative institutions, we see that they changed frequently in the period before 1528, but there is clear indication of a strong and increasing influence of government creditors over time. Heers (1961) provides a detailed picture of the workings of Genoese political institutions in the fifteenth century. Day-to-day control was exercised by a council of eight magistrates who served for terms of four months. These magistrates met almost daily and made all important decisions, in addition to nominating key administrative officials. In their meetings the magistrates were very frequently accompanied by the eight Protectors of San Giorgio, who thus exercised a very direct degree of control over the Genoese state. In the case of major decisions, Genoa also had a larger assembly, the Magnum Consilium, which included the magistrates in addition to between 300 and 400 citizens. This was apparently not a regular institution, nor did it have regular procedures determining who would participate in its deliberations.

In 1528 a series of dramatic reforms were enacted, giving Genoa a new set of political institutions that would last until 1798. A new form of aristocratic government was established based on 28 clans, or *alberghi*. From the list of all adult males from the *alberghi*, four hundred were individuals selected by lot to participate in the Maggiore Consiglio. From within this body one hundred individuals were chosen by lot to participate in a smaller council, the Minore Consiglio, which nominated the key officials who managed Genoese affairs on a daily basis.[20] In 1547 a

---

[20] See Epstein (1996b: 315–16).

constitutional reform was passed that reduced the element of lot in this selection process and that interestingly gave the Protectors of San Giorgio a partial right to nominate certain councillors.[21] Jacques Heers interprets the Andrea Doria reforms as the triumph of Genoa's mercantile class over both artisans and those nobles whose wealth was based primarily on land.[22] Epstein concurs with this analysis to the extent that the reforms signalled a durable exclusion of popular (popolo) participation in Genoese politics. He suggests that "[f]or five centuries the nobles and the popolo had been contending for power, and in 1528 the nobles and some of the richer popolo abolished the political rights of everyone else" (1996b: 316).

Interest Rates in Genoa

Genoa presents a rare case where we have data available for interest rates on government debt that cover a particularly long time span involving several distinct episodes in the evolution of Genoa's political institutions. To the extent one believes that Genoa's financial success depended on the creation of the Casa San Giorgio in 1407, we should expect to see a downward shift in interest rates after this date. According to this interpretation, which was essentially Machiavelli's analysis, even if the Genoese Republic itself was subject to constant turmoil and popular revolts, the existence of the Casa would have ensured creditworthiness by insulating the management of public finances from these developments. In an alternative interpretation that would be closer to the core argument of this book, Genoa's creditworthiness as a borrower depended more broadly on the extent to which creditor interests could establish lasting political dominance in Genoa. This may have been facilitated by the establishment of the Casa di San Giorgio, but the most dramatic break in this regard occurred after the establishment of the Andrea Doria Republic in 1528.

Figure 6.1 reports long-term interest rates on the Genoese public debt from three separate sources. It also places a vertical line at the date of the creation of the Casa di San Giorgio and at the creation of the Andrea Doria Republic. The series of data from 1340 to 1407 was collected by John Day (1963), and it corresponds to the period immediately prior to the establishment of the Casa di San Giorgio. The series that runs from 1445 to 1466 was compiled by Heers (1961). It covers a period when the Casa

---

[21] See Kirk (2005: 56–57).
[22] See in particular Heers (1961: 610).

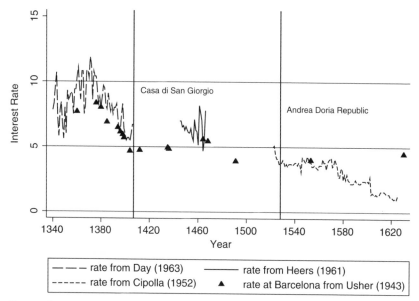

Figure 6.1. Interest rates on the public debt in Genoa. See text for a full description of calculations.

di San Giorgio had already established control over much of Genoa's consolidated debt, and when the Protectors of the Casa were incorporated into the decision-making institutions of the Republic. This was also a period when noble and popular revolts continued to occur with high frequency. Heers (1961: 160–61) suggests that during this period the market price for shares of the Casa was heavily influenced by the occurrence of these revolts. Finally, the series that runs from 1522 to 1625 was constructed by Carlo Cipolla (1952). This corresponds closely with the first century of the Andrea Doria Republic, which was established in 1528.

The interest rates in each of the three series depended on a nominal interest rate, but they were also conditioned on the level of customs receipts received by the Republic in a given year. The latter two series also take explicit account of the secondary market price of government debt, so as to present an actual yield on government debt.[23] Much of the movement in these series, particularly the short-term movements, would have depended on changes in trade flows that influenced revenues. However, their long-term trends would also have depended on the

---

[23] It is not clear from Day (1963) whether he also took into account the secondary market price when constructing his series.

nominal interest rate on government debt and its market price. A government judged to be more creditworthy should have been able to offer a lower nominal interest rate on its debt. Holding other factors constant, market prices should also have been higher for a more creditworthy government, resulting in a lower yield on debt. In a final step of the exercise, figure 6.1 also reports several data points on market interest rates for government debt issued by the city of Barcelona. As a self-governing maritime city located in a similar Mediterranean location, Barcelona makes for a comparison that we might expect to help control for a number of other potential determinants of the level of interest rates.[24]

It is inevitably a risky exercise attempting to establish inferences across the three different interest rate series for Genoa, given that they are not constructed using identical methods or sources, and that we also have two sizeable gaps where there are no data available. Nonetheless, if we do use this data to investigate change in Genoa over time, we conclude that interest rates were lower after the establishment of the Casa San Giorgio than before. But the sharpest drop in Genoese interest rates appears to have occurred only after the establishment of the Andrea Doria Republic in 1528. It was also only after this point that we have a clear indication that the Genoese republic was able to borrow at a lower rate of interest than the city of Barcelona.

Summary

Events in Genoa lead to us to several conclusions that fit with the core argument of this book. Representative political institutions of this city-state were critical for assuring access to credit to the extent that these institutions gave government creditors a very direct degree of control over the Republic's affairs. This degree of control increased over time, and it was associated with a notable decline in interest rates on Genoa's long-term debt. At the same time, the presence of significant popular protest over debt suggests that the Genoese Republic's ability to borrow was not something that was guaranteed by its status as a major center of commerce. Access to credit ultimately depended on the political dominance of one social group and on the fact that this group was able to use Genoese political institutions to control public finance. Once again, merchant oligarchy seems to have been a key ingredient in assuring access to credit.

[24]The interest rates for Barcelona are drawn from Usher (1943).

SIENA UNDER THE RULE OF THE NINE

The fourteenth-century experience of the Italian city-state of Siena provides a third important opportunity to investigate the reasons why city-states enjoyed a financial advantage over territorial states in Europe. Unlike Genoa and Cologne, Siena appears at first glance not to fit with my core argument. While Siena gained access to credit at an early date, the city did not succeed in establishing a consolidated long-term debt until 1430, which was later than most other Italian city-states. During the first half of the fourteenth century Siena had a stable system of public finance, and the commune found it relatively easy to gain access to credit. In the second half of the fourteenth century this changed as the commune found it increasingly difficult to attract loans and faced prolonged fiscal crisis. The core institutions of Sienese finance remained the same across these two periods. One thing that did change after mid-century was that Siena suffered a number of serious shocks. These involved both the Black Death and incursions by armed bands of mercenaries. But other Italian city-states also faced these same shocks, and in many cases without it adversely affecting their access to credit. I will also emphasize a further critical difference: during the first half of the fourteenth century Siena was governed by a merchant oligarchy, whereas after this point it was governed by several more short-lived regimes that involved significant popular participation and in which Siena's merchants played a less dominant role. There is direct evidence that this reduction in the political influence of merchants had significant adverse effects on public credit. Precisely because it allows us to observe the financial consequences of a merchant oligarchy losing power (the opposite of what happened in Genoa), Siena provides evidence of how political control by merchants was critical to the ability of city-states to gain access to credit. In the absence of merchant political control, the Sienese commune found it far more difficult to gain access to credit. It is possible to use events in fourteenth-century Siena to improve our understanding of the link between political representation and public credit thanks to the important work of William Bowsky (1970, 1981), who examined Sienese politics and finance under the regime of the Nine (1287–1355), and to the recent work of William Caferro (1998), who provides a view of the crisis of Sienese public finance during the half-century that followed.[25]

---

[25] In addition to work by these two authors, I have also relied on the contributions by Wainwright (1987) and Ascheri (1994), along with considering the earlier interpretations of events in Siena offered by Douglas (1902) and Schevill (1909).

Evolution of Sienese Public Finance

Siena at the outset of the fourteenth century was not as large as the most prominent Italian city republics, but it was still a very significant urban center, numbering around 50,000 individuals before the Black Death.[26] Though it was not a port and did not lie on a navigable river, Siena did lie on the principal road route from France to Rome, and it is known that merchants from Siena were pioneers in Europe, both with regard to long-distance trade and banking. Given Siena's early prominence, it seems necessary to explain why it declined during the course of the fourteenth century, becoming a second-rate power in Italy. To raise revenue, Siena relied on a wide number of indirect taxes, but the municipal government also relied significantly on a direct tax, the *dazio*. For this reason Bowsky (1970) has suggested that the tax structure in Siena was, at least initially, less regressive than that of numerous other Italian city-states. Faced with a need to raise funds quickly, particularly in response to military threats and opportunities, from an early date Siena also relied on loans. Like other Italian republics it raised money through forced loans that paid interest, and there is evidence of these being used at different points throughout the fourteenth century. However, the commune also relied extensively on voluntary loans contracted with residents of the city. Bowsky (1970: ch.8) presents evidence to show that these voluntary loans were particularly well secured with future revenues and that the government of the commune went to extensive lengths to see that interest and principal on both forced and voluntary loans were repaid. This included provisions requiring that new expenditures be authorized by the Nine (magistrates who managed the commune's affairs) and the city council (the Council of the Bell). It also seems clear that the Council of the Bell was an institution that met frequently, making it possible for the group to monitor public finances. A reform in 1332 reduced the frequency of council sessions by specifying that it should meet no more than once a week, which Bowsky (1981: 98–99) interprets as reducing the city council's influence on policymaking. Even if council meetings in Siena occurred only once per week, this was still a much more intensive form of representative activity than was observed in any European territorial state at this time.

During the first half of the fourteenth century, the ruling magistrates in Siena had frequent recourse to borrowing, and there is little indication

---

[26]This population estimate was produced by by Bowsky (1964).

from the extensive evidence in Bowsky (1970) that the commune faced significant constraints on its ability to raise funds. The interest rates on loans contracted by the commune of Siena were not low, settling to a habitual rate of 10% during this time.[27] However, this rate was not especially high compared to those paid by other city-states in the period before the Black Death, or with rates currently prevailing in Genoa.

What is most striking about Siena's public debt during the fourteenth century is that its early development was not followed by a successful effort to develop a consolidated debt with a secondary market, as happened in Florence, Genoa, and Venice. Nor does it appear that interest rates on Sienese debt fell after 1350, as was the case elsewhere.[28] By this point in time, the commune found itself faced with a need to defend itself against raids by marauding mercenary companies, but as it tried to fund its defense, Siena had increasing difficulty obtaining access to voluntary loans in particular. The analysis by Caferro (1998) provides detailed evidence on Siena's increasing difficulties after 1350 in obtaining credit through voluntary loans. He also documents the numerous temporary expedients that the regime was forced to use, which included frequent arbitrary actions taken to reschedule debts or suspend interest payments.[29] Faced with a proliferation of obligations to different creditors, the commune attempted to consolidate its loans into a single fund in the same manner that had been achieved in Genoa. It was unsuccessful in this effort. One might be tempted to argue that the absence of a consolidated debt provides an institutional explanation for Siena's troubles, but even when Siena did eventually succeed in establishing a consolidated debt (in 1430), there were few investors. A final sign of Siena's difficulty in obtaining credit during this period was that despite the commune's desperate need for finance, the total stock of Sienese debt at the end of the fourteenth century was actually significantly smaller than it had been during the first half of the century.[30]

---

[27]The most common rate during this period was 10%, but Bowsky (1970) reports that loans in some cases were made for nominal amounts that were less than what the commune actually received. This was a practice equivalent to selling a bond below its par value, and it would have implied that in these cases lenders were earning even higher returns.

[28]Wainwright (1987: 137) reports that during the fiscal crisis of 1369 the commune was forced to pay rates of between 16 and 20% on its loans. To the extent that these interest rates are representative, they would reflect a very sizeable increase compared with those that prevailed before 1350.

[29]Caferro (1998: 135–36).

[30]The conclusion is based on the figures presented by Caferro (1998: 154) who draws on Bowsky (1970: 295) for the debt stock before 1355.

Political Representation in Siena

Political factors provide an important explanation as to why Siena enjoyed access to credit prior to 1355 while lacking it thereafter. During the period from 1287 to 1355 Siena was controlled by an oligarchical regime in which the city's merchants were particularly well represented. During the decades after 1355, the commune was instead controlled by a sequence of regimes, several of which had much heavier popular participation and none of which was characterized by the same degree of merchant control.

Siena gained its independence as a commune during the twelfth century. After this point, like Genoa, it had a consular regime followed by rule of a podesta. Ultimate political authority in Siena rested with the city council (the Council of the Bell), which existed from 1176, and which intervened in all types of issues faced by the commune. From 1287 to 1355, while ultimate legitimacy remained with the Council of the Bell, the affairs of the commune were controlled by a committee of nine magistrates who held the title of the Nine Governors and Defenders of the Sienese Commune. More commonly, these individuals were simply referred to as the Nine. The Nine was actually a body of officials each of whom served a two-month term. The election procedure for these officials was intricate and was modified on several occasions between 1287 and 1355. There were two constants to this procedure though. First, there was always significant formal weight given to Siena's merchant guild in selecting both the members of the Nine and the members of the Council of the Bell. Second, there were specific restrictions on the types of individuals who could serve on the Nine.[31] By a statute of 1287 it was stated that the Nine "are and must be of the merchants and of the number of the merchants of the city of Siena, or indeed, of the middle people." This excluded members of the landed nobility, doctors, lawyers, and artisans.[32] Bowsky (1981: 87) notes that during the period of rule by the Nine, the same group of individuals eligible to serve as one of the Nine also typically held a significant fraction of the hundred seats on the Council of the Bell.

Historians have had sharply differing normative assessments of the regime of the Nine. For early-twentieth-century observers like Ferdinand Schevill (1909) and Langton Douglas (1902), this was an oligarchical regime from which Siena's mercantile elite drew profit for itself while

[31]Bowsky (1981: 58–61).
[32]Bowsky (1981: 63).

exploiting the popular classes, an opinion that reflects much historiography of city-states from this period. In Schevill's opinion, "In their greed of power the merchants did not hesitate to discard the whole theoretical basis of the early commune."[33] The work of William Bowsky has been fundamental in revising this interpretation. For Bowsky, the regime of the Nine was an oligarchical one that favored the wealthiest elements of Sienese society, but it was also one that made very considerable contributions to the commune. He further emphasizes that throughout the period between 1287 and 1355, the members of the Nine made it a practice frequently to consult the Council of the Bell for opinions and in its decision-making. Irrespective of the normative judgment they make about the regime of the Nine, what all historical observers seem to agree on was that the regime of the Nine was one in which merchants were particularly well represented. After an extensive investigation of all individuals who served as one of the Nine, Bowsky (1981: 74) found that "members of the merchant guild—bankers and international merchants in many commodities—predominate."

The regime of the Nine came to an end in 1355 as a result of a popular revolt, and it was followed by a series of short-lived regimes including the Dodici government of 1355–68, the Riformatori of 1368–85, and the Priori of 1385–99. While the social basis of the dominant individuals in each of these regimes varied, one conclusion that seems difficult to dispute is that they were each characterized by greater popular representation in government and commensurately less direct control by merchants than had been the case under the Nine. One historian has referred to the Riformatori government as "the most widely represent[ative] government in the history of the Tuscan communes."[34]

The Fall of the Nine as a Cause of Financial Crisis

What interpretation can we attach to the apparent link between the fall of Siena's merchant oligarchy and the commune's subsequent difficulty in obtaining access to credit? One possibility, and a plausible one, is that the Sienese experience does not demonstrate the importance of merchant political power, it merely shows that when a state is subject to a particularly severe set of exogenous crises, this may lead simultaneously to a financial

[33] Schevill (1909: 196).
[34] Caffero (1998: 22–23).

crisis and to the ouster of a sitting regime. One might emphasize here the combined effect of the Black Death, which reduced Siena's population by a half; the series of mercenary raids that began in 1342; and the increased burden of taxation necessary to defend against these raids (or in many cases to bribe the raiders). There would, however, be weaknesses with such an interpretation. First, Siena was hardly alone in experiencing a very high rate of mortality as a result of the plague. Second, the mercenary incursions to which Siena was subject during this period were not a purely exogenous development. The city became a target precisely because outsiders knew that the commune was experiencing a period of political instability. The fact that the city was subject to outside raids and that it had such difficulty defending itself was attributable at least in part to the difficulties experienced by the communal government in raising funds. This inability to raise funds was something that can, in turn, be directly linked to the composition of Siena's political regimes during this period.

In comparing late-fourteenth-century Florence with Siena during the same period, Caferro argues that Florence's greater ability to obtain access to credit was attributable to the fact that the Albizzi regime in Florence (which extended from 1382 to 1434) was a patrician regime dominated by the wealthiest Florentine citizens. He suggests that this is a striking difference from the case of Siena after 1355 as, for example, the Riformatori regime was a popular one whose own members were quite poor and which "represented the antithesis of the contemporary Florentine Albizzi regime." What this implies is that if Florence was largely immune to mercenary raids during this period while Siena was not, then this was not something that occurred by accident. Siena's military vulnerability was linked precisely to the political weakness of its merchants at this time.

As a final point, we can also suggest with some plausibility that the fall of the merchant oligarchy of the Nine in 1355 was triggered in part by an exogenous event, as opposed to an endogenous development such as an underlying fiscal crisis. The visit to the city by the Holy Roman Emperor Charles IV helped serve as a catalyst for revolt against the Nine, but there is little indication that the overthrow of the sitting Sienese government constituted a significant initial motivation for the emperor's trip to Italy (Schevill 1909: 213).

Overall, the fourteenth-century experience of Siena provides further support for the idea that oligarchic control by merchants was critical in facilitating the development of public credit. The Sienese case is so interesting precisely because it allows us to observe what happened when a merchant oligarchy lost political power. This gives us further confidence that it was political control by, and not simply the presence of, mercantile groups that was crucial for public credit.

SUMMARY

In this chapter, I have presented detailed evidence on the joint evolution of public credit and political representation in the city-states of Cologne, Genoa, and Siena to complement the broader analysis of the previous chapters. In each of these three cases we find that a municipal government was, at least initially, able to gain access to credit and that this access was associated with the creation of institutions through which creditors could exert a degree of control over public finances. In all three instances these institutions took the form of what can be called a merchant oligarchy. We also see evidence consistent with my core argument that the evolution and behavior of these institutions was influenced by a geographic factor (small size) and by the presence of an elite holding liquid wealth. Finally, these three cases also contribute to the analysis because they allow us to investigate more thoroughly the effect of changes within individual states over time. We can see clear evidence that access to credit was particularly strong during periods of firm merchant control.

CHAPTER SEVEN

Three Territorial State Experiences

As with the previous chapter on city-states, the objective of this chapter is to ask whether detailed historical evidence supports the conclusions that I have drawn about territorial states. I have argued that territorial states found it more difficult to gain access to credit because of the weakness of their representative assemblies. The contribution of this chapter will be to confront the following question: if having a representative assembly with strong control over finance had major advantages, then why could territorial states not emulate the institutions present in their city-state neighbors? To answer this question I will consider the experiences of France, Castile, and Holland.

While territorial states as a group may have been starkly different from city-states, there were, of course, also important differences between them. The Dutch Republic has traditionally been presented as a model in terms of the development of public credit, whereas France and Castile have been seen as prototypical examples of states that lacked creditworthiness. These differing outcomes have often been attributed to political institutions. It is said that the Dutch Republic had a powerful representative assembly and a constrained executive, whereas neither of these two conditions prevailed in the "absolutist" monarchies of France and Castile. I will argue that simple arguments about the presence or absence of absolutism ignore an important fact. On paper, France and Castile both had institutional mechanisms whereby government creditors could gain representation, and the formal parallel between Castilian and Dutch representative institutions is particularly striking. The problem was that in France and Castile these mechanisms simply did not produce the same outcome as in the Dutch Republic. I will argue that these differing outcomes illustrate the importance of geographic scale and merchant representation in determining whether it was possible to maintain an intensive form of political representation in which an assembly could exert control over public finances.

FRANCE AND THE *RENTES SUR L'HÔTEL DE VILLE*

There is a vast quantity of scholarship on the evolution of both representative institutions and royal finances in France during the medieval and early modern period. In this short subsection I cannot pretend to provide a major advance on these debates. What I instead propose is to consider one particular episode in the history of France's royal finances and explore how the early history of the rentes sur l'Hôtel de Ville set the stage for the French monarchy's frequent difficulty in later obtaining access to credit. The basic question I seek to answer is why during the initial period of the rentes sur l'Hôtel de Ville did the monarchy succeed early on in attracting investment and regularly serviced its *rentes*, whereas by the end of the sixteenth century it defaulted on its obligations and had difficulty attracting new investment.

Creation and Evolution of the Rentes sur l'Hôtel de Ville

In 1522 king François I, at the suggestion of his chancellor Antoine du Prat, initiated a new form of royal borrowing.[1] The municipality of Paris would sell up to 100,000 livres tournois of perpetual annuities, or rentes, with the proceeds forwarded to the king. In exchange the king would sign a contract pledging specific future revenues to be used to service these annuities. The annuities were redeemable, and they could also be sold to third parties. This first issue of the rentes sur l'Hôtel de Ville carried an interest rate of 8.33%. The future taxes with which the 1522 rentes were to be repaid all involved indirect taxes on goods sold in or near Paris. As a result, the *bureau de ville* of Paris (equivalent to the city council) was in a very good position to monitor revenue collection.[2] Since the bureau de ville also directly administered annuity payments, it could further help ensure that the rentes were serviced in a timely fashion.

The initial motivation for the creation of the rentes sur l'Hôtel de Ville was that François I was engaged in a series of expensive military conflicts in Italy, and he faced a desperate need for money to finance these actions.

---

[1] After completing this section I discovered the fascinating doctoral dissertation written by Camila Vam Malle (2008), who makes similar arguments to those I express here regarding the rentes sur l'hôtel de ville. In the discussion that follows I have drawn heavily on the work of Cauwès (1895), which remains the best source on the early evolution of the rentes sur l'hôtel de ville, as well as the study on annuities in sixteenth-century France by Schnapper (1956). I refer also to Jean Bodin's journal of the Estates General of 1576, to the recent study by Hamon (1994) on royal finances under François I, as well as to the discussion in Wolfe (1972) and Ulph (1947), and to the treatments of the institutions of Paris by Babelon (1986) and Doucet (1948).

[2] Since taxes in France were farmed out, neither the municipality nor royal officials collected them directly.

There was nothing radically new, though, about the monarchy agreeing to the payment of a rente, a long-term commitment to forgo a future part of its future revenues. As noted in chapter 1, from medieval times French monarchs had established the principle of alienating part of their future revenues in the form of an annuity paid to certain individuals or institutions. The creation of the rentes in 1522 occurred during a period when François I made heavy demands on a number of French cities to contribute to the war effort. In some cases this involved forced loans with uncertain promises of repayment. More frequently, municipal contributions were negotiated between individual city councils and the king as part of a grant. These grants held the memorable title of a *don gratuit* or "free gift." It would be inaccurate to presume, however, that a don gratuit could be unilaterally or costlessly imposed. A grant was actually a negotiated outcome that often came to a resolution only after very costly delays for the monarchy, which generally needed funds to be provided as quickly as possible. This appears to have been particularly true with regard to large and politically powerful municipalities like Paris. Given this fact, the practice of issuing rentes via the municipality of Paris is best seen as an alternative mechanism for generating finance that would meet with less resistance, precisely because it provided a reasonable expectation of a decent return for investors.

The study by Paul Cauwès (1895), which is the most detailed account of the rentes sur l'Hôtel de Ville during the sixteenth century, divides the history of the rentes into three periods. In the initial period, from 1522 to 1546, the monarchy regularly serviced its obligations while making relatively sparing use of this financing mechanism. François I preferred instead to raise funds through a variety of other means including advances from international bankers and forced loans. After the initial sale of rentes in 1522, there was not another issue until 1536, followed by three further issues in 1544, 1545, and 1546. The relative size of annual rentes issues is shown in figure 7.1 [3] In 1545 the king had initially sought to levy the sum of 120,000 livres tournois as a grant, and subsequently as a forced loan, but after protests by the *prévôt des marchands* (an elected official who had most of the powers of a mayor or senior magistrate), the municipality succeeded in negotiating that the sum would be raised through the sale of rentes . In all cases at this time when rentes sur l'Hôtel de Ville were

---

[3]It is expressed in terms of silver content in order to take account of the steady devaluation of the livre tournois over this period.

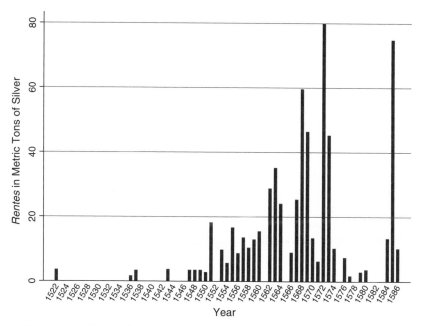

Figure 7.1. Issues of *Rentes sur l'Hôtel de Ville*. Source: Schnapper (1956).

issued they were backed with taxes collected in or near Paris. It was logical that the municipality would prefer to have the rentes backed with taxes collected nearby. These could be more easily monitored, helping to ensure timely payment of the rentes.[4]

In the second period, from 1547 to 1561, the monarchy began to make greater use of the sale of rentes, with new issues occurring on at least an annual basis. In these years the rentes continued to be regularly paid, and Cauwès (1895: 865) argues that this outcome was attributable to the repeated interventions by the bureau de ville. The bureau was thus acting very much in the same fashion as a representative body within a city-state. There was, however, one new feature of these rentes that would pose future problems. While all rentes issued before 1551 were guaranteed by taxes collected in or near Paris, beginning in 1551 the municipality of Paris was asked to sell rentes backed by taxes collected in more distant destinations, including a large number of destinations throughout northern France, and even, in one case, Marseille.[5]

[4]See the discussion in Schnapper (1956: 155) on this issue.
[5]See Schnapper (1956: 155).

The third period of the rentes, from 1561 to 1588, was one in which the monarchy sought to expand issues to unprecedented levels, as can be seen from figure 6.1. During this period, France was suffering from increased civil conflict, the authority of the crown was challenged across much of France's territory, and a new monarch, Henri III, was quickly demonstrating a reputation for fiscal profligacy. New issues of rentes were backed by a very wide range of taxes from different geographic locations, often without the same degree of initial verification that had existed in previous periods. A further complication involved a decision made in 1561 to involve France's clergy in the system for paying the rentes. This development contributed further to the general tendency of having the rentes reimbursed with revenues that could not be as easily monitored or controlled by municipal authorities in Paris. In the end, the massive increase in rentes issues, combined with the drastic drop in revenue collections as a result of the mounting tensions, led to a situation where, by the mid-1570s, the municipality of Paris was forced to suspend payments on many rentes. This, of course, made it increasingly difficult for the crown to obtain access to new finance. The suspension of payment was triggered in part by the fact that much of the money contracted to pay rentes never actually made it to Paris. In different locales the revenues were instead often used to pay troops or to fortify cities, or in other cases money was seized at the local level by the crown for "urgent affairs."[6]

One final issue to consider is who purchased the rentes sur l'Hôtel de Ville and whether they did so based on the expectation that they would make a profit or because they felt pressure to purchase. Analyzing the identity of subscribers for two issues of rentes in 1553 and 1554, Schnapper (1956: 160) finds that royal officials in particular were prominently represented. Members of the upper nobility also appear to have made large purchases. We might therefore conclude that the rentes sur l'Hôtel de Ville were equivalent to forced loans that paid interest, except for the fact that it was individuals over whom the crown had particular influence who made contributions. The complication for this picture is that the initial purchasers of rentes often sold them very quickly, and the rentes came to be used in a wide variety of transactions, particularly for purchasing real estate.[7] So, for example, Schnapper (1956: 163) cites the case of a lawyer

---

[6]Schnapper (1956: 266–267).
[7]This aspect is emphasized by both Cauwès (1895) and Schnapper (1956).

from the Parlement of Paris who was an initial subscriber to a rentes issue on June 23rd, 1554, but who then sold this annuity to a third party on July 2nd of the same year. Even if those who initially purchased rentes often had a relationship with the king, the willingness of third parties to subsequently purchase these annuities suggests there was an expectation that purchasers would be repaid. This situation clearly changed with the massive increases in rentes issues from the 1560s onward. During this period the general public grew noticeably more reluctant to purchase rentes, and Parisian municipal officials complained that the market could not bear further issues.

Local Institutions for Creditor Representation

The rentes sur l'Hôtel de Ville system nominally provided for representation of creditors in a way that very closely paralleled the institutional arrangements of city-states.[8] There was an elaborate process for verifying the initial rentes contract, followed by close subsequent monitoring of rentes payments by the bureau de ville. With regard to the bureau de ville, Schnapper (1956: 153) argues that while the king fundamentally lacked creditworthiness, "the municipality of Paris, in contrast, was a veritable creditors syndicate, always ready to defend the rentiers and very capable of succeeding." The full bureau de ville was composed of the *prévôt des marchands;* the *échevins*, or alderman, of the city; 24 councillors; and finally the prosecutor, clerk, and the *receveur* of the Hôtel de Ville. The latter official was the individual most directly charged with monitoring payment of the rentes. The prévôt and échevins were elected for two-year terms based on a complicated system involving sixteen different neighborhoods of the city. These officials then nominated the 24 councillors. Despite the formal openness of the election system, R. Doucet (1948: 270) observes that in practice it functioned as a system of cooptation where outgoing officials nominated incoming officials for election. In this way, Paris resembled many of the city-states considered in this study. In terms of their background, the principal elected officials in Paris initially came from the city's mercantile elite. However, during

---

[8] There were arrangements at the provincial level in France that can be seen in the same vein. The case of royal borrowing via the intermediary of the Estates of Burgundy has been studied by Potter and Rosenthal (1997, 2002), Potter (2003), and Swann (2003), demonstrating that the Estates had better direct access to credit than did the Crown.

the course of the sixteenth century the merchants were increasingly supplanted by royal officials, especially lawyers.[9] French monarchs during this period attempted to halt this process by preventing their officials from taking such municipal offices, but they were largely unsuccessful in doing so.[10]

There were two obvious potential obstacles to the effective functioning of the rentes system. First, unlike the city council in such places as Cologne, the municipality of Paris was not a sovereign body, and French kings retained many opportunities for intervening in Parisian affairs, as in regard to the election of principal magistrates. With this said, there seems to be little doubt from the historical record that at least in its initial phase, the arrangement of borrowing indirectly via the municipality of Paris increased the king's cost of taking an action like reassigning revenues allocated to pay rentes. The historical record makes clear that all efforts by the monarchy to take such action could occur only after a series of protracted negotiations, in which the prévôt des marchands and the bureau de ville would offer significant resistance.

The second limitation of the rentes sur l'Hôtel de Ville system was that it could not be scaled up to the national level. As long as the revenues to pay the rentes were collected in or near Paris, the municipality could play an effective role in ensuring that revenues collected were used to pay rentes as contracted. This was no longer the case once the system of rentes was expanded after 1551. As noted, after this point many new issues were guaranteed by royal revenues collected throughout northern France, or even in more distant locations from Paris. The expansion of the system in 1561 to includes rentes backed by revenues from the clergy, but still monitored by the municipality of Paris, had a similar effect. During the fiscal crisis between 1561 and 1588, there were few cases where the Crown unilaterally reassigned revenues that had already arrived Paris, but the wide geographic dispersion of the taxes to pay rentes resulted in the Crown's agents frequently making use of revenues at the local level for alternative purposes.[11]

---

[9]This was apparently a general movement in French cities at the time. Major (1960: 12) reports that in Dijon prior to 1550 the typical official had been a merchant, but between 1588 and 1594 the ratio was fourteen to six in favor of the lawyers.

[10]This is the conclusion drawn by Major (1960: 12–13). Babelon (1986: 269) refers to direct efforts by the Crown to impose merchants as municipal officials in Paris over royal officials.

[11]See Schnapper (1956) on these points.

In sum, France had a set of institutions that could increase commitment to repay debt, and thus facilitate access to credit, but these institutions functioned effectively only at the local level.

National Institutions for Creditor Representation

If one of the problems with the expanding issues of rentes was that the Parisian municipal authorities, could not effectively monitor or influence revenue collection in distant localities, then the next logical question is why France lacked a national institution that could serve this function. France's national representative institution, the Estates General, had existed in one form or another since 1302. One could imagine a number of different mechanisms whereby the Estates General might have played a direct role in monitoring either revenue collection or annuities payments so as to increase the credibility of debt servicing. The fact that it never did this might be seen as a failure on the part of French monarchs to understand the virtues of credible commitment. In what follows I will argue that more fundamentally, there were two underlying obstacles to the Estates General playing this type of role. First, France was simply too big. It was too large to sustain a representative assembly that would meet with high frequency, given early modern transport and communication conditions. It is difficult to imagine how under these conditions the Estates could have effectively monitored royal finances. A second obstacle, independent of geographic scale, involved the social composition of the Estates. This helped ensure that when they did meet, the Estates showed little inclination to defend the interests of state creditors. To support these arguments I will draw on events that took place during the Estates General of 1576.

The Estates General met at Blois in 1576 in a context of acute fiscal crisis and impending civil war between Catholics and Protestants. The Estates were convened by King Henri III both as a means of seeking a religious settlement and with the hope that the Estates would respond to the crisis by agreeing to new taxation. Before dealing with the financial problem, however, the Estates sought first to see (or hear) a full accounting of the current state of royal finances. Failing to satisfy the Estate's demands (Henri III's representative provided only a brief summary of the monarchy's financial situation), the Estates soon realized that, as Jean Bodin remarked, they had no way of knowing whether even this summary information was accurate. The problem of the Estates being unable to verify the true state of royal finances was not a one-off occurrence.

In 1588, the next occasion when the Estates met, they reached a similar conclusion about the vagueness of the monarchy's initial assessment of its financial situation. The Estates delegated a representative to travel to Paris to conduct a more detailed investigation of the state of finances, but this proved to be such a time-consuming process that the meeting of the Estates actually ended before this individual could produce a full report.[12]

These two cases certainly provide an illustration of royal resistance to providing a full financial accounting, and as such they fit closely with the pattern described by Philippe Hamon (1994), whereby French monarchs from the beginning of the sixteenth century made increasing attempts to make state finances a secretive domain. Beyond the attitude taken by French monarchs, however, it also seems clear that an assembly meeting less than once a decade would inevitably find it difficult to establish an accounting of royal finances. For each new Estates General this involved, in effect, trying to conduct an audit without any initial information.

If the problem was infrequent meetings, however, then why couldn't the Estates simply meet more frequently? One explanation is that a previous Estates General in 1560 had refused to consent to new taxation, and there was little incentive for a monarch to call such an assembly anew if it was expected that the response would be similar.[13] Adding to this problem, there were very significant obstacles to holding frequent assembly meetings in a polity the size of France, increasing the reluctance of individuals to attend. At the conclusion to the 1468 meeting, the assembled Estates actually stated that they could not meet as frequently as in the past.[14] An even more direct implication of the effect of polity size is that in many meetings of the Estates General, one of the significant points of contention was how to pay the costs of attendance, an issue that was not a point of political contention, for example, in the English parliament.[15] Finally, we also know that in strong contrast to the Estates General, within the regions of France provincial estates met on a much more frequent basis, usually once a year or once every two years. It seems logical that

---

[12]Cauwès (1895: 448–49).

[13]The studies by Major (1951, 1960) suggest that the Estates General was not convened more frequently because it repeatedly refused to consent to new taxation, which limited its usefulness to French monarchs.

[14]Blockmans (1998).

[15]See Major (1955) on this issue.

provincial estates would meet more frequently given the smaller size of these territories.[16]

Irrespective of how frequently the Estates General met, the episode of 1576 demonstrates that when the Estates did meet, creditor interests were poorly represented within the institution.[17] During the discussion of the Crown's financial situation, the Parisian delegation, which was part of the Third Estate, argued vociferously that any financial decisions made should not prejudice the interests of those who owned rentes issued on behalf of the king. Magistrates from the municipality of Paris, including the prévôt des marchands, were members of the parisian delegation and given the municipality's involvement with the rentes sur l'Hôtel de Ville, it is hardly surprising that they took this position. All available evidence suggests that these officials were, of course, themselves also significant holders of rentes. Given the clear lack of support within the Estates General for the king's proposal of raising new taxes, the Parisian delegation threw its weight behind an alternative proposal to sell off Crown lands in order to raise money.[18] Observers of the 1576 meeting reported that this attitude was directly motivated by the fact that without such a sale, the king would feel obliged to suspend payments on all or part of the rentes sur l'Hôtel de Ville.

The position of the Parisian delegation was opposed by the majority of Third Estate deputies, one of whom placed a sign at the entrance to the meeting chamber that called for seizing the revenues dedicated to paying the rentes sur l'Hôtel de Ville.[19] The outcome of the debate was greatly influenced by Jean Bodin (later famous as a political philosopher) who managed to establish himself as president of the Third Estate.[20] Bodin opposed the idea of new taxes, particularly as this might have been used to support a war against France's Protestants, an effort he did not support. Bodin also strongly objected to the idea of the sale of Crown lands as a

---

[16]Lewis (1962) rejects the idea that the "failure" of the French Estates General was attributable to the size of the polity, emphasizing instead the obstacle of provincial particularism. But the fact that provincial particularism was so strong in France (as opposed to England, for example) might ultimately have been endogenous to the size of the polity.

[17]The attitude taken by the deputies in 1576 also parallels the attitude anticipated by those in 1715 who argued for calling the Estates General in order to trigger a default. See Stasavage (2003) for this episode.

[18]Cauwès (1895: 455).

[19]Cauwès (1895: 456).

[20]On Bodin's role in the Estates General of 1576, see Wolfe (1972: 162–65) and Ulph (1947), as well as Bodin's journal of events at the Estates.

solution to the monarchy's financial problems. In the end, by refusing to sanction the proposal to sell Crown lands, the Estates General declared that "[i]f the affairs of the king are so desperate, he could make use of half of the rents constituted on both the cities and communities of the kingdom, he could tax the financiers who have lent to him, or he could sell off church lands."[21]

Why did the deputies of the Third Estate directly suggest that the king take actions equivalent to a default? For the vast majority of Third Estate deputies, who came from the provinces, there was a clear reluctance to jump to the defense of a group of creditors based in Paris. Cauwès (1894: 455) attributes Bodin's stance with regard to the rentes to a provincial attitude. The study by Martin Wolfe (1972: 167) argues that Bodin saw that proposals to raise new taxes were "an attempt to transfer money from the purses of the provincials into those of the Parisians." More generally, we know that other cities in France had been forced to make extra contributions to royal finances through mechanisms like forced loans and the don gratuit rather than the more advantageous option of selling rentes.

Summary

To briefly repeat the conclusions of the above analysis, we can suggest that France did in fact have institutions that creditors could use to monitor public finances. The problem was that these institutions existed and functioned effectively only at the local and not the national level. The institutional arrangement for using the Paris municipality to manage the rentes sur l'Hôtel de Ville closely resembled arrangements within city-states. The problem was that this institution could not effectively be scaled up. There were two fundamental reasons for this. First, the large size of the French polity made it difficult to maintain an intensive form of political representation. Second, even when the Estates General did meet, given their social composition, the Estates showed very little interest in defending the prerogatives of public creditors. This was very different from a merchant dominated city-state.

REVISITING ABSOLUTISM IN CASTILE

The final two historical cases that I consider in this chapter are those of Castile and the Dutch Republic, two states that were at war with each

---

[21]Cauwès (1895: 456).

other almost continuously during the period between the beginning of the Dutch revolt against Habsburg control in 1568 and the Peace of Westphalia in 1648. The prolonged conflict between the two states created a need for high levels of debt finance, and it is generally judged that the Dutch Republic was more successful in this regard, precisely because it was more creditworthy as a borrower. The Spanish monarchy paid significantly higher interest rates than the Dutch Republic on its loans. There is also evidence of the Spanish monarchy failing to gain access to adequate credit. It was at several points forced to suspend military operations against the Dutch due to borrowing constraints. The question that needs to be asked is why there was such a sharp difference in the evolution of public credit in these two states.

One potential response to the question is to refer to differences in political institutions. The Dutch Republic had strong representative assemblies at the general, the provincial, and the municipal levels that exercised control over public finances. In strong contrast, it has often been observed that Castile was an absolutist monarchy. The problem with such an argument emphasizing absolutism is that it is not supported by the last thirty years of historical research on the Cortes. This research has demonstrated how, up to the 1630s, the Castilian Cortes remained a very significant obstacle to the unilateral exercise of power by monarchs in the area of state finances.[22] The Cortes, which experienced a revival in its power during the late sixteenth and early seventeenth centuries, could pose considerable obstacles in the face of royal attempts to raise taxes or create new taxes.

A close look at Castilian and Dutch political institutions during the late sixteenth and early seventeenth centuries shows that they actually had more similarities than one might think.[23] In each state the central representative assembly was dominated by urban representatives from a similar number of cities. The Cortes of Castile was composed of representatives from eighteen towns.[24] These town representatives enjoyed

[22] See Thompson (1982, 1984, 1993a,b, 1994a,b), Jago (1981, 1985), Mackay (1999), and Lovett (1987), as well as Carretero Zamora (1988) on the relationship between cities, Crown, and Cortes.

[23] This point has been emphasized by Koenigsberger (1992) as well as Tracy (2002: 302).

[24] Since the middle of the sixteenth century, the Cortes of Castile had been composed exclusively of urban representatives. With nobility and clergy legally exempted from direct taxation, their participation was less critical. In 1597 the number of cities that sent representatives to the Cortes was set at 18. It included Burgos, Toledo, Leon, Granada, Seville, Cordoba, Jaen, Murcia, Guadalajara, Soria, Cuenca, Segovia, Avila, Toro, Zamora, Salamanca, Valladolid, and Madrid (Beneyto 1966: 465).

control over the approval of new taxation and the administration of taxes, and it is also known that the towns in each case were governed by merchant oligarchies whose members themselves invested in government debt. If we look at the structure of the Estates of Holland, the assembly of the dominant province within the Dutch Republic, we see that it, too, was controlled by representatives from the principal towns of the province (in this case eighteen). These towns were also controlled by merchant oligarchies who invested in public debt.[25] Given such similarities, instead of arguing that Castile and Holland had different outcomes with public credit because of fundamental differences between their political institutions, the more appropriate question to pose may be why were the financial histories of these two states so different despite their apparent institutional similarities?

I will suggest that the greater geographic scale of Castile was a critical factor in limiting the possibility for sustaining an intensive form of political representation. In both Castile and Holland the individual towns that sent representatives to the national-level assembly insisted these individuals be constrained by strict mandates. In the Netherlands this was not an obstacle to having an active assembly that met frequently. Deputies could shuttle back and forth between the assembly and their home towns. The situation in Castile was much different. As the historian H. G. Koenigsberger observed, "where the deputies of Flanders or Holland could travel back and forth to their nearby cities and often on comfortable inland waterways, the much greater distances and the much more difficult traveling conditions of the Castilian *meseta* made frequent reference back impossible" (1992: 641).

Castilian Public Credit in the Seventeenth Century

During the sixteenth and seventeenth centuries the Spanish crown's system of borrowing was based on two pillars: *asiento* contracts, which most closely resembled short-term debt, and *juro* contracts, which represented perpetual or term annuities.[26] Issuance of *juro* contracts was subject to legal limits imposed by the Cortes. There was no such limit on *asiento* contracts. Royal debt policy then frequently involved the issuance of

---

[25] In drawing this conclusion, the subsequent discussion is based in particular on Tracy (1985, 1990) 't Hart (1993, 1999), and Gilissen (1966).

[26] See Castillo (1963a, 1963b) for overviews of the system of Spanish public borrowing during this period.

asientos to meet extraordinary war financing needs, followed by subsequent efforts to convert *asientos* into *juros*. In some cases this was done by using contingent clauses contained in *asiento* contracts allowing for conversion into *juros* in case of non-repayment, albeit with a reduction in the principal owed. When conversions led the Crown to reach its limit for issuance of *juros*, it could then use a strategically declared bankruptcy to force further conversions and to pressure the Cortes to raise the limit for issuing *juros*. Debt conversions occurred with sufficient frequency that they were an integral (and anticipated) part of the financial system.[27] Under Philip II (1556–98) the anticipated nature of these conversions suggests that their existence alone cannot be taken as evidence that lending to the Spanish Crown was a foolish enterprise.[28]

Despite a dramatically more dire fiscal situation after the end of Philip II's reign, there continued to be significant investment in Spanish *juros* throughout the seventeenth century. Castillo (1963a,b) suggests that as the Castilian economy experienced a more general financial crisis during the seventeenth century, investment in *juros* may have become increasingly attractive. I.A.A. Thompson (1984: 161–64) argues that there was particularly wide ownership of *juros*, and most notably by the members of the oligarchies of the principal Castilian cities.[29] He also suggests that through the 1590s, juros traded at near par on the secondary market, but after the 1630s, and in particular after a suspension of interest payments in 1633, this was no longer the case.

Just how much of a premium did the Spanish monarchy pay on its debt when compared to the Dutch Republic? This question raises inevitable problems of measurement. Ideally one would compare the two states using the same interest rate measure. For Castile, Ruiz Martín (1975) reports an interest rate on *juros*, calculated as a fiscal interest rate proxy, taking annual interest payments on this form of debt as a percentage of the total stock of debt. Based on his data, from an interest rate of 10% at the beginning of the sixteenth century, the cost of long-term borrowing for the Castilian monarchy declined in a steady fashion, reaching a low of 5.8% in 1598. Mauro and Parker (1977) provide fiscal data, compiled from several different sources, from which one could estimate a cost of

[27] See also Conklin (1998) and Drelichman and Voth (2008a,b) on these backruptcies, as well as their discussion of the important role of Genoese investors in providing short-term credit to the Crown.

[28] A point that has been made with force by Drelichman and Voth (2008a,b).

[29] See also Jago (1981: 324) on this point.

borrowing of 5% in 1623 and 7% in 1667. One advantage of using a fiscal proxy for the interest rate on *juros* is that this would reflect actual costs of borrowing, whereas a measure based on the nominal interest rate would be biased if the Castilian monarchy unilaterally lowered this rate.

Three different sources can be used to provide a picture of the costs of borrowing for the Dutch republic during this same period. Wantje Fritschy (2003b) provides information on the interest rate for perpetual annuities issued by the Estates of Holland for various dates between 1569 and 1655. These data suggest that from an initial maximum of 8.33%, the annuities declined to a rate of 4% by the middle of the seventeenth century. Following data collected by Marjolein't Hart (1999), by the middle of the seventeenth century the Estates of Holland were able to sell annuities at rates as low as 3%.[30] Fiscal data from the province of Holland, which can be used to calculate a proxy measure for the interest rate, are available on an annual basis for the period after 1632.[31] The cost of borrowing calculated in this manner very closely tracks the overall trend in interest rates reported by Hart (1999) and Fritschy (2003b).

Remembering the potential limitations of these data series in allowing for a comparison between the two states, the information just presented suggests that it was not until the 1630s that the young Dutch Republic had costs of borrowing significantly lower than those prevailing in Castile. One reason for this is no doubt that Dutch debt was initially made more risky by uncertainty whether the republic would succeed in maintaining independence from Spain. After the 1630s, however, interest rates in Holland dropped very significantly, and by the end of their long period of conflict in 1648, it was clear that the Dutch Republic faced much lower costs of borrowing than did Castile.

If the Dutch Republic had access to less expensive credit than did the Habsburg monarchy, the extent to which Castile was at a disadvantage with regard to credit can also be seen by the fact that the Crown was, on several occasions, obliged to suspend military operations in the Netherlands. This was notably the case after the bankruptcy of 1607 when the Spanish Crown was forced to conclude a truce, which lasted twelve

---

[30] It may seem surprising that as a state which has been cited as an example of a financial revolution, there is not a more complete series of interest rates on annuities of the Estates of Holland. Fritschy (2003b: 63) provides the main reason for this; in 1725 most of the archives of Holland's Chamber of Audit were disposed of due to lack of storage space.

[31] Source: electronic file deposited by Wantje Fritschy with the European State Finance Database.

years (Ehrenberg 1928: 335). This implies quite a serious constraint on Crown policy.

Control of Public Finances by the Cortes

Compared with other assemblies in large monarchies, the Castilian Cortes of the late sixteenth and seventeenth centuries was actually able to establish extensive formal powers with regard to public finance. This was particularly true with regard to consent for taxation and the administration of tax collection. It is also true, though, that the Cortes never succeeded in establishing a high degree of control over royal spending decisions, despite several efforts to the contrary.

While the Cortes had a lengthy history as an institution, the short-term cause of the revival of the Cortes at the end of the sixteenth century was the defeat of the Spanish Armada in 1588, which prompted King Philip II to turn to the Cortes in order to seek new finance.[32] After lengthy negotiations, the Crown finally persuaded the individual Castilian cities that sent representatives to the Cortes to agree to a new tax, which came to be known as the *millones* (first voted in 1590). This came at a significant price; the individual cities would retain the sole authority to administer the tax as they saw fit. In addition, the principle was established that the Cortes could, in advance of agreeing to new taxes, request specific legislative initiatives by the Crown. This episode illustrates the extent to which a monarch who has been seen as a prototypical example of absolutism faced formidable constraints from a representative assembly.[33]

The millones was initially a one-off grant by Castilian cities to the monarchy. It quickly evolved into a more permanent arrangement that resembled a new system of taxation and that represented an increasingly large share of overall state revenues. The millones were administered by a committee controlled by the Cortes consisting of four *procuradores*—the name used for the city representatives to the Cortes. These individuals had substantial powers in terms of auditing (Jago 1981: 316). Over time, the royal Council of Finance (*Consejo de Hacienda*) succeeded in establishing a fair degree of control over the management of the millones, but José Ucendo (2001) argues that as an institution with a staff of only 150 people in a country with a population of several millions, the Consejo was obliged

---

[32] See Lovett (1987) and Gelabert (1999) for descriptions of this episode.

[33] On the negotiations that led to this outcome, and how they were indicative of the constraints faced by Philip II, see Lovett (1987).

to rely heavily on local authorities for tax collection. Moreover, on each occasion where the Crown launched negotiations to renew the *millones*, the cities of Castile used this as an opportunity to attempt to gain new concessions from the monarchy. This includes pledges regarding servicing of debt and reductions in expenditures, particularly war expenditures in Flanders.[34]

It is important to highlight the boundaries of influence of the Cortes. The institution established clear control over the administration of taxes thanks to the *comision de millones*. It also played a direct role in monitoring short-term indebtedness to the extent that it had a degree of oversight of *asiento* contracts. There is less evidence that the Cortes ever succeeded in exerting control over spending despite efforts to the contrary. Moreover, as I will next describe, the individual Castilian cities gradually lost control over their representatives to the Cortes. As a consequence, the representatives failed to effectively use even those formal powers that they did have at their disposal.

Explaining the Demise of the Cortes

While the Cortes succeeded under the regime of the millones in establishing a significant degree of formal control over royal finances, in practice after the first few decades of the seventeenth century it grew noticeably more pliant in the face of royal demands. It entered a period of decadence as an institution, and after 1665 the monarchy did away with the institution entirely. It instead chose to bargain on an individual basis with Castilian cities. Until recent years, the most popular interpretation has been to see the Cortes as a victim of steadily increasing royal authority. One problem with this explanation, as argued by I.A.A. Thompson (1982), is that the final decision of 1665 not to reconvene the Cortes occurred under one of the weakest of Habsburg monarchs. Rather than being triggered by the steady advance of royal power, the final demise of the Cortes, Thompson argues, was instead triggered by the cities of Castile, which grew increasingly dissatisfied with the functioning of the institution.

Underlying the increasing dissatisfaction of the cities with the Cortes was a fundamental agency problem—the cities of Castile had little effective means of controlling their individual procuradores. The procuradores to the medieval Cortes had been elected by city councils, but in a response

---

[34] See Gelabert (1999: 215–16).

to the way in which this electoral competition bred underlying factional conflict within cities, by the sixteenth century all but one of the 18 towns that sent representatives to the Cortes had done away with election as a method of selection.[35] They instead specified either a rotation of a set of individuals, or, more frequently, selection by lot.[36] While selection by lot might limit internal conflict over choice of representatives, it also had a further effect of removing the ability of cities to select individuals who they thought would best represent their interests. The response of the cities was to attempt to constrain their procuradores by giving them strict mandates, a move that was also designed to reduce potential royal influence through corruption. As argued previously, this reliance on mandates was not a particularity of the Cortes; it also was present in the Dutch Republic, and in fact many other early modern assemblies. But in the Dutch Republic a mandate system was consistent with an intensive form of political representation because of the polity's small scale. In Castile this was not the case. Seeking a Cortes that would be both more compliant and that could arrive at decisions more efficiently, the Crown repeatedly sought instead to have the procuradores granted full powers to make decisions regarding taxation. After 1632 the Crown finally succeeded in obtaining the consent of the cities to this change.

A proximate explanation for why the Castilian cities lost control of their *procuradores* is that the Crown was able to use the distribution of offices and bribes to obtain favorable decisions. A more fundamental explanation may have been that the cities that sent representatives to this assembly were simply too geographically dispersed to be able to monitor the activities of their procuradores in Madrid. Certainly, for earlier occasions we have evidence that Spanish monarchs were willing to use their country's geographic scale in order to weaken the ability of towns to control their representatives to the Cortes. In 1520, just after being elected Holy Roman Emperor, Charles V convened a meeting of the Cortes in the remote location of Santiago de Compostela. Before the proceedings began, he then transferred the meeting to the even more remote location of La Coruña, motivated by a desire to increase his leverage over the procuradores.[37] This ultimately aided in the king's effort to prompt the Cortes into approving the expenses entailed in the trip that Charles conducted to claim the imperial Crown.

[35] The exception was Burgos.
[36] See Thompson (1993a: 6–9).
[37] Drelichman (2003).

Summary

To repeat my core conclusions from this section, the argument that Castile lacked creditworthiness because it had absolutist institutions is insufficient—Castilian representative institutions actually had many formal similarities to those of the Dutch Republic. Moreover, in both cases representative institutions were dominated by urban groups. The crucial difference between the two cases was that in Castile the cities that sent *procuradores* to the Cortes eventually lost control of these representatives, whereas in the Dutch Republic this was never the case. The much larger size of Castile and its unfavorable geography may provide a crucial explanation for this outcome.

ACCOUNTING FOR HOLLAND'S FINANCIAL REVOLUTION

Existing scholarship emphasizes how the period when the United Provinces established their independence from Spain also witnessed a revolution in public credit. James Tracy has argued convincingly that there was an important political foundation to Holland's financial revolution, and it involved the fact that within the republic, the same individuals who lent to the government also held political control.[38] In what follows I will draw upon Tracy's conclusion while also attempting to suggest why the ultimate financial outcome in Holland was so different from that in Castile despite the superficial similarities in their political institutions.

Public Credit in Holland

The important work of James Tracy has emphasized how, in an attempt to obtain more finance from its Dutch possessions, the Habsburg monarchy consented to a series of measures, beginning first by allowing the sale of annuities at the provincial level in 1515, and continuing with the establishment of provincial-level taxes during the 1540s and 1550s. For centuries, cities in the Low Countries had sold their own annuities serviced with municipal taxes, but this innovation of selling annuities guaranteed by provincial revenues was something new. The irony of the story is that this same financial machinery was eventually turned against the Habsburgs

---

[38]Tracy (1990, 1985, 2002).

when the Dutch provinces revolted against Habsburg rule. Numerous authors have suggested that the structure of Dutch financial and political institutions helps explain why a relatively small state like the Dutch Republic was able to prevail in a military struggle with a much larger enemy.

Despite the innovations of the 1540s and 1550s, as well as those that occurred after the revolt against the Habsburgs which began in 1568, the Dutch republic's system of public finance and of decision-making was never fully centralized. The generality of the Netherlands sold debt, as did the different constituent provinces, of which Holland was the most prominent. At the provincial level, the sale of both annuities and obligations was conducted by receivers, the same individuals charged with collecting taxes, involving either the overall provincial receiver or receivers from individual tax districts.[39] Finally, individual cities also continued to sell their own annuities.

Fritschy (2003a) has offered a significant correction to the interpretation of James Tracy (1985), though her account does not alter his broader conclusions about the role played by representative assemblies. If there was a revolution in provincial finance, Fritschy suggests that in the first few decades after the revolt against Habsburg control, this was first and foremost a tax revolution. War expenditures were funded by a massive increase in taxation, first at the municipal level and subsequently at the provincial level, and it was only after this point that borrowing became a major source of war finance.[40]

Representative Assemblies in the Dutch Republic

The representative institutions of the Dutch Republic were highly developed, and they gave state creditors an effective way to monitor public finances. There were three separate levels of representation.[41]

At the summit of the system, although not necessarily in terms of power, stood the States General, which was composed of deputies from

---

[39] See 't Hart (1993: ch.6; 1999) for a concise description.

[40] While Tracy (1985) emphasized the importance of sales of annuities as a form of public credit, Fritschy (2003a) emphasizes the importance of *obligaties*, which were initially short-term loans that evolved into long-term loans over time and which had the advantage of being more easily marketable. She suggests that for this reason the *obligaties* were preferred by merchants.

[41] See Gilissen (1966) and Grever (1982) for overviews.

the seven provinces of the Republic. The States General sat more or less permanently after gaining its independence from the Habsburg Empire, with meetings occurring almost daily, the exceptions being Sundays and holidays.[42] It made decisions regarding defense, foreign policy, and other matters, in addition to setting overall levels of taxation and spending for the Republic. The States General was also a forum where individual provincial delegations had relatively little latitude with regard to decisions. Following a tradition known as "hearing and reporting," before any significant decision was taken, each provincial delegation would need to consult its respective provincial estates.[43]

A very similar pattern of decision-making existed at the provincial level. If we take the example of Holland, the Republic's most important province, we observe that the States of Holland was a sovereign body but one in which representatives were obliged continuously to refer back to individual town councils before making decisions. A formal rule introduced in 1585 stated that nothing could be placed on the agenda of the States of Holland unless it had previously been circulated among all voting town governments. The other salient feature of the States of Holland is that its representatives were overwhelmingly urban. After independence the States were composed of representatives from eighteen towns, of which Amsterdam was the most prominent, in addition to the *ridderschap*, which represents the nobility and countryside (Israel 1995: 278–79). While the ridderschap always expressed its opinion first, political power in the States of Holland clearly rested with town councils. It also seems clear that this pattern of town dominance was the case for the majority of the provinces of the Dutch Republic.[44]

Moving down a level, we can examine the pattern of representation within the town councils of Dutch cities.[45] The day-to-day affairs of government in Dutch cities were typically conducted by a small number of burgomasters selected for one-year terms together with a small group of aldermen. These officials were elected by a larger council called the *vroedschap* (the wisdom), whose members were chosen for life by cooptation.[46] The cities of the Northern Netherlands had, for the most part, not experienced the guild revolutions that occurred elsewhere in the

---

[42] See Grever (1982) for a detailed description of the procedures of the States General.
[43] Gilissen (1966).
[44] See Gilissen (1966: 432).
[45] See Tracy (1990; 1985: 150–51) and 't Hart (1993).
[46] See Tracy (1990: ch.1) for a concise description.

Low Countries from the beginning of the fourteenth century. As a result, they retained an oligarchic character, and this closed oligarchic character would become accentuated over time.

The final critical factor in understanding the implications of Dutch representative institutions for public credit is that those who held public office, at either the provincial level or at the municipal level, were themselves major investors in public annuities. This has been demonstrated in the most detailed fashion by Tracy (1985: ch.5) for the case of the Estates of Holland. It should come as no surprise then that the Estates of Holland would eventually establish a firm reputation for creditworthiness. While town magistrates were heavily engaged in commerce, Tracy's detailed evidence on owners of public annuities in the city of Amsterdam does point to a certain degree of separation between the city's political and commercial elite. Many of the largest merchants most heavily engaged in commerce were not significant purchasers of public annuities.[47] One explanation he offers for this is that over time, serving as a magistrate became increasingly time consuming, and it may have necessitated divesting oneself of commercial activities. The other explanation offered by Tracy for this separation is that many of the individuals most actively engaged in trade were recent arrivals to the city. Over time, they or their children would move into a political career. If accurate, this would correspond closely to the process described by Michael Postan (1952) cited in chapter 1 of this book.

Accounting for the Political Structure of the Dutch Republic

The foregoing discussion points to the formal similarity between the Dutch representative institutions and those in Castile. Assemblies in both countries during the late sixteenth and early seventeenth centuries were dominated by urban representatives from a fixed and similar number of towns. In each case these assemblies had significant power, and the member towns placed their representatives under strict mandates. The Cortes, however, never succeeded in establishing the same monitoring role as did its Dutch counterpart, and it suffered from serious agency problems in the relationship between cities and *procuradores*. This raises the question of how the Dutch cities were able to overcome both of these problems.

---

[47] See also Tracy (1990: 196) on this subject.

One possible interpretation is that Dutch representative institutions became dramatically stronger only after the provinces had successfully revolted against Habsburg rule. In other words, an intensive form of representation could occur only after a republic was established. Jonathan Israel (1995: ch.13) argues that it was only after 1572 that both the Estates General and the Estates of Holland were able to transform themselves into institutions that met continuously and that no longer depended on the whim of a prince to be convened.[48] While the activities of each of these bodies did increase after the revolt, all of the evidence suggests that the Estates General of the Netherlands and the States of Holland were already extremely active well before the revolt of 1572. From the first meeting of the Estates General, which took place at Bruges in 1464, through 1576 there were 160 separate meetings of the assembly according to John Gilissen (1966: 408). For the States of Holland, Tracy (1990: 124) reports that there were 285 meetings held between 1542 and 1562, during a period of Habsburg rule, an average of 13.5 meetings a year.[49] By general European standards this points to a very intensive form of representation existing well prior to the revolt.

We can conclude that if the Dutch Republic was similar to city-states in having a very intensive form of political representation, this was because it shared the same underlying features. It was a polity dominated by merchants and that covered a small territory. It also had relatively oligarchic political institutions.

SUMMARY

The experience of France, Castile, and the Dutch Republic helps illustrate the obstacles faced by most territorial states in establishing an intensive form of political representation, and thus in gaining access to credit. The seventeenth-century evolution of the Spanish Cortes and the failed attempt to expand the system of the rentes sur l'Hôtel de Ville each illustrate the difficulties of sustaining a system of creditor representation in a large polity, just as the Dutch Republic demonstrates how a territorial state could sustain a more intensive form of representation, provided that

---

[48] See in particular Israel (1995: 278, 292).

[49] The first historical reference to the "States of Holland" in fact dates from 1428 (Tracy 1990: 14).

it was small. Geographic size was not the only critical factor, however. Outcomes in each of the three states examined also hinged critically on the extent to which mercantile groups—those with liquid wealth who would invest in debt—were dominant within an institution. This was clearly the case in the Dutch Republic whereas it was not the case in France. As a result, even in those instances where the French Estates General did meet, it demonstrated little interest in supporting government creditors.

CHAPTER EIGHT

Implications for State Formation and Development

I have attempted in this book to provide a broad picture that allows for a better understanding of two phenomena that observers since at least the eighteenth century have seen as somehow being linked—the development of a representative form of government and the establishment of a system of public credit. An enhanced appreciation of the intertwined history of representation and public credit in Europe can in turn inform us about broader scholarly debates on related subjects. In making these arguments I have been heavily influenced by the work of several key scholars. Like Charles Tilly, I emphasize that there was more than one path of state development in Europe. Following Douglass North, I consider the constraining effects of representative assemblies. Drawing on the insight of Wim Blockmans, I have stressed the idea that geographic scale was a fundamental constraint on the ability to sustain an intensive form of political representation. The originality of my contribution lies in the fact that unlike either North or Tilly, I provide an account suggesting exactly how political representation mattered, and at the same time I demonstrate how the emergence of this institution was endogenous to a specific set of underlying conditions involving geographic scale and merchant power. I then offer a political account of city-state origins that differs from existing theories. I have made all these arguments by using extensive new data. These data are necessarily imperfect and are clearly subject to error, but they also improve very substantially on previous efforts of this type. Recognizing that my quantitative evidence can take us only so far, I have also presented qualitative evidence on a broad range of polities.

In what follows, rather than summarize my principal conclusions, a task that was fulfilled in the introduction, I will instead consider the implications of this book for three broad debates concerning the following topics: (1) the role of warfare in the process of state formation, (2) the possibility of using institutional change to solve commitment problems, and finally (3) the sources of early modern growth.

THE DEBATE ON WAR AND STATE FORMATION

At least since Otto Hintze (1906), war has been seen as a determinant force driving the development of state institutions in Europe. Since the important work directed by Charles Tilly (1975), more contemporary scholars have also attached a singular importance to war when attempting to explain varieties of state development over time and across polities. In scholarly work on war and state formation, it is commonly argued that external threats helped condition the relationship between rulers and citizens and that the need for money led to concessions involving the creation of representative assemblies with important powers (see note 4 in chapter 1). In addition, it is claimed that external threats created incentives to create strong bureaucratic institutions. Finally, many suggest that the nature of military technology also had a critical effect on the type of states that emerged. As the introduction of new technologies and new styles of fighting led to the creation of larger armies, the city-states of Europe were increasingly imperiled by the continent's larger territorial powers.

Drawing upon this body of work, scholars specializing in other world regions have then drawn the conclusion that a relative absence of recent interstate conflict in regions such as Africa may explain the failure to develop state institutions characterized by high administrative capacity.[1] Likewise, if in medieval Europe external threats prompted rulers to seek support of their citizens and as a concession to grant authority to a representative assembly, then the absence of similar external threats in post-independence Africa may explain why African rulers have often felt less compelled to seek the consent of their citizens or to establish institutions through which they may be held accountable.[2]

The empirical evidence that I have presented in this book suggests that war actually had considerably more ambiguous effects on state formation in Europe than is commonly believed.

Yes, it was the case that the demands of war often led European rulers to call representative assemblies as a means of negotiating for new taxes, but in states spanning a large swath of territory this process could only go so far. In large states it was possible to have a form of accountability in which an assembly could, at infrequent intervals, exert a veto over tax policies. What was not possible to achieve was having a further power that characterizes modern representative assemblies—the ability to intervene at high frequency and to actively manage affairs of state.

---

[1] For a well-argued example, see Herbst's (2000) claim that an absence of interstate war has led to weak state capacity in Africa.

[2] This is an argument made in Bates (2001).

Yes, it was also true that within early modern Europe the demands of war led to the development of administrative capacity—but this too must logically have been conditioned by geographic scale.

Finally, yes there is also no doubt that changes in what Samuel Finer (1975) called the "format of the military forces" over time implied an increased cost of fighting war. This in turn influenced state development. But the way in which these changes (which may or may not have been due to exogenous technological change) influenced state development is more complex than is commonly suggested. Territorial states had an advantage in this new military environment because they could draw on larger populations for revenues and manpower. But city-states also had an advantage to the extent that they could support the political institutions necessary to raise abundant credit at low cost. It was arguably this access to credit that was one of the keys to their survival.

The above conclusions are important for their own sake, but they also have broader implications, because authors have drawn upon a particular reading of the European experience to inform our understanding of state formation in other contexts. If war had a more muted effect on state formation in Europe than is so frequently presented, then we might want to reconsider whether the weakness of such institutions in a region like contemporary Africa is necessarily the product of an absence of interstate conflict. It still may be the case that early modern European experience can provide lessons for understanding state development in Africa, but the principal lesson may lie elsewhere. The lesson may instead be that it is inherently difficult to establish institutions of accountability in large territories with high communications costs.[3]

INFORMATION, COMMITMENT, AND DEMOCRACY

Throughout this book I have emphasized how in medieval Europe geographic scale posed a fundamental constraint on the possibility of maintaining an intensive form of political representation. If we accept this conclusion as accurate, then we can draw one immediate implication from my results—a representative institution thought to solve a specific commitment problem could be established in only certain types of societies. But one might then suggest that my conclusions are historically bounded, given that since the invention of the railroad and the telegraph,

---

[3] This is a point that is also emphasized by Herbst (2000) in his work on Africa.

geographic scale is no longer as serious a constraint on maintaining an intensive form of political representation. In fact, I wish to argue that my particular historical conclusions have implications for a much broader range of contexts. They support the idea that if there are many situations in politics in which conceding control may be useful to solve a commitment problem, it is also the case that the effective exercise of control often depends upon costly information acquisition. If, for exogenous reasons, these costs are sufficiently high, then the solution to the problem may simply not be feasible.

It has been suggested that in politics there are many reasons why the Coase theorem may not apply; in other words, it is not realistic to expect that two parties will be able to agree on a bargain that achieves a socially efficient outcome irrespective of the initial distribution of property rights. Chief among these is the fact that in the absence of third-party enforcement, holders of political power face an inherent commitment problem—they can act in contravention to previous statements or agreements.[4] With regard to economic development, where security of property is an issue, it is widely argued that the best feasible solution to this problem may then be for a ruler to concede a degree of control to an institution, such as a representative assembly in the historical European case, in which property holders play a significant role.[5] In more recent years it has been suggested that conceding control may help to solve a different sort of political commitment problem: a wealthy elite may choose to democratize in order to avoid a revolution. In this case the choice to democratize involves a potential cost for the elite in terms of redistributive taxation (a decision that at one time was seen as a violation of property rights) in exchange for avoiding the sort of full-scale expropriation that might ensue with revolutionary upheaval.[6]

Implicit in both of these claims is the assumption that for those to whom power is granted, it is costless to exercise this prerogative. But whether we are considering the propertied (in the former example) or the propertyless (in the latter), the ability to exercise power effectively is likely to depend upon having information, and the acquisition of information may be costly. As long as these two groups are exercising power via

---

[4]This general point is emphasized in Acemoglu (2003) in a contribution where he considers the multiple reasons for the absence of a political Coase theorem.

[5]North and Thomas (1973), North and Weingast (1989), and Acemoglu, Johnson, and Robinson (2005).

[6]Acemoglu and Robinson (2006, 2000) and Boix (2003).

representatives, then information about potential representatives will need to be acquired to aid in choosing the individual best suited for the task. It will also be necessary to obtain information about what a representative does once he or she is selected. Political scientists since Anthony Downs (1957) have emphasized that there may be endogenous reasons why citizens may find it optimal not to acquire information. But there may also be exogenous reasons why it is too costly to acquire information, a fact that Downs himself also clearly recognized. In the medieval and early modern era, costs of acquiring information were heavily influenced by geographic scale. Today, for many areas of the globe, geographic scale no longer poses as much of a constraint to the transmission of information. There are, however, certainly many regions where geographic scale does still matter, in particular if individuals are too poor to make use of the most up-to-date travel and communications technologies. Poorer individuals will be less likely to have access to the Internet, they may be unable to read a newspaper (if they can find one), and they may not even have easy access to a radio. Careful empirical studies in areas as diverse as present-day Uganda, India, and the United States in the 1930s have demonstrated that improvements in citizen access to information can have dramatic effects on the relationship between representatives and constituents.[7]

We can see then that there is a clear conclusion that emerges both from my account emphasizing geographic scale and from more recent accounts of access to media. The ability to hold a ruler to account does not only depend on the fixed costs of formal institutional change; it also involves important ongoing costs involving the acquisition of information. If these costs are sufficiently high, it may not be possible to maintain the institution. Alternatively, it may be possible to maintain the institution but without it serving its intended purpose. Here one can see clear parallels between assemblies in very different historical contexts. Compare, for example, the Cortes of Castile in the seventeenth century to the Ugandan Parliament in the twenty-first century. In each case an institution has arguably failed to function as intended because of exogenous factors that have made it costly for constituents in controlling their representatives.[8] Finally, my conclusions about exogenous costs of information acquisition may also help tell us what was truly revolutionary

---

[7] See Besley and Burgess (2002), Stromberg (2004), and Humphreys and Weinstein (2010).

[8] For the Castilian case, see the detailed discussion in chapter 7 and the associated references. For the Ugandan case, see Humphreys and Weinstein (2010).

about the change that occurred in British politics after 1688. Certainly the formal extent of parliamentary control increased after this point, but there were also other very important changes at this time that arguably lowered the exogenous costs for constituents in acquiring information about the actions of their representatives. First, the invention of modern political party organizations gave constituents a new technology for monitoring their representatives.[9] Second, the development of a very active print news culture also certainly lowered costs of information acquisition.[10] These changes helped ensure that the British Parliament did not follow the same course as the Cortes of Castile, an assembly that acquired very significant prerogatives but in which representatives at the center eventually escaped control by their distant constituents.

UNDERSTANDING EARLY MODERN GROWTH

Though I have not directly considered the sources of early modern growth as part of this study, my conclusions may nonetheless aid our understanding of this phenomenon. If previous work has suggested that the city-state was a political organization favorable to growth, it has generally not considered how these small entities could survive against territorial states with larger populations. My conclusions about representation, credit, and oligarchic control help shed light on this question. Of equal importance, my work may also help us to understand why the political institutions of many city-states initially produced economic dynamism while subsequently favoring economic decadence.

   To begin this story, we need to consider the political determinants of growth within European city-states. Scholars have long suggested that European cities were important engines of economic growth during the medieval and early modern periods. Among European cities those that enjoyed substantial political autonomy may have been particularly likely to fulfill this function. As described in the introductory chapter, we know that many significant technological innovations during the early modern period emerged within autonomous cities. We also know from the evidence presented by Bosker, Buringh, and van Zanden (2008)

---

[9]Rather than attempt to monitor actions of their representatives directly, they could use the leadership of the Whig or Tory parties as an enforcement mechanism. See Stasavage (2003) on this point.

[10]See Knights (2005) and Pincus (2009) on this point.

that during the centuries between 1000 and 1800, those European cities that had the status of independent communes experienced faster rates of population growth on average than did cities that were more politically subservient to territorial rulers. This pattern may be attributable to a faster growth of trade and industrial production in these cities, undergirded by technological innovations in both of these domains. These economic developments may in turn have been favored by the independent political status of these cities. However, we should be cautious before drawing a definitive conclusion, because cities with dynamic economies may also have found it easier to assert their independence in the first place.[11]

Why might political autonomy for a city favor economic dynamism? There are many features of cities—independent or not—that may make them sites for technological development, such as the ease with which information can be transmitted within them. But in medieval and early modern times, political autonomy may have created further economic benefits.[12] For one, governance by a city council dominated by merchants and the consequent insulation from the whim of an outside monarch may have made for a more stable legal environment in which to conduct business. Second, governance by a group of individuals meeting regularly face to face may have facilitated the sort of commitment mechanisms described by Avner Greif (2006). In an environment characterized by these two conditions individuals would logically have been more likely to make the sort of investments necessary for economic growth.

But if there are reasons to think that political autonomy should favor economic dynamism, there are also cogent claims that would lead us to expect the opposite outcome. Any city council with sufficient power to assure the security of property rights for inhabitants would also have the power to create barriers to entry that would protect incumbent interests and that would hinder the arrival of entrants with fresh innovations.[13] It

---

[11]We also have evidence suggesting that individual territorial capitals could have dynamic economies, at least for a time. See the evidence on Paris in Slivinski and Sussman (2009).

[12]On this question, see Mokyr (1995, 1990), Bosker, Buringh, and van Zanden (2008), Hicks (1969), and Delong and Shleifer (1993). Many of the assumptions about city-states and economic performance can be traced back to Max Weber's idea on the subject (Weber [1921] 1958), though he did not make as explicit a claim about the economic dynamism of autonomous cities relative to other cities.

[13]This was recognized by both Mokyr (1995, 1990) and Hicks (1969). See Epstein (2000) for a forceful argument that political autonomy for city-states may actually have hindered growth.

was very common for the councils of city states to establish regulations prohibiting foreigners from engaging in certain activities, and similar restrictions often applied to inhabitants of surrounding rural areas controlled by a city. The same can be said of the guild institutions that were particularly strong within certain city-states. By restricting entry to a market, guild institutions might encourage individuals to make costly investments necessary to acquire skills, but ultimately guild restrictions might also be used to deter new entrants offering to produce a product at lower cost. There is not as yet a scholarly consensus over which of these two effects of guilds predominated, when, and why.[14]

So it would seem that there are equally persuasive arguments in favor of both the optimistic and pessimistic views of city-state growth. In fact, my conclusions regarding oligarchic control and access to credit within city-states can help us to understand better why an autonomous city controlled by a merchant oligarchy might survive for a lengthy period, initially enjoying a dynamic phase of growth while subsequently entering a period of decadence as the city became a rentier republic.

A common interpretation of how city-states emerged is that they began as acts of usurpation of authority by groups located in a specific place engaging in a specific type of activity who sought to manage their own affairs rather than having them be managed by a feudal ruler.[15] It is easy to see how in an initial phase of development this successful usurpation of power may have led to a more predictable environment for business and to faster economic growth. As my conclusions show, several features of a city-state environment then made it likely that a city could survive as an autonomous entity by being able to borrow large sums and on short notice in order to meet defense needs. City-states were small. This meant that merchants who engaged in trade and industry and who had accumulated fortunes could lend to the city with the knowledge that they could easily monitor public finances. Within an autonomous city merchants would be likely to find themselves in a predominant position within any assembly or council. Thus they would be able to ensure that decisions were taken consistent with the need to reimburse debts. This would be all the more likely if merchants could establish a form of oligarchic control in which other groups (members of craft guilds and popular classes) would be excluded from power. It appears indeed that the most oligarchic city-states

---

[14]See in particular the contrasting views of Epstein and Prak (2008), Dessi and Ogilvie (2004), and Ogilvie (2007) on this subject.

[15]Epstein (2000) gives this interpretation following Weber ([1921] 1958).

had the best access to credit. But if oligarchic control increased chances of survival, ultimately it may have had ambiguous, and perhaps negative, consequences for economic growth.

At an initial stage of a city-state's development, an oligarchic political regime might not be a hindrance to growth. If those with the most up-to-date techniques in trade or production were responsible for establishing independence, then they would very likely also be part of a ruling oligarchy. Over time, however, this situation might change for two distinct reasons.

First, if continued growth depended on the arrival of outsiders bringing new techniques, then an oligarchical regime might be less likely to accept such entrants, particularly if this would pose a challenge to established positions of members of the oligarchy. In a more abstract setting Daron Acemoglu has considered how an oligarchic regime might initially have a high level of growth by virtue of its protection of property rights, but if politics is controlled by family dynasties, and subsequent generations of dynasties tend to be less skilled than their predecessors, then over time economic growth would decelerate within an oligarchic regime.[16]

A second possible mechanism would be for the policy preferences of a family dynasty to change over time as a result of diversification out of high-risk commercial and industrial activities. The fortunes of many great merchants in European city-states were made in the area of long-distance trade, a high-risk activity. Once a merchant had accumulated wealth in this sort of activity, there would be a logical incentive to diversify a portfolio by investing in lower-risk activities, such as land rents and government annuities (in the case of city-state annuities). Michael Postan (1952: 217) goes further, suggesting that many great merchants completely divested themselves from trading activities and became rentiers, leading to what he called a "process of financial degeneration." While contemporary historians might question the degree of uniformity that Postan implies for this phenomenon across major European cities, they would probably not dispute the notion that this was nonetheless a very common phenomenon.

---

[16]It could also be the case that subsequent generations have the same skills as their predecessors, but the type of skills required to sustain economic growth changes. In related work North, Wallis, and Weingast (2009) have distinguished between limited access orders that provide security of property for incumbents but which also involve substantial barriers to entry in both politics and economic markets, and open access orders that provide free entry into both politics and markets. Unlike Acemoglu, they seem to suggest that ultimately it is possible to avoid a trade-off between property rights protection and openness for new entrants.

Under any political regime this shifting of resources from high-risk to low-risk activities would have potential implications for growth. Under an oligarchic regime this might be magnified if members of an oligarchy had already divested out of high-risk activities, and they therefore sought to orient a city's policies toward the conservative goal of securing debt repayment as opposed to actively seeking new markets. Given that I have developed my core arguments by drawing an analogy from the literature on the allocation of control rights in corporate finance, it is worth pointing out that this literature acknowledges that granting control to investors can have both costs and benefits. It will increase access to finance, but it may also produce inefficiently conservative actions.[17] Supporting this point, it is common to encounter references to conflict within cities between more established families who had adopted a conservative outlook of rentiers and newer families still engaged in higher-risk trading activities.[18] Finally, it is interesting to note that a similar process has been hinted at for the Dutch Republic, the territorial entity that most closely resembled a city-state in terms of its politics. If in the seventeenth century the dynamism of the Dutch economy was something to be emulated, by the eighteenth century its stagnation was something to be avoided.

I should emphasize that the story I have just detailed is speculative and based on a number of assumptions for which we as of yet lack fully convincing evidence. Nonetheless, to the extent that this account is accurate it would point to a third broad implication of this study. It would suggest that for city-states the same political conditions that were key to the early success of these "states of credit" may have also ultimately set them on a path toward economic decline.

[17] See Bolton and Dewatripont (2005: ch.11) for a concise elaboration of the trade-offs involved.

[18] See Rotz (1977) for one particularly detailed study of such a conflict in the city of Lübeck, with a nuanced conclusion.

Bibliography

Acemoglu, Daron. 2003. "Why Not a Political Coase Theorem? Social Conflict, Commitment, and Politics." *Journal of Comparative Economics* 31: 620–52.

——— 2008. "Oligarchic Vesus Democratic Societies." *Journal of the European Economic Association.* 6: 1–44.

Acemoglu, Daron, Simon Johnson, and James Robinson. 2005. "The Rise of Europe: Atlantic Trade, Institutional Change, and Economic Growth." *American Economic Review* 95 (3): 546–79.

Acemoglu, Daron, and James Robinson. 2000. "Why Did the West Extend the Franchise?" *Quarterly Journal of Economics* 105: 1167–99.

———. 2006. *Economic Origins of Dictatorship and Democracy.* Cambridge: Cambridge University Press.

Aghion, Philippe, and Patrick Bolton. 1992. "An Incomplete Contracts Approach to Financial Contracting." *Review of Economic Studies* 59 (3): 473–94.

Airlie, Stuart. 1998. "Private Bodies and the Body Politic in the Divorce Case of Lothar II." *Past and Present* 161: 3–38.

Albers, Hermann. 1930. *Veroffentlichungen aus dem Staatsarchiv der freien Hansestadt Bremen.* Bremen: G. Winters Buchhandlung.

Allmand, Christopher. 1998. "War." In *The New Cambridge Medieval History*, vol.7. Cambridge: Cambridge University Press.

Anderson, Perry. 1974. *Lineages of the Absolutist State.* London: NLB.

Ascheri, Mario. 1994. "Siena in the Fourteenth Century: State, Territory, and Culture." In *The "Other Tuscany" Essays in the History of Lucca, Pisa, and Siena during the Thirteenth, Fourteenth, and Fifteenth Centuries,* edited by T. Blomquist and M. Mazzaou. Kalamazoo: Western Michigan University.

Babelon, Jean-Pierre. 1986. *Paris au XVIe Siècle.* Paris: Hachette.

Bairoch, Paul. 1988. *Cities and Economic Development : From the Dawn of History to the Present.* Chicago: University of Chicago Press.

Bairoch, Paul, Jean Batou, and Pierre Chèvre. 1988. *The Population of European Cities from 800 to 1850.* Geneva: Librairie Droz.

Bardach, Juliusz. 1977. "La formation des assemblées polonaises au XVème siècle et la taxation." In *Anciens pays et assemblées d'états.* Kortrijk: UGA.

Barzel, Yoram, and Edgar Kiser. 1992. "The Rise and Fall of Jewish Lending in the Middle Ages." *Journal of Law and Economics* 35 (1): 1–13.

——— 2002. "Taxation and Voting Rights in Medieval England and France." *Rationality and Society* 4 (4): 473–507.

Bates, Robert. 2001. *Prosperity and Violence: The Political Economy of Development.* New York: W.W. Norton.

Bates, Robert, and Donald Lien. 1985. "A Note on Taxation, Development and Representative Government." *Politics and Society* 41 (1): 53–70.

Bean, Richard. 1973. "War and the Birth of the Nation-State." *Journal of Economic History* 33 (1): 203–21.

Beard, Charles, and John Lewis. 1932. "Representative Government in Evolution." *American Political Science Review* 26: 223–40.

Beck, Nathaniel, Jonathan Katz, and Richard Tucker. 1998. "Taking Time Seriously: Time-Series Cross-Section Analysis with a Binary Dependent Variable." *American Journal of Political Science* 42 (4): 1260–88.

Belfanti, Carlo Marco. 2001. "Town and Country in Central and Northern Italy, 1400–1800." In *Town and Country in Europe, 1300–1800*, ed. S. Epstein. Cambridge: Cambridge University Press.

Beneyto, Juan. 1966. "Les Cortès d'Espagne, du XVIème au XIXème siècles." In *Gouvernés et gouvernants*. Bruxelles: Éditions de la Librairie Encyclopédique.

Bergier, J. F. 1962. "Taux de l'intérêt et crédit à court terme à Genève dans la seconde moitié du XVI." In *Studi in onore di Amintore Fanfani*. Vol. 4. Milano.

Besley, Timothy, and Robin Burgess. 2002. "The Political Economy of Government Responsiveness: Theory and Evidence from India." *Quarterly Journal of Economics*. 117: 1415–52.

Besley, Timothy, and Torsten Persson. 2009. "The Origins of State Capacity: Property Rights, Taxation, and Politics." *American Economic Review*. 99 (4): 1218–44.

———. 2010. "State Capacity, Conflict, and Development." *Econometrica*. 78 (1): 1–34.

Bien, David. 1987. "Office, Corps, and a System of State Credit: The Uses of Privilege Under the Ancièn Régime." In *The French Revolution and the Creation of Modern Political Culture.*, edited by Keith Michael Baker. Oxford: Pergamon.

Bisson, Thomas. 1966. "The Military Origins of Medieval Representation." *American Historical Review* 71 (4): 1199–218.

———, ed. 1973. *Medieval Representative Institutions: Their Origins and Nature.* Hinsdale, Ill: Dryden.

Blockmans, Wim. 1976. "Le régime représentatif en Flandre dans le cadre européen au bas Moyen Âge avec un projet d'application des ordinateurs." In *Album Elémer Malyusz*. Bruxelles.

———. 1978. "A Typology of Representative Institutions in Late Medieval Europe." *Journal of Medieval History* 4: 189–215.

———. 1987. "Finances publiques et inégalité sociale dans les Pays-Bas au XIVe–XVIe Siècles." In *Genèse de l'État Moderne*. Paris: Éditions du CNRS.

——— 1994. "Voracious States and Obstructing Cities: An Aspect of State Formation in Preindustrial Europe." In *Cities and the Rise of States in Europe A.D. 1000 to 1800*, edited by C. Tilly and W. Blockmans. Boulder, Colo.: Westview.

———. 1998. "Representation (Since the Thirteenth Century)." In *The New Cambridge Medieval History*, edited by R. Mckitterick. Cambridge: Cambridge University Press.

———. 1999. "Flemings on the Move. A Profile of Representatives, 1384–1506. In *Secretum Scriptorum. Liber Alumnorum Walter Prevenier*, edited by W. P. Blockmans, M. Boone, & Th. Hemptinne. Leiden: Apeldoorn.

———. 1999. "The Low Countries in the Middle Ages." In *The Rise of the Fiscal State in Europe c.1200–1815*, edited by R. Bonney. Oxford: Oxford University Press.

Boix, Carles. 2003. *Democracy and Redistribution*. Cambridge: Cambridge University Press.

Boix, Carles, Bruno Codenotti, Giovanni Resta. 2006. "War, Wealth and the Formation of States." Mimeo, Princeton University.

Bolton, Patrick, and Mathias Dewatripont. 2005. *Contract Theory*. Cambridge: MIT Press.

Bonis, Gyorgy. 1965. "The Hungarian Feudal Diet." In *Gouvernés et gouvernants*. Bruxelles: Éditions de la Librairie Encylopédique.

Boone, Marc. 1990. *Geld en Macht: De Gentse Stadsfinanciën en de Bourgondische Staatsvroming (1384–1453)*. Ghent: Verhandelingen der maatschaapij voor Geschiedenis en Ovdheidkunde te Gent XV.

———. 1991. "Plus deuil que joie: Les ventes de rentes par la ville de Gand pendant la période bourguignonne: entres intérêts privés et finances publiques." *Bulletin Trimestriel (Crédit Communal de Belgique)* 176: 3–25.

Bosker, Maarten, Eltjo Buringh, and Jan Luiten van Zanden. 2008. "From Baghdad to London: The Dynamics of Urban Development in Europe and the Arab World, 800–1800." Mimeo, International Institute of Social History.

Boucoyannis, Deborah. 2006. Land, Courts, and Parliaments: The Hidden Sinews of Power in the Emergence of Constitutionalism. Ph.D. diss., University of Chicago.

Bougard, Pierre. 1988. "L'apogée de la ville (1191–1340)." In *Histoire d'Arras*. Dunkerque: Editions des Beffrois.

Bowsky, William. 1964. "The Impact of the Black Death Upon Sienese Government and Society." *Speculum* 39 (1): 1–34.

———. 1970. *The Finance of the Commune of Siena 1287–1355*. Oxford: Clarendon.

———. 1981. *A Medieval Italian Commune: Siena Under the Nine, 1287–1355*. Berkeley: University of California Press.

Brandt, A. von, and W. Koppe. 1953. *Stadtewesen und Burgertum als Geschichtliche Krafte*. Lubeck: Max Schmidt-Romhild.

Braudel, Fernand. 1988. *The Identity of France*. New York: Harper and Row.

Brewer, John. 1989. *The Sinews of Power*. London: Hutchinson.

Caferro, William. 1998. *Mercenary Companies and the Decline of Siena*. Baltimore: Johns Hopkins University Press.

Calabria, Antonio. 1991. *The Cost of Empire: The Finances of the Kingdom of Naples in the Time of Spanish Rule.* Cambridge: Cambridge University Press.

Carboni, Mauro. 1995. *Il debito della città: Mercado del credito, fisco, e società a Bologna fra Cinque e Seicento.* Bologna: Società Editrice il Mulino.

Carlotto, N. 1993. *La città custodita. Politica e finanza a Vicenza dalla caduta di Ezzelino al vicariato imperial (1259–1312),* Milano.

Carlos, Ann, and Larry Neal. 2006. "The Micro-Foundations of the Early London Capital Market: Bank of England Shareholders During and After the South Sea Bubble, 1720–1725." *Economic History Review* 59 (3): 498–538.

Carniello, B. R. 2002. "The Rise of an Administrative Elite in Medieval Bologna: Notaries and Popular Government, 1282–1292." *Journal of Medieval History* 28: 319–47.

Carretero Zamora, Juan Manuel. 1988. *Cortes, monarquia, ciudades.* Madrid: Siglo Veintiuno.

Carsten, F. L. 1954. *The Origins of Prussia.* Oxford: Clarendon Press.

———. 1959. *Princes and Parliaments in Germany: From the Fifteenth to the Eighteenth Century.* Oxford: Clarendon Press.

———. 1965. "The German Estates in the Eighteenth Century." In *Gouvernés et gouvernants.* Bruxelles: Éditions de la Librairie Encyclopédique.

Caselli, Fausto Piola. 2003. "Public Debt, State Revenue and Town Consumption in Rome (16th–18th Centuries)." In *Urban Public Debts: Urban Government and the Market for Annuities in Western Europe (14th–18th Centuries),* edited by M. Boone, K. Davids, and P. Janssen. Turnhout: Brepols.

Castillo, Alvaro. 1963a. "Dette flottante et dette consolidée en Espagne de 1557 à 1600." *Annales* 18: 745–59.

———. 1963b. "Los juros de castilla. Apogeo y fin de un instrumento de credito." *Hispania* 23: 43–70.

Cauwès, Paul. 1895. "Les commencements du crédit publique en France: Les rentes sur l'Hôtel de Ville au XVIeme siècle." *Revue d'Economie Politique* 9 (10): 96–123, 825–65, 407–77.

Cipolla, Carlo. 1952. "Note sulla storia des saggio d'interesse." *Economia Internazionale* 2: 255–72.

Clark, Gregory. 1988. "The Cost of Capital and Medieval Agricultural Technique." *Explorations in Economic History* 25: 265–94.

———. 1996. "The Political Foundations of Modern Economic Growth: England, 1540-1800." *Journal of Interdisciplinary History* 26 (4): 563–88.

———. 2007. *A Farewell to Alms: A Brief Economic History of the World.* Princeton: Princeton University Press.

Clarke, M.V. 1926. *The Medieval City State.* New York: Barnes and Noble.

Conklin, James. 1998. "The Theory of Sovereign Debt and Spain under Philip II." *Journal of Political Economy* 106 (3): 483–513.

Contamine, Philippe. 1984. *War in the Middle Ages.* New York: Basil Blackwell.

Corteguera, Luis R. 2002. *For the Common Good: Popular Politics in Barcelona, 1580–1640*. Ithaca: Cornell University Press.

Dahl, Robert, and Edward Tufte. 1973. *Size and Democracy*. Stanford: Stanford University Press.

Day, John. 1963. *Les douanes de gênes, 1376–1377*. Paris: SEVPEN.

de Boislisle, A. M. 1875. *Le budget et la population de la France sous Philippe de Valois*. Paris.

de Lagarde, Georges. 1937. "Individualisme et corporatisme au Moyen Âge." In *L'Organisation corporative du Moyen Âge à la fin de l'Ancien Régime*. Louvain: Bibliothèque de l'Université.

———. 1939. "La structure politique et sociale de l'Europe au XIVème siècle." In *L'Organisation corporative du Moyen Âge à la fin de l'Ancien Régime*. Louvain: Bibliotheque de l'Universite.

de Luca, Giuseppe. 2006. "Government Debt and Financial Markets: Pro-Cycle Effects in Northern Italy During the XVIth and the XVIIth Centuries." Paper presented to the International Economic History Congress, Helsinki.

de Vries, Jan. 1984. *European Urbanization 1500–1800*. Cambridge: Harvard University Press.

Decoster, Caroline. 2002. "La convocation à l'assemblée de 1302, instrument juridique au service de la propagande royale." *Parliaments, Estates and Representation* 22: 17–35.

DeLong, J. Bradford, and Andrei Shleifer. 1993. "Princes and Merchants: European City Growth before the Industrial Revolution." *Journal of Law and Economics* 36 (2): 671–702.

Derycke, Laurence. 2003. "The Public Annuity Market in Bruges at the End of the 15th Century." In *Urban Public Debts: Urban Government and the Market for Annuities in Western Europe (14th–18th Centuries)*, edited by M. Boone, K. Davids, and P. Janssens. Turnhout: Brepols.

Dessì, Roberta, and Sheilagh Ogilvie. 2004. "Social Capital and Collusion: The Case of Merchant Guilds." Mimeo, Cambridge University.

Dhondt, Jan. 1950. "Les origines des États de Flandre." In *Anciens pays et assemblées d'états*. Louvain: E. Nauwelaerts.

———. 1966. "Les assemblées d'états en Belgique avant 1795." In *Gouvernés et gouvernants*. Bruxelles: Éditions de la Librairie Encyclopédique.

Dickson, P.G.M. 1967. *The Financial Revolution in England*. London: Macmillan.

———. 1987. *Finance and Government under Maria Theresia 1740–1780*. 2 vols. Oxford: Oxford University Press.

Dincecco, Mark. 2009. "Fiscal Centralization, Limited Government, and Public Revenues in Europe, 1650–1913." *Journal of Economic History* 69: 48–1003.

Dollinger, Philippe. 1954. "Les villes allemandes au Moyen Age: leur statut juridique, politique et administratif." In *La Ville*. Bruxelles: Éditions de la Librairie Encyclopédique.

———. 1955. "Les villes allemandes au Moyen Age: les groupements sociaux." In *La Ville*. Bruxelles: Éditions de la Librairie Encyclopédique.

———. 1971. *The German Hansa*. Stanford: Stanford University Press.

Doucet, R. 1948. *Les institutions de la France au XVI siècle*. 2 vols. Paris: Éditions A. et J. Picard.

Douglas, Langton. 1902. *A History of Siena*. London: John Murray.

Downing, Brian. 1992. *The Military Revolution and Political Change: Origins of Democracy and Autocracy in Early Modern Europe*. Princeton: Princeton University Press.

Downs, Anthony. 1957. *An Economic Theory of Democracy*. New York: Harper.

Downs, George, and David Rocke. 1994. "Conflict, Agency, and Gambling for Resurrection: The Principal-Agent Problem Goes to War." *American Journal of Political Science* 38 (2): 362–80.

Doyle, William. 1996. *Venality: The Sale of Offices in Eighteenth-Century France*. Oxford: Clarendon Press.

Drelichman, Mauricio. 2003. "All the Glitters: Precious Metals, Rent Seeking and the Decline of Spain." Mimeo, University of British Columbia.

Drelichman, Mauricio, and Hans-Joachim Voth. 2007. "Institutions and the Resource Curse in Early Modern Spain." In *Institutions and Economic Performance*, edited by Elhanan Helpman. Cambridge: Harvard University Press.

———. 2008. "The Sustainable Debts of Philip II: A Reconstruction of Spain's Fiscal Position, 1560–1598." Mimeo, University of British Columbia.

———. 2008. "Lending to the Borrower from Hell: Debt and Default in the Age of Philip II, 1556–1598." Mimeo, University of British Columbia.

Dumont, François, and Pierre-Clément Timbal. 1966. "Gouvernés et gouvernants en France (période du Moyen Âge et du XVIème siècle)." In *Gouvernés et gouvernants*. Bruxelles: Editions de la Librairie Encyclopédique.

Dunbabin, Jean. 1999. "West Francia: The Kingdom." In *The New Cambridge Medieval History*, edited by T. Reuter. Cambridge: Cambridge University Press.

Ehrenberg, Richard. [1928] 1963. *Capital and Finance in the Age of the Renaissance*. New York: Augustus M. Kelley.

Eltis, David. 1989. "Towns and Defence in Later Medieval Germany." *Nottingham Medieval Studies* 33: 91–103.

Epstein, S. R., and P. Maarten Prak, eds. 2008. *Guilds, Innovation, and the European Economy, 1400–1800*. Cambridge: Cambridge University Press.

Epstein, Stephan. 1993. "Town and Country: Economy and Institutions in Late Medieval Italy." *The Economic History Review* 46 (3): 453–77.

————. 1996a. "Taxation and Political Representation in Italian Territorial States." In *Public and Private Finances in the Late Middle Ages*, edited by M. Boone and W. Prevenier. Leuven: Garant.

————. 2000. *Freedom and Growth: The Rise of States and Markets in Europe, 1300–1750*. London: Routledge.

Epstein, Steven A. 1996b. *Genoa and the Genoese, 958–1528*. Chapel Hill: University of North Carolina Press.

Ertman, Thomas. 1997. *Birth of the Leviathan: Building States and Regimes in Medieval and Early Modern Europe*. Cambridge: Cambridge University Press.

Espinas, Georges. 1902. *Les finances de la commune de Douai, des origines au XVe siècle*. Paris: Alphonse Picard.

Fawtier, Robert. 1953. "Parlement d'Angleterre et Etats Généraux de France au Moyen-Âge." *Comptes Rendus de l'Académie des Inscriptions et des Belles Lettres*. Paris.

Felloni, Giuseppe. 1977. "Italy." In *An Introduction to the Sources of European Economic History 1500–1800*, edited by C. Wilson and G. Parker. Ithaca: Cornell University Press.

Finer, Samuel. 1975. "State- and Nation-Building in Europe: The Role of the Military." In *The Formation of National States in Western Europe*, edited by C. Tilly. Princeton: Princeton University Press.

Finer, Samuel. 1995. *The History of Government*. 3 vols. Oxford: Oxford University Press.

Folz, Robert. 1965. "Les Assemblées d'Etats dans les principautés allemandes (fin XIIIème–début XVIème siècle)" In *Gouvernés et gouvernants*. Bruxelles: Editions de la Librairie Encyclopédique.

Font y Rius, José M. 1954. "Les villes dans l'Espagne du Moyen Âge—l'histoire de leurs institutions admnistratives et judiciaires." In *La Ville: Première Partie: Institutions Administrative et Judiciaires*. Bruxelles: Éditions de la Librairie Encyclopédique.

Forbonnais, François Véron Duverger de. 1758. *Recherches et considérations sur les finances de France depuis l'année 1595 jusqu'à l'année 1721*. Basel: Frères Cramer.

Fox, Edward Whiting. 1971. *History in Geographic Perspective*. New York: W.W. Norton.

Fratianni, Michele. 2006. "Government Debt, Reputation and Creditors' Protections: The Tale of San Giorgio." *Review of Finance* 10 (4): 487–506.

Fried, Johannes. 1995. "The Frankish Kingdoms, 817–911: The East and Middle Kingdoms." In *The New Cambridge Medieval History: Volume II c.700–c.900*, edited by R. Mckitterick. Cambridge: Cambridge University Press.

Fritschy, Wantje. 2003a. "A Financial Revolution Reconsidered: Public Finance in Holland during the Dutch Revolt, 1568–1648." *Economic History Review* 56 (1): 57–89.

————. 2003b. "Three Centuries of Urban and Provincial Public Debt: Amsterdam and Holland." In *Urban Public Debts: Urban Government and the Market for Annuities in Western Europe (14th–18th Centuries)*, edited by M. Boone, K. Davids, and P. Janssens. Turnhout: Brepols.

Fryde, E. B. 1955. "Loans to the English Crown, 1328–31." *English Historical Review* 70 (275): 198–211.

Fryde, E. B., and M. M. Fryde. 1963. "Public Credit, with Special Reference to North-western Europe." In *The Cambridge Economic History of Europe: Volume III Economic Organization and Policies in the Middle Ages*, edited by M. M. Postan, E. E. Rich, and E. Miller. Cambridge: Cambridge University Press.

Ganshof, F. L. 1971. "On the Genesis and Significance of the Treaty of Verdun (843)." In *The Carolingians and the Frankish Monarchy: Studies in Carolingian History*, edited by F. L. Ganshof. Ithaca: Cornell University Press.

Gelabert, Juan. 1999. "Castile, 1504–1808." In *The Rise of the Fiscal State in Europe*, edited by R. Bonney. Oxford: Oxford University Press.

Gilissen, John. 1954. "Les villes en Belgiques: Histoire des institutions administratives et judiciaires des villes belges." In *La Ville*. Bruxelles: Editions de la Librairie Encyclopédique.

————. 1966. "Les États Généraux en Belgique et aux Pays-Bas sous l'Ancien Régime." In *Gouvernés et gouvernants*. Bruxelles: Éditions de la Librairie Encyclopédique.

————. 1969. "Les rapports entre gouvernés et gouvernants, vus à la lumière de l'histoire comparative des institutions. Synthèse générale." In *Gouvernés et gouvernants*. Bruxelles: Éditions de la Librairie Encyclop édique.

Gilliard, François. 1965. "Gouvernés et gouvernants dans la Confédération Helvétique, des origines à la fin de l'Ancien Régime." In *Gouvernés et gouvernants*. Bruxelles: Éditions de la Librairie Encyclopédique.

Gilomen, Hans-Jörg. 2003. "La prise de décision en matière d'emprunts dans les villes suisses au 15e siècle." In *Urban Public Debts: Urban Government and the Market for Annuities in Western Europe (14th–18th Centuries)*, edited by M. Boone, K. Davids and P. Janssens. Turnhout: Brepols.

Goldberg, Eric J. 2006. *Struggle for Empire: Kingship and Conflict under Louis the German, 817–876*. Ithaca: Cornell University Press.

Grassby, Richard. 1970. "English Merchant Capitalism in the Late Seventeenth Century. The Composition of Business Fortunes." *Past and Present* (46): 87–107.

Graves, Michael. 2001. *The Parliaments of Early Modern Europe*. London: Longman.

Greif, Avner. 1994. "On the Political Foundations of the Late Medieval Commercial Revolution: Genoa during the Twelfth and Thirteenth Centuries." *Journal of Economic History* 54 (2): 271–87.

————. 2006. *Institutions and the Path to the Modern Economy*. Cambridge: Cambridge University Press.

————. 2005. "Commitment, Coercion and Markets: The Nature and Dynamics of Institutions Supporting Exchange" Pp. 727–89 in *Handbook of New Institutional Economics*. edited by Claude Ménard and Mary M. Shirley. Dordrecht, Netherlands: Springer.

Grever, John H. 1982. "The Structure of Decision-Making in the States General of the Dutch Republic 1660–68." *Parliaments, Estates and Representation* 2 (2): 125–54.

Guiso, Luigi, Paolo Sapienza, and Luigi Zingales. 2008. "Long-Term Persistence." Mimeo, University of Chicago, Booth School of Business.

Guizot, M. 1838. *Histoire de la civilisation en Europe depuis la chute de l'Empire Romain*. Paris: Emile Perrin.

Hall, John. 1992. *Powers and Liberties: The Causes and Consequences of the Rise of the West*. Berkeley: University of California Press.

Hamilton, Earl J. 1947. "Origin and Growth of the National Debt in Western Europe." *American Economic Review* 37 (2): 118–30.

Hamon, Philippe. 1994. *L'argent du roi: Les finances sous François Ier*. Paris: Comité pour l'Histoire Économique et Financière de le France.

————. 1999. *"Messieurs des finances." Les grands officiers de finance de la France de la Renaissance*. Paris: Comité pour l'Histoire Économique et Financiè re de le France.

Hart, Oliver, and John Moore. 1998. "Default and Renegotiation: A Dynamic Model of Debt." *Quarterly Journal of Economics* 113 (1): 1–42.

Hart, Marjolein 't. 1993. *The Making of a Bourgeois State: War, Politics and Finance During the Dutch Revolt*. Manchester: Manchester University Press.

————. 1999. "The United Provinces, 1579–1806." In *The Rise of the Fiscal State in Europe c.1200–1815*, edited by R. Bonney. Oxford: Oxford University Press.

Hayton, David. 2002. Introductory survey in *The History of Parliament: The House of Commons: 1690–1715*. Cambridge: Cambridge University Press.

Heckman, James. 1979. "Sample Selection Bias as a Specification Error." *Econometrica* 47: 153–161.

Heers, Jacques. 1961. *Gênes au XVe siècle*. Paris : SEVPEN.

Henneman, John. 1967. "Financing the Hundred Years' War: Royal Taxation in France in 1340." *Speculum*. 42 (2): 275–98.

Herb, Michael. 2003. "Taxation and Representation." *Studies in Comparative International Development* 38 (3): 3–31.

Herbst, Jeffrey. 2000. *States and Power in Africa: Comparative Lessons in Authority and Control*. Princeton: Princeton University Press.

Hicks, John. 1969. *A Theory of Economic History*. Oxford: Oxford University Press.

Hintze, Otto. 1906 [1975]. "Military Organization and the Organization of the State." In *The Historical Essays of Otto Hintze*, edited by Felix Gilbert. New York: Oxford University Press.

———. [1931] 1975. "The Preconditions of Representative Government in the Context of World History." In *The Historical Essays of Otto Hintze*, edited by Felix Gilbert. New York: Oxford University Press.

Hoffman, Philip, and Jean-Laurent Rosenthol. 1997. "The Political Economy of Warfare and Taxation in Early Modern Europe: Historical Lessons for Economic Development." In *The Frontiers of the New Institutional Economics*. New York: Academic Press.

Hoffman, Philip, and Kathryn Norberg, eds. 1994. *Fiscal Crises, Liberty, and Representative Government 1450–1789*. Stanford: Stanford University Press.

Holmstrom, Bengt, and Jean Tirole. 1997. "Financial Intermediation, Loanable Funds, and the Real Sector." *Quarterly Journal of Economics* 112 (3): 663–91.

Homer, Sidney, and Richard Sylla. 1996. *A History of Interest Rates*. New Brunswick, N.J.: Rutgers University Press.

Hui, Victoria Tin-bor. 2005. *War and State Formation in Ancient China and Early Modern Europe*. Cambridge: Cambridge University Press.

Humphreys, Macartan, and Jeremy Weinstein. 2010. "Policing Politicians: Citizen Empowerment and Political Accountability in Uganda." Mimeo, Columbia University.

Innes, Matthew. 2000. *State and Society in the Early Middle Ages: The Middle Rhine Valley, 400–1000*. Cambridge: Cambridge University Press.

Israel, Jonathan. 1995. *The Dutch Republic: Its Rise, Greatness, and Fall 1477–1806*. Oxford: Clarendon Press.

Jago, Charles. 1981. "Habsburg Absolutism and the Cortes of Castile." *American Historical Review* 86 (2): 307–26.

———. 1985. "Philip II and the Cortes of Castile: The Case of the Cortes of 1576." *Past and Present* 109: 24–43.

Jedruch, Jacek. 1982. *Constitutions, Elections and Legislatures of Poland, 1493–1993*. New York: Hippocrene.

Jespersen, Leon. 2000. "The Constitutioinal and Administrative Situation." In *A Revolution from Above? The Power State of 16th-and 17th-Century Scandinavia*, edited by L. Jespersen. Odense: Odense University Press.

Johnstone, Hilda. 1951. *Annals of Ghent*. London: Thomas Nelson.

Jones, E. L. 1981. *The European Miracle: Environments, Economies, and Geopolitics in the History of Europe and Asia*. New York: Cambridge University Press.

Jones, Phillip. 1997. *The Italian City-State: 500–1300: From Commune to Signoria*. Oxford: Clarendon.

Keir, D. L. 1938. *The Constitutional History of Modern Britain, 1485–1937*. London: Adam and Charles Black.

Kingra, Mahinder S. 1993. "The Trace Italienne and the Military Revolution during the Eighty Years' War, 1567–1648." *Journal of Military History* 57 (3): 431–46.

Kirk, Thomas Allison. 2005. *Genoa and the Sea: Policy and Power in an Early Modern Maritime Republic, 1559–1684.* Baltimore: Johns Hopkins University Press.

Kirshner, Julius. 2006. "States of Debt." Paper presented to the Mellon Sawyer Seminar on Debt, Sovereignty, and Power, Cambridge University, November 18, 2006.

Klessman, Eckart. 2002. *Geschichte der Stadt Hamburg.* Hamburg: Die Hanse.

Knights, Mark. 2005. *Representation and Misrepresentation in Later Stuart Britain.* Oxford: Oxford University Press.

Knipping, Richard. 1894. "Das Schuldenwesen der Stadt Köln im 14. und 15. Jahrhundert." *Westdeutsche Zeitschrift für Geschichte und Kunst* 13: 340-97.

———. 1898. *Die Kölner Stadtrechnungen des Mittelalters mit einer Darstellung der Finanzverwaltung.* Bonn: Herm. Behrendt.

Koenigsberger, H. G. 1971. "The Parliament of Piedmont during the Renaissance, 1460–1560." In *Estates and Revolutions: Essays in Early Modern European History,* edited by H. G. Koenigsberger. Ithaca: Cornell University Press.

———. 1977. "The Italian Parliaments from Their Origins to the End of the 18th Century." In *Anciens Pays et Assemblées d'États.* Kortrijk: UGA.

———. 1992. "Review of José Ignacio Fortea Pérez, Monarquía y Cortes en la Corona de Castilla: Las Ciudades ante la Politica Fiscal de Felipe II, Valladolid, Cortes de Castilla y León, 1990." *European History Quarterly* 22: 639–41.

———. 2001. *Monarchies, States Generals and Parliaments: The Netherlands in the Fifteenth and Sixteenth Centuries.* Cambridge: Cambridge University Press.

Kohn, Meir. 1999. "Finance Before the Industrial Revolution: An Introduction." Mimeo, Dartmouth College.

———. 2008. "How and Why Economies Develop and Grow: Lessons from Preindustrial Europe and China." Mimeo, Dartmouth College.

Korner, Martin. 1995. "Expenditure." In *Economic Systems and State Finance,* edited by R. Bonney. Oxford: Clarendon.

Lane, Frederic C. 1966. "The Funded Debt of the Venetian Republic, 1262–1482." In *Venice and History: The Collected Papers of Frederic C. Lane.* Baltimore: Johns Hopkins University Press.

———. 1973. *Venice: A Maritime Republic.* Baltimore: Johns Hopkins University Press.

Lane, Frederic C., and Reinhold Mueller. 1985. *Money and Banking in Medieval and Renaissance Venice.* Baltimore: Johns Hopkins University Press.

Langford, Paul. 1989. *A Polite and Commercial People: England 1727–1783.* Oxford: Oxford University Press.

Levi, Margaret. 1988. *Of Rule and Revenue.* Berkeley: University of California Press.

Lewis, P. S. 1962. "The Failure of the French Medieval Estates." *Past and Present* 23: 3–24.

Liebeskind, W. A. 1937. "Le souverain des anciennes républiques suisses." In *Histoire des Assemblées d'États,* Bulletin of the International Committee of Historical Sciences, Edition Anastatique, Brussels.

———. 1939. "Les Assemblees d'État de l'Ancienne Suisse." In *L'Organisation corporative du Moyen Age à la fin de l'Ancien Régime*. Louvain: Bibliothèque de l'Université.

Lopez, Robert S. 1971. *The Commercial Revolution of the Middle Ages, 950–1350*. New York: Prentice Hall.

Lönnroth, Erik. 1966. "Government in Medieval Scandinavia." In *Gouvernés et Gouvernants*. Bruxelles: Éditions de la Librairie Encyclopédique.

Lousse, Émile. 1937. "La formation des ordres dans la société médiévale." In *L'Organisation corporative du Moyen Âge à la fin de l'Ancien Régime*. Louvain: Bibliothèque de l'Université.

———. 1943. "Assemblees d'états." In *L'Organisation corporative du Moyen Âge à la fin de l'Ancien Régime*. Louvain: Bibliothéque de l'Université.

———. 1966. "Gouvernés et gouvernants en Europe Occidentale durant le bas Moyen Âge et les Temps Modernes, rapport général." In *Gouvernés et gouvernants*. Bruxelles: Éditions de la Librairie Encyclopédique.

Lovett, A. W. 1987. "The Vote of the *Millones* (1590)." *Historical Journal* 30: 1–20.

Lynn, John A. 1991. "The Trace Italienne and the Growth of Armies: The French Case." *Journal of Military History* 55 (3): 297–330.

Macdonald, James. 2003. *A Free Nation Deep in Debt: The Financial Roots of Democracy*. New York: Farrar, Strauss, and Giroux.

MacHardy, Karin J. 2003. *War, Religion, and Court Patronage in Habsburg Austria: The Social and Cultural Dimensions of Political Interaction*. New York: Palgrave Macmillan.

Mackay, Ruth. 1999. *The Limits of Royal Authority: Resistance and Obedience in Seventeenth-Century Castile*. Cambridge: Cambridge University Press.

Maclean, Simon. 2003. *Kingship and Politics in the Late Ninth Century: Charles the Fat and the End of the Carolingian Empire*. Cambridge: Cambridge University Press.

Major, J. Russell. 1951. *The Estates General of 1560*. Princeton: Princeton University Press.

———. 1955. "The Payment of the Deputies to the French National Assemblies, 1484–1627." *Journal of Modern History* 27 (2): 217–29.

———. 1960. *Representative Institutions in Renaissance France 1421–1559*. Madison: University of Wisconsin Press.

Mallett, Michael E. 1994. "The Art of War." In *Handbook of European History, 1400–1600 Volume 1*, edited by T. J. Brady, H. Oberman, and J. D. Tracy. Leiden: E. J. Brill.

Manin, Bernard. 1995. *Principes du gouvernement représentatif*. Paris: Calmann-Lévy.

Mann, Michael. 1986. *The Sources of Social Power: Volume 1 A History of Power from the Beginning to A.D. 1760*. Cambridge: Cambridge University Press.

Marongiu, Antonio. 1968. *Medieval Parliáments: A Comparative Study*. London: Eyre and Spottiswoode.

Mauro, Frédéric, and Geoffrey Parker. 1977. "Spain." In *An Introduction to the Sources of European Economic History 1500–1800*, edited by C. Wilson and G. Parker. Ithaca: Cornell University Press.

Mckitterick, Rosamond. 1983. *The Frankish Kingdoms under Carolingians: 751–987*. London: Longman.

Mitchell, B. R. 1988. *Abstract of British Historical Statistics*. Cambridge: Cambridge University Press.

Mitchener, Kris, and Marc Weidenmier. 2010. "Supersanctions and Sovereign Debt Repayment." *Journal of International Money and Finance*. 29: 19–36.

Mohlo, Antonio. 1971. *Florentine Public Finances in the Early Renaissance, 1400–1433*. Cambridge: Harvard University Press.

Mokyr, Joel. 1990. *The Lever of Riches: Technological Creativity and Economic Progress*. Oxford: Oxford University Press.

———. 1995. "Urbanization, Technological Progress and Economic History." In *Urban Agglomeration and Economic Growth*, Herbert Giersch. New York: Springer.

———. 1994. "Cardwell's Law and the Political Economy of Technological Progress." *Research Policy* 23: 561–574.

Mousnier, Roland. 1966. "La participation des gouvernés à l'activité des gouvernants dans la France du XVIIème et du XVIIIème siècles." In *Gouvernés et gouvernants*. Bruxelles: Éditions de la Librairie Encyclopédique.

Mueller, Reinhold. 1997. *The Venetian Money Market: Banks, Panics, and Public Debt 1200–1500*. Baltimore: Johns Hopkins University Press.

Munro, John H. 2003. "The Medieval Origins of the Modern Financial Revolution: Usury, Rentes, and Negotiability." *International History Review* 25 (3): 505–562.

Murray, James. 2005. *Bruges, Cradle of Capitalism, 1280–1390*. Cambridge: Cambridge University Press.

Nelson, Janet. 1995. "The Frankish Kingdoms, 814–898: The West." In *The New Cambridge Medieval History: Volume II c.700–c.900*, ed. R. Mckitterick. Cambridge: Cambridge University Press.

———. 1999. "Rulers and Government." In *The New Cambridge Medieval History: Volume III 900–1024*, edited by T. Reuter. Cambridge: Cambridge University Press.

North, Douglass. 1981. *Structure and Change in Economic History*. New York: W. W. Norton.

North, Douglass, and Robert Paul Thomas. 1973. *The Rise of the Western World: A New Economic History*. Cambridge: Cambridge University Press.

North, Douglass C., and Barry R. Weingast. 1989. "Constitutions and Commitment: The Evolution of Institutions Governing Public Choice in Seventeenth-Century England." *Journal of Economic History* 49 (4): 803–32.

North, Douglass, John Wallis, and Barry Weingast. 2009. *Violence and Social Orders: A Conceptual Framework for Interpreting Recorded Human History.* Cambridge: Cambridge University Press.

Nussli, Christos. 2003. *Periodic Historical Atlas of Europe.* Yverdon, Switzerland: Euratlas.

O'Brien, Patrick. 2001. "Fiscal Exceptionalism: Great Britain and Its European Rivals: From Civil War to Triumph at Trafalgar and Waterloo." Mimeo, Department of Economic History, London School of Economics.

O'Brien, Patrick, and Philip A. Hunt. 1999. "England, 1485–1815." In *The Rise of the Fiscal State in Europe c.1200–1815,* edited by R. Bonney. Oxford: Oxford University Press.

Ogilvie, Sheilagh. 2007. "'Whatever Is, Is Right'? Economic Institutions in Pre-industrial Europe." *Economic History Review* 60 (4): 649–84.

Ormrod, W. M. 1995. "The West European Monarchies in the Later Middle Ages " In *Economic Systems and State Finance,* edited by R. Bonney. Oxford: Clarendon.

———. 1999. "England in the Middle Ages." In *The Rise of the Fiscal State in Europe c.1200-1815,* edited by R. Bonney. Oxford: Oxford University Press.

Outhwaite, R. B. 1966. "The Trials of Foreign Borrowing: The English Crown and the Antwerp Money Market in the Mid-Sixteenth Century." *Economic History Review* 19 (2): 289–305.

Parisot, Robert. 1898. *The Royaume de Lorraine sous les Carolingiens (843–923).* Paris.

Parisse, Michel. 1999. "Lotharingia." In *The New Cambridge Medieval History,* edited by T. Reuter. Cambridge: Cambridge University Press.

Parker, Geoffrey. 1974. "The Emergence of Modern Finance in Europe, 1500–1750." In *The Fontana Economic History of Europe: Volume 2, The Sixteenth and Seventeenth Centuries,* edited by C. Cipolla. Hassocks: Harvester.

———. 1988. *The Military Revolution: Military Innovation and the Rise of the West 1500–1800.* Cambridge: Cambridge University Press.

Partner, Peter. 1980. "Papal Financial Policy in the Renaissance and Counter-Reformation." *Past and Present* (88): 17–62.

———. 1999. "The Papacy and the Papal States." In *The Rise of the Fiscal State in Europe c.1200–1815,* edited by R. Bonney. Oxford: Oxford University Press.

Payne, Stanley. 1973. *A History of Spain and Portugal.* Madison: University of Wisconsin Press.

Petit-Dutaillis, Ch. 1947. *Les communes françaises: caractères et évolution des origines au XVIIIe siècle.* Paris: Albin Michel.

Pezzolo, Luciano. 2001. "Economic Policy, Finance, and War." Mimeo, ca' Foscari: University of Venice.

———. 2003a. "The Venetian Government Debt, 1350–1650." In *Urban Public Debts: Urban Government and the Market for Annuities in Western Europe (14th–18th Centuries),* edited by M. Boone, K. Davids, and P. Janssens. Turnhout: Brepols.

————. 2003b. "Italian Monti: The Origins of Bonds and Government Debt." Mimeo, ca' Foscar: University of Venice.

————. 2006. "Government debt and the State in Italy, 1300–1700." Mimeo, ca' Foscar: University of Venice.

Pincus, Steve. 2009. *1688: The First Modern Revolution*. New Haven: Yale University Press.

Piola Caselli, Fausto. 2003. "Public Debt, State Revenue and Town Consumption in Rome (16th–18th Centuries)." In *Urban Public Debts: Urban Government and the Market for Annuities in Western Europe (14th–18th Centuries)*, edited by M. Boone, K. Davids, and P. Janssens. Turnhout: Brepols.

Pirenne, Henri. 1909. "The Formation and Constitution of the Burgundian State (Fifteenth and Sixteenth Centuries)." *American Historical Review* 14 (3): 477–502.

————. 1910. *Les anciennes démocraties des Pays-Bas*. Paris: Flammarion.

————. 1925. *Medieval Cities: Their Origins and the Revival of Trade*. Princeton: Princeton University Press.

————. 1936. *Histoire de l'Europe des invasions au XVIe siècle*. Paris: Félix Alcan.

————. 1914. *Les périodes de l'histoire sociale du capitalisme*. Bruxelles: Académie Royale de Belgique.

Pitkin, Hanna. 1967. *The Concept of Representation*. Berkeley: University of California Press.

Postan, Michael. 1952. "The Trade of Medieval Europe: The North." In *The Cambridge Economic History of Europe*, edited by M. M. Postan and E. E. Rich. Cambridge: Cambridge University Press.

Potter, Mark. 2003. *Corps and Clienteles: Public Finance and Political Change in France, 1688–1715*. Aldershot: Ashgate.

Potter, Mark, and Jean-Laurent Rosenthal. 1997. "Politics and Public Finance in France: The Estates of Burgundy, 1660–1790." *Journal of Interdisciplinary History* 27: 577–612.

————. 2002. "The Development of Intermediation in the French Credit Markets: Evidence from the Estates of Burgundy." *Journal of Economic History* 62: 1024–49.

Reincke, H. 1953. "Die alte Hamburger Stadtschuld der Hansezeit, 1300–1563" in A. von Brandt et W. Koppe. *Städtewesen und Bürgertum als geschichtliche Kräfte*, Lübeck.

Reyerson, Kathryn. 1998. "Commerce and Communications." In *New Cambridge Medieval History: Volume V c.1198–c. 1300*, edited by David Abulafia. Cambridge: Cambridge University press.

Reynolds, Susan. 1984. *Kingdoms and Communities in Western Europe: 900–1300*. Oxford: Oxford University Press.

Riché, Pierre. 1983. *Les Carolingiens: Une famille qui fit l'Europe*. Paris: Hachette.

Riley, James. 1987. "French Public Finances, 1727–1768." *Journal of Modern History*. 59: 209–243.

Robinson, James. 1998. "Debt Repudiation and Risk Premia: The North-Weingast Thesis Revisited." Mimeo, University of California, Berkeley.

Rokkan, Stein. 1973. "Cities, States, and Nations: A Dimensional Model for the Study of Contrasts in Development." In *Building States and Nations: Models and Data Resources*. Beveriy Hills, Calif.: Sage Publications.

———. 1975. "Dimensions of State Formation and Nation Building: A Possible Paradigm for Research on Variations Within Europe." In *The Formation of National States in Western Europe*, edited by Charles Tilly. Princenton: Princenton University Press.

Rosenthal, Jean-Laurent. 1998. "The Political Economy of Absolutism Reconsidered." In *Analytic Narratives*, edited by R. Bates, A. Greif, M. Levi, J.-L. Rosenthal, and B. Weingast. Princeton: Princeton University Press.

Roth, Cecil. 1987. *A History of the Jews in England*. Oxford: Clarendon.

Rotz, Rhiman. 1977. "The Lübeck Uprising of 1408 and the Decline of the Hanseatic League." *Proceedings of the American Philosophical Society* 121 (1): 1–45.

Rousseau, Jean-Jacques. 1964 *Considérations sur le Gouvernement de Pologne*. Éditions Pléiade Oeuvres Complètes, Vol. 3, Paris: Gallimard Paris.

Rubinstein, Nicolai. 1966. *The Government of Florence under the Medici (1434 to 1494)*. Oxford: Clarendon.

Ruiz-Martin, F. 1975. "Crédito y banca, comercio y transportes en la época del capitalism mercantile." In Actas de las I jornadas de metodologia aplicada a las ciencias históricas. Vol. 3. Historia moderna. Santiago de Compostela.

Rystad, Goran. 1987. "The Estates of the Realm, the Monarchy, and Empire, 1611–1718." *The Riksdag: A History of the Swedish Parliament*. New York: St. Martin's Press.

Schevill, Ferdinand. 1909. *Siena: The Story of a Medieval Commune*. New York: Charles Scribner's.

Schib, Karl. 1954. "Les institutions urbaines suisses." In *La Ville*. Bruxelles: Éditions de la Librairie Encyclopédique.

Schnapper, Bernard. 1956. *Les rentes au XVIe siècle*. Paris: SEVPEN.

Schneider, Jean. 1954. "Les villes allemandes au Moyen Âge: compétence administrative et judiciaire de leurs magistrats." In *La Ville*. Bruxelles: Éditions de la Librairie Encyclopédique.

———. 1955. "Les villes allemandes au Moyen Âge: les institutions économiques." In *La Ville*. Bruxelles: Éditions de la Librairie Encyclopédique.

Schuck, Herman. 1987. "Sweden's Early Parliamentary Institutions from the Thirteenth Century to 1611." *The Riksdag: A History of the Swedish Parliament*. New York: St. Martin's Press.

Schumpeter, Joseph. [1918] 1954. "The Crisis of the Tax State." In *International Economic Papers: Translations Prepared for the International Economic Association*, edited by A. Peacock. New York: Macmillan.

Schwarzwalder, Herbert. 1965. *Reise in Bremens Vergangenheit*. Bremen: Carl Schunemann Verlag.

Scribner, Robert. 1976. "Why Was There no Reformation in Cologne?" *Bulletin of the Institute of Historical Research* 49 (120): 217–41.

———, ed. 1996. *Germany A New Social and Economic History: Volume 1, 1450–1630.* New York: Arnold.

Sidgwick, Henry. 1903. *The Development of European Polity.* London: Macmillan.

Slivinski, Al, and Nathan Sussman. 2009. "Taxation Mechanisms and Growth in Medieval Paris." Mimeo, Hebrew University of Jerusalem.

Société Jean Bodin, ed. 1954. *La Ville: Première partie: institutions administratives et judiciaires. Recueils de la Société Jean Bodin.* Bruxelles: Éditions de la Librairie Encyclopédique.

———, ed. 1955. *La Ville: Deuxième partie: Institutions économiques et sociales. Recueils de la Société Jean Bodin.* Bruxelles: Éditions de la Librairie Encyclopédique.

———, ed. 1965. *Gouverné et gouvernants: Quatrième partie: Bas Moyen Âge et Temps Modernes. Recueils de la Société Jean Bodin.* Bruxelles: Éditions de la Librairie Encyclopédique.

———, ed. 1966. *Gouverné et gouvernants: Troisième partie: Bas Moyen Âge et temps modernes. Recueils de la Société Jean Bodin.* Bruxelles: Éditions de la Librairie Encyclopédique.

———, ed. 1969. *Gouverné et gouvernants: Première partie synthèse générale: Civilisations archaiques, islamiques et orientales. Recueils de la Société Jean Bodin.* Bruxelles: Éditions de la Librairie Encyclopédique.

Sonenscher, Michael. 2007. *Before the Deluge: Public Debt, Inequality, and the Intellectual Origins of the French Revolution.* Princeton: Princeton University Press.

Soule, Claude. 1965. "Les pouvoirs des députés aux États Généraux en France." In *Anciens pays et assemblées d'états.* Leuven: U. Nauwelaerts.

Spruyt, Hendrik. 1994. *The Sovereign State and Its Competitors: An Analysis of Systems Change.* Princeton: Princeton University Press.

Spufford, Peter. 2002. *Power and Profit: The Merchant in Medieval Europe.* New York: Thames and Hudson.

Stasavage, David. 2003. *Public Debt and the Birth of the Democratic State: France and Great Britian 1688–1789.* Cambridge: Cambridge University Press.

———. 2010. "When Distance Mattered: Geographic Scale and the Development of European Representative Assemblies." *American Political Science Review* 104:625–43.

Strait, Paul. 1974. *Cologne in the Twelfth Century.* Gainesville: University of Florida Press.

Strayer, Joseph R. 1970. *On the Medieval Origins of the Modern State.* Princeton: Princeton University Press.

———, ed. 1989. *Dictionary of the Middle Ages.* New York: Charles Scribner's.

Stromberg, David. 2004. "Radio's Impact on Public Spending." *Quarterly Journal of Economics* 119 (1): 189–212.

Sussman, Nathan, and Yishay Yafeh. 2006. "Institutional Reforms, Financial Development and Sovereign Debt: Britain 1690–1790." *Journal of Economic History* 66 (4): 906–35.

Swann, Julian. 2003. *Provincial Power and Absolute Monarchy: The Estates General of Burgundy, 1661–1790.* Cambridge: Cambridge University Press.

Thompson, I.A.A. 1982. "Crown and Cortes in Castile, 1590–1665." *Parliaments, Estates and Representation* 2 (1): 29–45.

———. 1984. "The End of the Cortes in Castile." *Parliaments, Estates and Representation* 4 (2): 125–33.

——— 1993a. "Cortes, Cities and Procuradores in Castile." In *Crown and Cortes: Government, Institutions and Representation in Early-Modern Castile,* edited by I.A.A. Thompson. Aldershot: Variorum (Ashgate).

———. 1993b. "Absolutism in Castile." In *Crown and Cortes,* edited by I.A.A. Thompson. Aldershot: Variorum (Ashgate).

———. 1994a. "Castile: Absolutism, Constitutionalism, and Liberty." In *Fiscal Crises, Liberty, and Representative Government 1450–1789,* edited by P. H. a. K. Norberg. Stanford: Stanford University Press.

———. 1994b. "Castile: Polity, Fiscality, and Fiscal Crisis." In *Fiscal Crises, Liberty, and Representative Government 1450–1789,* edited by Philip Hoffman & Kathryn Norberg. Stanford: Stanford University Press.

Thompson, James Westfall. 1935. *The Dissolution of the Carolingian Fisc in the Ninth Century.* Berkeley: University of California Press.

Tilly, Charles. 1975. "Reflections on the History of European State Making." In *The Formation of National States in Western Europe,* edited by C. Tilly. Princeton: Princeton University Press.

———. 1990. *Coercion, Capital, and European States.* Cambridge: Blackwell.

Tilly, Charles, and Wim Blockmans, eds. 1994. *Cities and the Rise of States in Europe A.D. 1000 to 1800.* Boulder, Colo.: Westview.

Timbal, Pierre-Clément. 1954. "Les villes de consulat dans le Midi de la France: Histoire de leurs institutions administratives et judiciaires." In *La Ville.* Bruxelles: Éditions de la Librairie Encyclopédique.

Tirole, Jean. 1999. "Corporate Governance." *Econometrica* 69:1–35.

———. 2006. *The Theory of Corporate Finance.* Princeton: Princeton University Press.

Toch, Michael. 1995. "The Medieval German City under Siege." In *The Medieval City Under Siege,* edited by I. A. Corfis and M. Wolfe. Woodbridge: Boydell.

Tomz, Michael. 2007. *Reputation and International Cooperation: Sovereign Debt Across Three Centuries.* Princeton: Princeton University Press.

Tracy, James. 1985. *A Financial Revolution in the Habsburg Netherlands: Renten and Renteniers in the County of Holland, 1515–1565.* Berkeley: University of California Press.

———. 1990. *Holland under Habsburg Rule, 1506–1566: The Formation of a Body Politic.* Berkeley: University of California Press.

———. 1994. "Taxation and State Debt." In *Handbook of European History, 1400–1600* , ed. H. O. Thomas Brady, and J. D. Tracy. Leiden: E. J. Brill.

———. 2002. *Emperor Charles V, Impresario of War: Campaign Strategy, International Finance, and Domestic Politics*. Cambridge: Cambridge University Press.

———. 2003. "On the Dual Origins of Long-Term Urban Debt in Medieval Europe." In *Urban Public Debts: Urban Governbment and the Market for Annuities in Western Europe (14th–18th centuries)*, edited by M. Boone, K. Davids, and P. Janssens. Turnhout: Brepols.

Ucendo, José Ignacio Andrés. 2001. "Castile's Tax System in the Seventeenth Century." *Journal of European Economic History* 30 (3): 597–617.

———. 2006. "Government Policies and Financial Markets: The Madrid XVIIth-Century Case." Paper Presented to the International Economic History Association, World Congress, Helsinki.

Ulph, Owen. 1947. "Jean Bodin and the Estates-General of 1576." *Journal of Modern History* 19 (4): 289–96.

Usher, Abbott Payson. 1943. *The Early History of Deposit Banking in Mediterranean Europe*. Cambridge: Harvard University Press.

Vam Malle-Sabouret, Camila. 2008. "De la naissance de la dette publique au plafond souverain: Rôle des gouvernements régionaux dans l'évolution de la dette publique." Doct. diss., Institut d'Études Politiques de Paris.

van der Burg, Martijn, Laurence Derycke, and Manon van der Heijden. 2006. "Annuity Buyers and Urban Debt: A Comparison Between 15th-Century Bruges, 16th-Century Dordrecht, and 17th-Century Rotterdam." Paper Presented to the International Economic History Association, World Congress, Helsinki.

van der Burg, Martijn, and Marjolein 't Hart. 2003. "Renteniers and the Recovery of Amsterdam's Credit (1578–1605)." In *Urban Public Debts: Urban Government and the Market for Annuities in Western Europe (14th–18th Centuries)*, ed. M. Boone, K. Davids, and P. Janssens. Turnhout: Brepols.

van der Heijden, Manon. 2003. "Renteniers and the Public Debt of Dordrecht (1555–1572)." In *Urban Public Debts: Urban Government and the Market for Annuities in Western Europe (14th–18th Centuries)*, edited by M. Boone, K. Davids, and P. Janssens. Turnhout: Brepols.

van der Wee, Herman. 1977 "Money, Credit, and Banking Systems." In *The Cambridge Economic History of Europe: Volume V*, edited by E. E. Rich, and C. H. Wilson. Cambridge: Cambridge university Press.

———. 1963. *The Growth of the Antwerp Market and the European Economy*. 3 vols. The Hague: Martinsus Nijhoff.

van Houtte, Jan. 1967. *Bruges: Essai d'histoire urbaine*. Bruxelles: Renaissance du Livre.

van Nieuwenhuysen, A. 1984. *Les finances du duc de Bourgogne Philippe le Hardi (1384–1404)*. Bruxelles: Éditions de l'Université de Bruxelles.

van Werveke, Hans. 1934. *De Gentsche Stadsfinancien in de Middeleeuwen*. Bruxelles: Académie Royale de Belgique.

———. 1946. *Gand: Esquisse d'histoire sociale*. Bruxelles: La Renaissance du Livre.

———. 1963. "The Rise of the Towns." In *The Cambridge Economic History of Europe: Volume III Economic Organization and Policies in the Middle Ages*, edited by E. E. Rich and Michael Poston, and Edward Miller. Cambridge: Cambridge University Press.

van Zanden, Jan Luiten. 2006. "Economic Growth in a Period of Political Fragmentation, Western Europe 900–1300." Manuscript, International Institute of Social History, Utrecht University.

Velde, François. 2004. "Government Equity and Money: John Law's System in 1720 France." Unpublished ms., Federal Reserve Bank of Chicago.

Velde, François, and David Weir. 1992. "The Financial Market and Government Debt Policy in France: 1746–1793." *Journal of Economic History*. 52:1–39.

Verbruggen, J. F. [1954] 1997. *The Art of Warfare in Western Europe during the Middle Ages*. Woodbridge: Boydell.

Verhulst, Adrian. 1989. "The Origins of Towns in the Low Countries and the Pirenne Thesis." *Past and Present* 122: 3–35.

———. 1999. *The Rise of Cities in North-West Europe*. Cambridge: Cambridge University Press.

Voigtlaender, Nico, and Hans-Joachim Voth. 2009. "The Three Horsemen of Riches: Plague, War, and Urbanization in Early Modern Europe." Mimeo, University of California Los Angeles.

Wainwright, Valerie. 1987. "The Testing of a Popular Regime: The Riformati and the Insurrections of 1371." *I Tatti Studies: Essays in the Renaissance* 2: 107–70.

Waley, Daniel. 1969. *The Italian City-Republics*. New York: Mcgraw Hill.

Weber, Max. [1921] 1958. *The City*. New York: Free Press.

Wickham, Chris. 2005. *Framing the Early Middle Ages: Europe and the Mediterranean*. Oxford: Oxford University Press.

Wilson, Peter H. 1992. "The Power to Defend, or the Defence of Power: The Conflict between Duke and Estates over Defence Provision, Wurttemberg 1677–1793." *Parliaments, Estates, and Representation* 12 (1): 25–45.

Wolfe, Martin. 1972. *The Fiscal System of Renaissance France*. New Haven: Yale University Press.

Wood-Leigh, K. L. 1932. "The Knights' Attendance in the Parliaments of Edward III." *English Historical Review* 47: 398–413.

Zagarri, Rosemarie. 1987. *The Politics of Size: Representation in the United States, 1776–1850*. Ithaca: Cornell University Press.

Index

Acemoglu, Daron, 4n.5, 5n.9–10, 159n.4–6, 164
Airlie, Stuart, 98–99
Amsterdam, 64
Arras, 32, 59
assemblies. *See* representative assemblies

Babelon, Jean-Pierre, 138n.10
Bairoch, Paul, 79–80, 100
Barcelona, 32–33, 36, 62n.33, 124
Batou, Jean, 79, 100
Blockmans, Wim, 1n, 27n.4, 51–52, 55n, 65, 156
Boccanegra, Guglielmo, 120
Boccanegra, Simone, 118, 120
Bodin, Jean, 139, 141–42
Bosker, Maarten, 161
Boucoyannis, Deborah, 52n.15
Bowsky, William, 26, 60, 125–29
Braudel, Fernand, 98
Britain: costs of information acquisition and post-1688 political development in, 160–61. *See also* England; Great Britain
Bruges, 42–43, 45, 64, 90
Buringh, Eltjo, 161

Caferro, William, 125, 127, 129–30
Carlos, Ann, 38
Carlotto, N., 31n.12
Carolingian Empire, 19, 96–99
Castile: absolutism and representation, 143–44; administration of public finance, 60–61; assembly meetings, problems associated with, 52–53; as a case study, 23–24; control of public finance by the Cortes, 147–48; demise of the Cortes as a representative institution, 148–49; the Dutch Republic and, comparison of, 142–44,

150; geographic scale and representation, 149; interest rates paid by the Dutch Republic and, comparison of, 145–46; long-term debt, establishment of, 10, 30n.8, 31–32; merchants' political power, 144; public credit in the seventeenth century, 144–47; sales tax, 27; selection of representatives by lot, 62n.33. *See also* Spain
Castillo, Alvaro, 145
Cauwès, Paul, 23, 134–35, 142
Charles IV (Holy Roman Emperor), 130
Charles V (Holy Roman Emperor), 149
Chèvre, Pierre, 79, 100
Cipolla, Carlo, 123
city-states: assemblies in, origins of, 48–50; case studies of, 20–22, 110–11, 131 (*see also* Cologne; Genoa; Siena); changing fortunes of, date of exit from the sample and, 36–37; definition of, 6, 32–33; economic explanations for the financial advantages enjoyed by, 43–46; endogeneity problems with the city-state advantage claim, reassessment of, 106–8; form of government and access to credit, relationship of, 2–3; merchant representation, cost of borrowing and, 90–93; municipal debt in Northern Europe as model for long-term debt, 33; origins of (*see* origins and development of city-states); political institutions and economic innovation, relationship of, 4–5; public debt, sophisticated management of, 59–60; representation, merchant-craftsmen conflict and variations in institutions of, 13–14; survival of, credit and, 4, 28–29; taxation by, 27; variation in, analysis of, 18. *See also* names of city-states

city-states vs. territorial states: credibility as borrowers, 35; geographic scale and representation, 14–15, 51–54 (*see also* geographic scale); interest rates, 38–43, 84–90; interest rates and merchant representation, 92–93; long-term public debt, timing of development of, 9–11, 29–38; meeting frequency of representative assemblies, 66–68; merchant representation, 62–63; prerogatives of representative assemblies, 57–61; public debt, probability of creating, 78, 81–84; representation, intensity of, 13; revenue volatility, 45–46; statistical analysis of, 17–18; wealth held by the political elite, types of, 15–16

Clark, Gregory, 40, 79

Coase theorem, 159

Cologne, 111–12, 117; as a case study, 21; distributional conflicts over public finance, 116–17; long-term debt, establishment of, 31; managing public debt, sophisticated system for, 59–60; military expenditure, 27n.4; political power of merchants, 90, 114–17; political representation, revolts and, 65, 113–16; political representation and debt ownership, relationship of, 64; public credit, development of, 112–13; the *Richerzeche,* 65n, 114–15

commitment problems: institutions as a response to, 5–6; representation as a response to, costs of information and, 158–61

community responsibility system, 11n

Contamine, Philippe, 26

control rights, 7–8, 72

credit: dataset for analysis of, 16; evolution and importance of, 9–11; hypotheses regarding access to, 70; importance of, 25–29; problem of for medieval and early modern political leaders, 6–8; representation and (*see* representation and credit, relationship of); supply of, 37–38 (*see also* mercantile interests); survival of city-states and, 4

Day, John, 120n.18, 122

debt: cost of (*see* interest rates); evolution and early forms of, 9–11; sold below par value, 42

debt, long-term: dates for first creation of, 9–11, 29–38; holders of, 63–64; results of regression estimating conditions for creating, 81–84; specification of regression estimating conditions for creating, 78–81

de Lagarde, Georges, 12, 50

democracy: costs of, solving commitment problems and the, 158–61; credibility of debt repayment and, 2–3; mercantile interests and, 2; in representative institutions, revolts/uprisings focused on expanding, 65. *See also* representative assemblies

Derycke, Laurence, 42–43, 64

de Vries, Jan, 80, 101

Dickson, P.G.M., 38

Dincecco, Mark, 56n

Dollinger, Philippe, 52, 114

Dordrecht, 64

Douai, 32, 60n.27, 90

Douglas, Langton, 128

Downing, Brian, 50

Downs, Anthony, 160

du Prat, Antoine, 133

Dutch Republic: as a case study, 23; Castile and, comparison of, 142–44, 150, 153; interest rates paid by Castile and, comparison of, 145–46; long-term debt, establishment of, 31; merchants' political power, 144; political foundation of the financial revolution, 150; political structure, accounting for, 153–54; province of Holland (*see* Holland); public credit, 150–51; public credit and representative assemblies, 153; representative assemblies, 151–53

economic development: in early modern city-states, 4–5, 161–65; state formation and, three debates regarding, 3–6

economic innovation: financial advantages of city-states, as an explanation for, 44; political institutions and, 3–5

Edward III (king of England), 9, 34

Ehrenberg, Richard, 4, 10, 28

Eltis, David, 27n.4, 28

England: attendance as a duty for the medieval Parliament, 53; the Magna Carta, 48; returns on land rent contracts, 40. *See also* Britain; Great Britain

Epstein, Stephan, 16, 29–31, 38, 87–88, 120, 122

Ertman, Thomas, 50n.8, 55n

Espinas, Georges, 27, 30n.9, 60n.27

Finer, Samuel, 3n.3, 50, 114n.9, 158

Florence, 64, 130

France, 132–33, 142; administration of public finance, 61; army, increased size of, 36; as a case study, 22–23; creditor representation, local institutions for, 137–39; creditor representation, national institutions for, 139–42; Estates General, payment for attendance at, 54, 140; extraordinary taxes, efforts to raise revenue through, 27–28; long-term debt, establishment of, 10–11, 30–31; national assembly, first meeting of, 49; Paris (*see* Paris); public debt, investment of nobility in, 38; *rentes sur l'Hôtel de Ville,* creation and evolution of, 133–37; *rentes sur l'Hôtel de Ville,* opposition of the Estates General to paying for, 141–42; *rentes sur l'Hôtel de Ville,* pressures on venal office-holders to purchase, 43; sale of debt below par in, 42n.32; travel during medieval times, assemblies and, 51–52

François I (king of France), 133–34

Fritschy, Wantje, 146, 151

Fryde, E. B., 10, 34–35, 112

Fryde, M. M., 10, 112

Genoa, 117–18, 124; assembly control of state finances, exception to, 59; the Casa di San Giorgio, 22, 59n, 64, 117–19, 122–24; as a case study, 21–22; distributional conflict over public finance, 119–20; interest rates, 122–24; long-term borrowing continued into the eighteenth century, 36; long-term (public) debt, establishment of, 31, 118–19; merchants' political power, 119, 122, 124; political instability and institutions, 120–22; political representation and debt ownership, relationship of, 64

geographic scale: intensity of political representation and, 66–68; as obstacle to exercising a control right, 8; political representation in Castile and Holland differentiated by, 144; representative assemblies and, 1, 14–15, 51–54; use of by the Castilian crown to undermine the Cortes, 149

Ghent, 27n.4, 32, 37, 43, 45, 65

Gilissen, John, 154

Goldberg, Eric J., 105

Great Britain: administration of debt by the assembly, 59; owners of public debt, 38. *See also* Britain; England

Greif, Avner, 4n.7, 11n, 119, 121, 162

Guiso, Luigi, 103

Guizot, M., 2n, 50

Habsburgs and the Habsburg Empire, 36, 150–52, 154

Hamilton, Earl J., 30n.8

Hamon, Philippe, 140

Hanseatic League, 52

Hart, Marjolein 't, 64, 146

Heckman, James, 88

Heers, Jacques, 22, 119, 121–23

Hennemann, John, 28

Henri III (king of France), 136, 139

Henry II (king of England), 26

Hintze, Otto, 55n, 156

Holland: administration of debt by the assembly, 59; the assembly in, 152–53; travel during medieval times, assemblies and, 51–52. *See also* Dutch Republic

information: about public finances,
assemblies and the distribution of, 60;
costs of acquiring, maintaining
representative institutions and the,
158–61

innovation. *See* economic innovation

intensity of representation: city-states vs.
territorial states regarding, 13; frequency
of assembly meetings as measure of,
65–68

interest rates: data on, 38–39;
determination of in a formal model,
75–76; differential between city-states
and territorial states, 39–43; differential
between city-states and territorial states,
regressions exploring source of, 84–90;
in Genoa, 122–24; land rents, returns
on, 40; life vs. perpetual annuities,
39–40; merchant representation and,
91–93; moral suasion or compulsion as
a factor in, 42–43; on public debt,
returns on land rents compared to,
40–42; in Siena, 127

Israel, Jonathan, 154

Italian city-states: public debt in, the
prestanza and, 33–34. *See also* names of
city-states

Jewish lenders, 9n.15, 34n.19

Johnson, Simon, 4n.5, 5n.9, 159n.5

Johnstone, Hilda, 51n.14

Jones, Phillip, 26

Kingra, Mahinder S., 36n

Kirshner, Julius, 33

Knipping, Richard, 59, 112–13

Koenigsberger, H. G., 144

land rents, 40–42, 79, 81

Levi, Margaret, 5n.9, 49n.5, 52n.15

Lewis, P. S., 52n.15, 141n.16

Lopez, Robert S., 119n.16

Lothar I (Holy Roman emperor),
96–97n.6, 98

Lothar II (king of Lotharingia), 99

Lotharingia, 96–100, 105

Lousse, Émile, 48

Lübeck: Circle Society, 65n, 114;
democratic representation,
revolts/uprisings seeking to expand, 65;
form of wealth held by older and more
recently established merchants, 37–38;
political divisions within the elite of,
117; political representation and debt
ownership, relationship of, 64

Lynn, John A., 36n

Macchiavelli, Niccolo, 122

Macdonald, James, 64n.35

Maclean, Simon, 96n.4

Mainz, 37

Major, J. Russell, 54, 138n.9–10, 140n.13

Mauro, Frédéric, 145

Mckitterick, Rosamond, 98n.7

mercantile interests: in city-state case
studies, 21–22, 110–11 (*see also*
Cologne; Genoa; Siena); public debt,
ownership of, 37–38; representation of,
interest rates and, 90–93; representative
assemblies and, 2–3, 50, 62–65; in
territorial state case studies, 132 (*see also*
Castile; Dutch Republic; France)

military technology: political organization
and, 3–4; post-1500 revolution in,
36, 50

Mitchener, Kris, 74n.4

Mokyr, Joel, 4

Munro, John H., 33n.15

Naples, Kingdom of, 38

Neal, Larry, 38

North, Douglass C., 156, 164n

origins and development of city-states,
18–20, 94, 107–9; the Carolingian
partition hypothesis, 95–100, 104–6;
the city-state advantage and, 106–8;
economic growth, dynamics of, 161–65;
empirical analysis of, 100–6; the
Rokkan/Tilly hypothesis, 95, 104

Ormrod, W. M., 26

Outhwaite, R. B., 35n.21

Paris: *rentes sur l'Hôtel de Ville*, creditor representation and administration of, 137–39; *rentes sur l'Hôtel de Ville*, system of, 23, 133–37; tax base provided by, 27. *See also* France

Parker, Geoffrey, 10, 36, 145

Pezzolo, Luciano, 64

Philip II (king of Spain), 145, 147

Philippe VI (king of France), 27

Phillip Augustus (king of France), 25–26

Phillip IV "the Fair" (king of France), 49

Pirenne, Henri, 2n, 50, 97

Pitkin, Hannah, 53

Postan, Michael, 37, 153, 164

public credit. *See* credit

public debt. *See* debt, long-term

representation and credit, relationship of, 1–3, 47, 63–65; case studies of city-states illustrating, 20–22, 110–11 (*see also* Cologne; Genoa; Siena); case studies of territorial states illustrating, 22–24, 132 (*see also* Castile; Dutch Republic; France); formal model of, assumptions/setup/play of the game in, 72–74; formal model of, equilibrium results in, 75–76; formal model of, predictions from, 77; interest rate differential between city-states and territorial states, regressions identifying factors in, 84–90; merchant representation and interest rates, 90–93

representative assemblies: as a commitment technology, 5; control right exercised by, 7–8; corporatist interpretation of medieval, 48; costs of, commitment problems and, 5–6, 158–61; creation of a public debt and, regression estimating probability of, 77–84; dataset for analysis of, 16–17; dichotomous typology of, 55n; evolution of, 11–14, 57–58; geographic scale and (*see* geographic scale); intensity of representation (*see* intensity of representation); meeting frequency, 65–68; membership of, social groups and, 61–65; mercantile interests in, 2,

50, 62–65, 90–93; necessary conditions for representation through, 1–2; origins of, causal mechanisms leading to, 48–50; prerogatives of, 57–61; public credit/creditors and, 1–3, 47, 63–65 (*see also* representation and credit, relationship of); questions for analysis of, 55–57; selection methods for, 62; sources for analysis of, 54–56

revenues: the financial advantage of city-states and, 44–46. *See also* taxation

Reynolds, Susan, 50

Robinson, James, 4n.5, 5n.9–10, 159n.5–6

Rokkan, Stein, 19, 95, 96n.3, 104

Roman Empire, 103

Rosenthal, Jean-Laurent, 56n, 74n.3

Rotz, Rhiman, 117

Ruiz-Martin, F., 145

Rystad, Goran, 52

Sapienza, Paolo, 103

Saxony, 31n.12

Schevill, Ferdinand, 128–29

Schnapper, Bernard, 136–37

Schneider, Jean, 59, 60n.26, 64

Scribner, Robert, 113–15

Sidgwick, Henry, 50, 114n.9

Siena, 125; as a case study, 22; credit, defense of the city and access to, 28–29, 130; interest rates, 30–31n.11, 127; long-term debt, establishment of, 30n.11, 31; managing public debt, sophisticated system for, 59–60; merchants' political power, 90, 125, 128–31; military expenditures, 26–27; political representation, 128–29; public finance, evolution of, 126–27; representation and credit, relationship of, 91, 125, 129–31; revolts/uprisings and the expansion of democratic representation, 65, 129

Société Jean Bodin, 54–55

Spain: increased size of the army, 36. *See also* Castile

Spufford, Peter, 51, 95

Stasavage, David, 68

state formation: economic development
and, three debates involving, 3–6; war
and, 3–4, 156–58 (*see also* war)

taxation: administration by assemblies, 57;
defense financed through, 27–28; veto
power of assemblies over, 55–56. *See
also* revenues
technological innovation. *See* economic
innovation
territorial states: administration of public
finances, 60–61; assemblies, rise and fall
of, 48–50; case studies of, 22–24, 132,
154–55 (*see also* Castile; Dutch
Republic; France; Holland); creation of
long-term debt, factors accounting for
the speed of, 35–36; economic
explanations for the financial
disadvantages faced by, 43–46;
long-term borrowing, explanations for
the late development of, 34–35; military
revolution in, 36; prerogatives of
assemblies, variation in, 59; short-term
borrowing, 34–35; taxation by, 27–28.
See also city-states vs. territorial states
Thompson, I.A.A., 145, 148
Thompson, James Westfall, 99
Tilly, Charles, 19, 95, 104, 156–57
Tirole, Jean, 7n
Toch, Michael, 28
Tomz, Michael, 74n.4
Tracy, James, 33n.15, 52, 64, 110n,
150–51, 153–54
Treaty of Meersen (870 A.D.), 19, 98–99
Treaty of Verdun (843 A.D.), 19, 96–99,
105

Ucendo, José, 147
urbanization, measures of, 79–80
Usher, Abbott Payson, 11

Vam Malle-Sabouret, Camila, 133n.1
van der Burg, Martijn, 64
van der Heijden, Manon, 64
Van Werveke, Hans, 50
van Zanden, Jan Luiten, 161
Venice, 4, 44
Verbruggen, J. F., 25
Verviers, 31n.12
Vicenza, 31n.12

Wainwright, Valerie, 127n.28
Wallis, John Joseph, 164n
war: budgetary stress caused by, 26–27;
debt finance and the sixteenth-century
military revolution, 36; the importance
of credit due to, 25–29; obligatory
service as feudal obligation, 25–26;
public finance and, 9; state formation
and, 3–4, 156–58; survival of city-states,
access to credit and, 11
wealth: liquidity of and investment in
public debt, merchants vs. landowners
regarding, 37–38; types of held by the
political elite, 15–16, 61
Weber, Max, 50, 162n.12
Weidenmier, Marc, 74n.4
Weingast, Barry R., 164n
Wolfe, Martin, 142
Württemberg, 59

Zagarri, Rosemarie, 51n.10
Zingales, Luigi, 103